New Hampshire Town Names

New Hampshire Town Names

And Whence They Came

ELMER MUNSON HUNT

NOONE HOUSE
PETERBOROUGH, NEW HAMPSHIRE
WILLIAM L. BAUHAN, *Publisher*

This book is set in Linotype Baskerville. Composed and printed at the Evans Printing Company, Concord, N. H. and bound at the Colonial Press, Inc., Clinton, Mass.

Maps are reproduced courtesy of the New Hampshire Department of Resources and Economic Development.

Library of Congress Catalog Card No. 79-125806
SBN: 87233-009-5

Contents

I • DARTMOUTH-LAKE SUNAPEE REGION

II • LAKES REGION

III • MERRIMACK VALLEY REGION

IV • MONADNOCK REGION

V • SEACOAST REGION

VI • WHITE MOUNTAIN REGION

Introduction

MANY OF US might easily assume that because a New Hampshire town is called Dover, or Nottingham, or Peterborough, the name was simply transplanted by the early settlers direct from a place in old England, or perhaps from southern New England. Such an assumption would be wrong most of the time. As the late Elmer Munson Hunt shows, the great majority of New Hampshire town names are indeed English in origin, but they were often brought here in varied and unexpected ways. How did these towns get their names? Where did they come from?

In some introductory notes to this book, left unfinished at the time of his death, the author wrote: "Like communities in other American states, New Hampshire towns took their names for the most part from *people*. Some of these people were leaders of groups of colonists to whom the provincial government gave grants on condition that they build houses, cultivate the land, construct bridges and roads, and maintain schools and churches. Many more of these people were leaders in the English Parliament, who had great political influence over colonial affairs, and London merchants who sponsored and promoted the process of colonization in New England."

"New Hampshire towns not only took English names," Mr. Hunt continues, "but adopted from England and older communities in southern New England, traditions of local self-government. Visiting America in the 1830's, the French political writer de Tocqueville observed: 'In New England political life had its origin in the township and it might be said that each of them formed an independent nation. In the American township power has been distributed with admirable skill for the purpose of interesting the greatest possible number of persons in the commonweal. They possess advantages which strongly excite the interest of mankind, namely independence and authority.' From their inception, New Hampshire towns were parcelled out to form fixed geographical squares or areas; what we call a 'town' here (and elsewhere in New England), would be a 'township' in other parts of the country. Until very recently, each New Hampshire town was allotted representation individually in the state legislature."

New Hampshire contains 235 incorporated towns and cities, plus another two dozen or so "unincorporated places" occupying officially defined geographical limits. The task of documenting the origins of their names — nearly 260 in all — had been virtually completed by Elmer Munson Hunt at the time of his death. It was a prodigious job, gathering the information about each of these separate and individual communities, delving into hundreds of separate town histories and genealogies, consulting original land grants, proprietors' records and other ancient documents — the handwriting often faded with age. In addition to the almost 260 "official" towns and places on the map of New Hampshire, there are numerous other villages, post offices, and localities, none of them incorporated and all of them part of larger "parent" towns or cities. Mr. Hunt had begun research on some of these places, and where possible, the origins of their names have been included along with the "parent" town. But it is with the origins of town names — as officially recognized — that this book is primarily concerned.

From Elmer Munson Hunt's account of the naming of New Hampshire's towns, we can see that the grants fall roughly into three historical periods: the first extending over a century, from the earliest settlements in the 1630's to the mid-1700's; next, the age of the Wentworth governors, beginning in 1741 — when New Hampshire was separated permanently from the administration of Massachusetts — and lasting until the Revolution; and finally the period of Revolution and statehood after 1775.

Up to the year 1741, only about fifty towns had been granted in New Hampshire, covering less than twenty percent of its present land area. The colony was for much of this time under the jurisdiction of the governors of Massachusetts, who often appointed deputies or "Lieutenant-Governors" to administer the affairs of the northern province. Development was slow, and most of the land was unsurveyed wilderness. In fact, until 1700, New Hampshire had chartered only six towns, a tiny enclave along the seacoast. Portsmouth, Exeter, Dover, and Hampton were the first four, and Kingston and New Castle were not added until the 1690's. After the first decade of the eighteenth century and the settlement of the Indian wars, development began to accelerate. Three men were mainly responsible for the New Hampshire towns chartered in this period. Under Samuel Shute, governor of Massachusetts from 1716 to 1723, seven towns were granted. Lieutenant-Governor John Wentworth, father and grandfather of the two Wentworth governors who were to dominate New Hampshire affairs in the late colonial period, established eleven more towns between 1723 and 1730. And in the subsequent decade, Governor Jonathan Belcher granted at least twenty-seven new towns. By the end of the period the towns had spread out from the seacoast, new communities were taking root along the Merrimack River Valley, and a few pioneer settlements had begun in the western wilderness along the Connecticut River.

But the greatest growth came during the relatively short span of thirty-five years when the New Hampshire province was governed by Benning Wentworth (1741-1766), and his nephew, John (1766-1775). Under the two Wentworth governors, well over half of our towns were granted and named. It was the beginning of a period of a great migration of new settlers that was to continue for three decades after the Revolution. Pioneer families came north to New Hampshire from Massachusetts and Connecticut, across the water from England, and "up country" from the seacoast towns of Portsmouth and Dover. The Wentworths, as Elmer Munson Hunt points out, were responsible for: "no fewer than 152 charters establishing new towns in New Hampshire and 128 in what is now Vermont (then part of New Hampshire), thus providing homes and farms in the hitherto undivided and unpopulated two million acres in northern New England for more than thirty thousand families."

A reading of this book will reveal that the Wentworths were related by blood or marriage not only to other prominent Amer-

ican colonial families, but — more importantly — to the English aristocracy. (Unravelling the tangled branches of the Wentworth family tree would discourage all but the most ambitious
genealogists.) Among their numerous relatives were prime
ministers, cabinet members, dukes, earls, soldiers, merchants,
bishops, and lesser gentry. If any family could be said to represent the "Establishment" in eighteenth century England, the
Wentworths would amply qualify.

It is no accident that the names of Wentworth cousins and
in-laws dot the New Hampshire landscape to this day: Atkinson,
Bennington, Claremont, Deering, Fitzwilliam, Francestown,
Hollis, Pelham, Warner, Wentworth are a sampling of the
towns so named. The original five counties of New Hampshire,
created in 1769 by Governor John Wentworth, reflect the family influence: Cheshire, probably for the estate of Sir George
Wentworth in Cheshire County, England; Grafton, to honor
a cousin, Augustus Henry Fitzroy, Duke of Grafton; Hillsborough for the Earl of Hillsborough; Rockingham for Charles
Watson-Wentworth, Marquess of Rockingham and twice prime
minister; and Strafford, in memory of Thomas Wentworth, first
Earl of Strafford, adviser to Charles I and progenitor of the
Wentworth clan.

If the Wentworths did not neglect their influential family
connections, they also paid honor to many others. While ever
loyal to the British crown, the two governors were nevertheless
strong upholders of colonial rights and interests. Thus, as Elmer
Munson Hunt states, towns were named for influential parliamentary leaders, especially those who espoused the cause of
the colonies. Five of our towns, for example, are named for
two great prime ministers: Walpole and Orford for Robert
Walpole, Earl of Orford; and Pittsfield, Pittsburg, and Chatham for William Pitt, Earl of Chatham. Merchants who might
help New Hampshire's trade and economy were remembered;
the towns of Keene and Jaffrey bear such names. The Wentworths did not forget outstanding settlers and surveyors at
home, and among the towns so named are Goffstown, Gilmanton, Hinsdale, Stoddard, Moultonborough, and Sanbornton.

When the colonies had thrown off the yoke of the British

crown, the pattern of names changed. There were, however, just over fifty new grants made in the Republican period — and so these names are in a distinct minority. Little more than twenty percent of the towns were named from the Revolution onward, though a number of the older Wentworth names were discarded in favor of more patriotic models. Prominent revolutionary patriots, generals and statesmen now replaced English lords, merchants and parliamentarians. Such towns as Langdon, Weare, Sullivan, Stark and Bartlett owe their names to New Hampshire revolutionary figures. Early presidents were honored: Mont Vernon and Washington for our first president; and Jefferson, Madison, and Monroe for his successors. The town of Adams was named in 1800, but enthusiastic Democrats re-named it Jackson following Andrew Jackson's victory in the election of 1828. There are even two towns named for presidential also-rans: Ashland for Henry Clay's estate in Kentucky; and Fremont for General John C. Fremont, the "great pathfinder" and first nominee of the Republican Party. As in colonial days, politics played its part in the naming of the towns. While New Hampshire honors its Daniel Webster, by a curious omission there is no town bearing the name of the state's only president, Franklin Pierce. Interesting exceptions to the post-revolutionary pattern of names are two towns named for Englishmen. Wilmot was named in the early 1800's for the English radical and intellectual, Dr. James Wilmot, and Nelson for the hero of the Battle of Trafalgar.

In documenting the sources of New Hampshire town names, Elmer Munson Hunt records some unexpected departures — even in colonial times — from the predominantly Anglo-Saxon names of our communities. Three of the state's best known towns have names of German derivation: Hanover, Franconia, and Berlin. And at one time there was a Heidelberg (now New London), Danzig (Newbury), and Dresden (re-named Hanover). Alstead commemorates J. H. Alsted, a German professor and scientist. Also from continental Europe come Lisbon and Piermont, the latter probably from the Italian *piemonte* or piedmont. Irish settlers left their imprint with Dublin, Lon-

donderry, Antrim, Kilkenny, Derry, Coleraine (now Brookfield), and Limerick (re-named Stoddard).

The Granite State, like many of its sister states, has a scat-
tering of biblical names. There are at least seven in New Hampshire: Canaan, Goshen, Lebanon, Hebron, Salem, Sharon, and
Bethlehem. In the early days of the Republic, writers and orators were fond of comparing America to ancient Greece and
Rome. Such towns as Troy and Laconia were named then —
in the same period when men were building houses and court-
houses in the Greek Revival style. Concord, Candia and Auburn
also have names derived from classical sources.

A few towns were named for literary figures. Marlow, named
for the poet Christopher Marlowe, was formerly called Addison
in honor of Joseph Addison. Wilton may have got its name
from Sir Joseph Wilton, an English sculptor, and Dryden was
the name first given to Colebrook. The little village of Whittier
honors one of New England's celebrated poets. Milton, on the
other hand, appears to have been named for its mills, and not
for the famous English poet.

Indian names are surprisingly few in number. Today only
four incorporated towns bear names from New Hampshire's
first inhabitants: Ossipee, Merrimack, Nashua, and Sunapee.
Some towns were formerly known by Indian names, including
Keene (Upper Ashuelot), New Durham (Cocheco), and Hollis (Nittisset), and Indian names survive in such unincorporated villages and towns as Penacook, Contoocook, Wonalancet, Chocorua, and Kearsarge. It is in the names of New
Hampshire's natural features — its rivers, mountains and lakes
— that the Indian receives his due. There is scarcely a lake or
river of any consequence that does not have a name of Indian
derivation.

Elmer Munson Hunt emphasizes that most of our towns were
named for people, but there are others whose names appear to
have come directly from towns in England. Manchester and
Portsmouth are certainly the most important representatives
of this group, and both bear similarities to their English counterparts. Among some of the other towns so named were Rye,
Epsom, Gosport, Croydon, and Exeter. But this group of towns

is relatively few in number. A larger group come by their names "second-hand", via older towns in southern New England. The pioneer settlers who trekked north up the Connecticut River Valley transplanted to New Hampshire such Connecticut town names as Danbury, Lyme, Enfield, Plainfield, Stratford, Coventry (now Northumberland) — in all, about twenty towns so named. Another twenty or so owe their names to Massachusetts, including Plymouth, Salem, Roxbury, Groton, New Boston, Deerfield and others. There seems to be only one town name derived from Maine, and that is Gorham. Alexandria appears to have been named not for the Egyptian city, but Alexandria, Virginia; and Troy and Albany were probably named for their counterparts in New York State.

Then among all the names derived from people or other places, there is the rarity — the name freshly minted for the occasion. One such original invention is Gilsum, named for two of its proprietors, Gilbert and Sumner. Settlers from Barnstable, Massachusetts and Hampstead, Long Island made a similar compromise and called their town Barnstead. There were a few names that were made to fit the local topography; Bow for a bend in the Merrimack River; Hooksett for a similar geological conformation (or was it just a good place to fish?); and such others as Seabrook and Sugar Hill. Two others were given to describe the optimistic feelings of the grantees: Freedom and Success. Perhaps the pleasantest sounding names are Plaistow, an old English country word, and Charming Fare, the old name for Candia.

But the great majority of our town names, however derived, have their English origin in common. As Mr. Hunt wrote in his notes, "these early English names are distinguished by such suffixes as *town* or *ton*, *borough* or *bury*, *village* or *ville* (transplanted from the French), *worth*, *dale*, *ham* and *stead*. A map of New Hampshire would also show such topographical endings as *ford*, *hill*, *vale*, *field*, *wood*, *land*, *mount*, and *brook*, and the term *chester*, derived from the Latin word *castra* or camp."

No introduction would be complete without a word about how this book came to be written. It is really the product of one man's "retirement." Soon after Elmer Munson Hunt came to Salisbury, New Hampshire, following a lifetime career in journalism and advertising, he was appointed director of the New Hampshire Historical Society. His new post opened up an interest in the historical lore of his adopted state, which continued unabated until his death in May 1968 at the age of eighty-five. During his eleven year tenure at the state historical society — from 1944 to 1955 — Mr. Hunt researched and wrote numerous articles and papers, many of which appeared in the society's magazine *Historical New Hampshire*. A descendant of several early New England settlers himself, Mr. Hunt was particularly interested in the settlement and development of New Hampshire in colonial days. Three of his booklets laid the groundwork for the present volume: *Family Names in New Hampshire Town Histories,* published in 1946; *The English Background of the Wentworth Town Grants,* 1950; and *The Origin of New Hampshire Mountain Names,* 1955.

Following his second "retirement" — in 1955 from the New Hampshire Historical Society — the project received further impetus when Mr. Hunt was invited by the *Manchester Union Leader* to write some articles on the origins of New Hampshire town and place names. The series grew into a regular column that appeared in the paper for a decade or more, and covered nearly every town name as well as many other mountain, river and place names. This volume incorporates the great majority of these articles, many of them revised and expanded for book publication.

In a letter written before his death, Elmer Munson Hunt acknowledged his gratitude to all those who had given him help and encouragement in the preparation of this book, and to the many readers who wrote in response to his articles in the *Manchester Union Leader*. He said it would not be possible to thank everyone individually, except for a very few who were most directly involved with his work. He mentioned especially: his wife, the late Clara K. Hunt, for her devotion and patience in typing, proofreading and editing the articles as they were written; Mr. William Loeb, publisher of the *Manchester Union Leader,* who not only lent his encouragement and support to the project, but kindly gave his permission to adapt and reprint the articles for this book; the staffs of the New Hampshire State Library and the New Hampshire Historical Society; and Miss Stella J. Scheckter of the State Library who gave unfailingly of her time and help in the research for the book.

To Mr. Hunt's acknowledgments, we would also add a word of appreciation to Mrs. Katherine deP. Gilbert for her assistance in editing and arranging the book, and to Polly Hunt Adams for her cooperation in making her father's book available for publication. Thanks also go to Miss Scheckter again, and to Norbert B. Lacy, for the painstaking and thorough job of compiling the index at the end of this volume. It should be pointed out that, due to limitations of space, it was not possible to include every proper name in the index — there are a vast number in this volume. But all persons or places of any significance in the naming of the towns have been included. It is suggested that those who wish to read further into the families of early settlers consult Mr. Hunt's *Family Names in New Hampshire Town Histories,* published by the New Hampshire Historical Society.

WILLIAM L. BAUHAN

I

Dartmouth-Lake Sunapee Region

ACWORTH

ACWORTH, New Hampshire, located in the hilly country bordering the Connecticut River valley, received its first charter in 1752. In that year it was named Burnet, after William Burnet (1688-1729) who became colonial governor of Massachusetts and New Hampshire in 1728 and died in office the following year. Burnet, who was the son of the famous Bishop Gilbert Burnet of Salisbury, England, had served for eight years previously as governor of New York and New Jersey. His record was a distinguished one, and he was known as "a friend of civil and religious liberty."

No settlements were apparently made under this charter, and the proprietors made a regrant in 1766 under the name Acworth, probably after Sir Jacob Acworth of the British admiralty, associated in the West Indies trade with Portsmouth shipping interests.

Many of the new grantees came from the town of Ashford in Windham County, Connecticut, and included members of the families of Harper, Silsby, Keyes, Grout, Dickey, and Chatterton. Later settlements were made by the McClures, McKeans and others from Londonderry, New Hampshire. The town was incorporated in 1772.

A community known for its "hills and hollows," it was at one time famous for the cultivation of flax. Its Congregational Church, built in 1821 and still in excellent repair, is reputed to be one of the most beautiful architecturally in New England. The ordination of its minister, Phineas Cooke, known throughout the countryside as the "High Priest of New Hampshire," is said to have attracted a throng of more than 2,500 people.

Acworth was one of a group of country towns denied individ-

3

ual representation in the early state legislatures, a matter over which they protested with ultimate success.

ANDOVER

THE TOWN of Andover appears to have had as its first settler in 1748 a physician named Anthony Emery. Dr. Emery came there from Hampton after graduating from Harvard in 1736 and from him the town took its earliest name, Emerystown.

Dr. Emery took a leading part in raising a colonial force to assist the British in the capture of Louisbourg on Cape Breton Island, and in that campaign he served as surgeon under Colonel Blanchard in 1758. Upon his return he secured from Governor Benning Wentworth grants of land in his neighborhood for sixty soldiers who took part in the expedition, renaming the town New Breton, after Cape Breton where they had made their successful campaign against the French.

Cape Breton, an island 110 miles long, was considered an important citadel by northern New England, second only to Quebec. Its capture was desired not only for its fisheries, but for the prevention of French colonial expansion to the west along the St. Lawrence.

The incorporation of New Breton under the new name of Andover took place in 1779 following the outbreak of the Revolution. The name Andover was probably selected by Dr. Emery, since in that year the academy at Andover, Massachusetts, endowed by John Phillips, was completed. Dr. Emery was related by marriage to Mr. Phillips, and was his college-mate at Harvard in the 1730's.

Andover includes the settlements of Cillyville, Gale, and Potter Place. The last was named for Richard Potter, a famous magician of the last century who built a handsome farm and estate near Andover. Potter Place was established in 1844 as a station of the Northern Railroad, which had to remove his grave to make way for its tracks. Potter's remains were removed to a new site and the station named in his honor.

BRADFORD

First called New Bradford and then Bradfordton, this town was granted by Governor John Wentworth in 1771. It assumed its present name in 1787, the year of the national constitutional convention, when state by state was called upon to decide whether America would adopt its constitution or not. Eight states had ratified and one more was needed when the New Hampshire delegation convened at Exeter that year. The Anti-Federalists were strongly opposed to the Constitution, and prospects for approval seemed dim. By a parliamentary maneuver, however, the convention was adjourned for several months and reconvened at Concord. There under the leadership of Colonel Thomas Stickney of Bradford, as moderator, it approved ratification and New Hampshire forced the decision which gave America its constitution.

Colonel Stickney is celebrated in New Hampshire history as being the donor in 1790 of land and forty pounds to build the Merrimack County Court House in Concord, and a tablet in front of the Elks building commemorates his memory.

The town of Bradford did not, as is sometimes assumed, get its name from the famous colonial governor, William Bradford, but from its parent town of Bradford, Massachusetts, which in turn took its name from the historic town in West Riding, Yorkshire, England, named Bradford, or originally Bradforth.

As Bradford, Massachusetts grew in population, people of the surrounding neighborhoods — Haverhill, Salisbury, Kingston and others — migrated to the north. Those of Bradford followed suit and applied for New Hampshire grants, which were given them at the close of the Revolution in Bradford, New Hampshire, these being readily made by the new government. The town of Bradford was formed out of what was known as Washington Gore and parts of Washington and Newbury.

Bradford today also contains the villages of Bradford Center and Melvin Mills. Among its outstanding natural features are Silver Hill (1940 feet) and Lake Massasecum on the town's eastern boundary.

CANAAN

CANAAN is one of several New Hampshire towns chartered in 1761. It probably got its name at the suggestion of early settlers who had come from Canaan, Connecticut, which had been established in 1738.

Most of the grantees of Canaan, New Hampshire were Connecticut natives with such names as Spencer, Peck, Rathbun, Cady, Lamphear, Whiting and Chamberlain, some of them represented by as many as six members of the same family. The first moderator was Thomas Gustin, whose name had been abbreviated from that of his ancestor, Jean Augustine, who had come from France in the early 1600s and engaged in shipping at Falmouth (Portland) Maine, and later in Lyme, Connecticut.

Not all the grantees became permanent settlers and the town had to be resurveyed in 1769 and a new charter issued. A majority of Canaan's early families, however, remained in New Hampshire and their names may be found in our town histories.

Canaan, in Connecticut, is one of a long list of towns in that state with biblical names, which include Bethany, Bethel, Bethlehem, Gilead, Goshen, Hebron, Lebanon, and Sharon.

CHARLESTOWN

IN 1753, Governor Benning Wentworth named this Connecticut River town in honor of his friend, Admiral Sir Charles Knowles of the British Navy, who was then governor of Jamaica.

Sir Charles had a distinguished career, having gone to sea at an early age, commanded a ship under Admiral Edward Vernon in the war with Spain during the blockade of the ports of Porto Bello and Cartagena and served at Louisbourg in 1745, becoming its first English governor in 1746.

Charlestown was originally Number Four in a line of numbered towns on the Connecticut River border established by Governor Jonathan Belcher as "trading posts," or forts, others among them being named Dummer, Howe, Hinsdale, Shattuck and Bridgman, all administered by Colonel Ebenezer Hinsdale. The Colonel had graduated from Harvard in 1727, and served as chaplain of the forts and "missionary to the Indians." He built "Fort Hinsdale" at his own expense.

In recent years efforts have been made for the restoration of old Fort Number Four at Charlestown. Although these "river trading posts" had occasional misunderstandings with the Algonquin Indians from the north, their traffic with them continued for several decades, and brought considerable prosperity to the early colonists.

Among the grantees of Charlestown were the moderator, Phineas Stevens, and the families of Willard, Farnsworth, Sartwell, Spofford, Weatherbee, Holden, Hastings, Amsden and Johnson, the last named being that of a trader who once lost the confidence of his Indian "customers" and was taken by them to Canada, where he was later ransomed and returned, as related in a popular best-seller called *Johnson's Captivity,* in the early 1800's. Charlestown was the birthplace of two governors: Henry Hubbard, elected in 1842; and Ralph Metcalf, elected in 1855.

CLAREMONT

THE ONLY CITY of Sullivan County derives its name from one of England's most famous palaces called Claremont Castle in Esher, Surrey. It was named in honor of the first Earl of Clare, John Holles (1564-1637), whose daughter, Lady Arabella Holles, married Thomas Wentworth, the Earl of Strafford, governor of Ireland under King James I, and ancestor of Governor Benning Wentworth.

Claremont Castle was built in 1710 under the direction of Thomas Pelham Holles, a descendant of John Holles, who succeeded to the Earldom of Clare, and later became Duke of Newcastle. One of the great landowners of eighteenth century England, he was also active in government, serving as Secretary of State, 1724 to 1754, and for a brief time as Prime Minister. His cousin, Governor Benning Wentworth, undoubtedly visited

Claremont Castle during his residence in England in the 1740s, prior to becoming New Hampshire's first provincial governor. The architect of Claremont Castle was Sir John Vanbrugh, who also designed Blenheim Castle, now one of England's most famous landmarks, for the Duke of Marlborough.

When Thomas Pelham Holles died in 1768 Claremont Castle became the home of Lord Clive of India, who rebuilt it. In the early 1800's it became a royal residence, as the home of Princess Charlotte, the ill-fated daughter of King George IV. Queen Victoria spent much of her girlhood on the estate. It was later occupied by King Louis Philippe, in exile from France; he died there in 1850. The castle was later acquired by the British government, and is now occupied by a girls' school.

Claremont, New Hampshire was granted as a town in 1764 to cover a "six mile square" area bordering the Connecticut River, and the original settlement contained "the governor's farm." As a result of its population and industrial growth, Claremont was incorporated as a city in 1947. Among its landmarks is the first Roman Catholic church in New Hampshire, still standing where it was built in 1823.

CORNISH

THIS HISTORIC TOWN, with its many stately mansions reminiscent of colonnaded Greek revival architecture, celebrated its two hundredth birthday in 1963.

Originally known as "Mast Camp," probably because it was a shipping point for the tall masts which the English government floated down the Connecticut River on the way to England for use by the Royal Navy, it was established in 1763, and named for one of the distinguished admirals of the navy, Sir Samuel Cornish.

Admiral Cornish began his career as a lieutenant in 1739, in the employ of the East India Company. He served under Admiral Vernon in the West Indies campaign against Cartagena, and under Admiral Matthews in the Mediterranean. Later he became a rear admiral in the fleet which took the Philippines from Spain, and was successively vice admiral of the "White," "Red," and "Blue" divisions of the British navy. His duties brought him into contact with the Portsmouth shipping projects in which the early New Hampshire governors were engaged.

A large number of the first grants of land at Cornish went to members of the church at Greenland, presided over by Reverend James McClintock, who is famous for having preached the inaugural sermon at the first session of the Legislature in 1784, receiving fifteen pounds for doing so. Among the Greenland families so honored were the names of McClintock, Weeks, Haynes, Brackett, Cate, Bryant, March, Johnson, Huggins, Neal and Berry, all well known in New Hampshire history.

One of the boundaries of Cornish named in its original charter, bears the picturesque name of "Blow-me-down Brook."

Cornish has acquired national fame as a summer resort and for the many well-known artists and writers who have lived there. Among its residents have been Maxfield Parrish and Kenyon Cox, the artists; Austin Corbin, the financier who established the Blue Mountain Reservation; and Winston Churchill, the New Hampshire author and candidate for Governor in 1906. Most notable of all was the sculptor, Augustus Saint-Gaudens, famed for his portrayals of Lincoln and Sherman, who settled in Cornish in 1885. His home and studio, now known as the Saint-Gaudens Museum, were declared a National Historic Site in 1964.

CROYDON

CROYDON, unlike so many towns in this state which were named for historic personages, got its name from Croydon, a well-known suburb of London, England. Founded in the ninth century, the English Croydon is famous for its palace under which several archbishops of Canterbury are buried.

Croydon, New Hampshire, received its charter from Governor Wentworth in 1763, the same year as its neighbor, Cornish.

Among the grantees were twelve members of the famous New England Chase family, from whom were descended Salmon P. Chase, Supreme Court justice and member of Lincoln's cabinet, and Bishop Philander Chase of Ohio.

Also among the grantees was Captain Stephen Hall, whose grandson, Samuel Read Hall, born in Croydon in 1795, achieved fame as one of the first men to work out plans which resulted in much of the present American school system. He is reputed to have been the first American school teacher to use a blackboard.

Beginning as a school teacher, Professor Hall, who had graduated from Kimball Union Academy at Meriden, became a Congregational minister. While engaged in "mission" work he established a school for teachers in Concord, Vermont, becoming convinced, as he said, that "the entire system of education in America is defective and in need of drastic reform."

Professor Hall was at one time principal of the teachers' seminary at Phillips Academy in Andover, Massachusetts, and later held a similar position at Plymouth in this state. He wrote several textbooks of wide circulation, establishing himself as a foremost American authority on teaching.

DANBURY

DANBURY was not one of the original Colonial grants, but was formed from part of its northern neighbor, Alexandria, in 1795, and was named and incorporated the same year. The town derives its name from Danbury, England, which had been known in its early history as "Danebury," after a Danish camp established there in the eleventh century by King Canute. Danbury, Connecticut, which dates back to 1687, took its name from the same English town when it was settled by the early New England colonists.

New Hampshire's Danbury owes its beginnings to Major Joshua Tolford (or Talford) originally of Londonderry. Tolford, accompanied by General John Stark and others, was sent

in 1754 to make a survey of the Coos country, and was rewarded
with other grants in Lancaster, Lempster, Livermore, Thornton,
New London, and Alexandria.

Major Tolford became the first moderator of Danbury. Another of the original grantees, Jonathan Taylor, a felt-maker
from "the hat city" of Danbury, Connecticut, appears to have
suggested the name. Others among the early grantees of the
town were the families of Hoyt, Minot, Corliss, Dudley, Ford,
Topliff, Colby and Broadstreet. In the middle of the last century Danbury annexed additional land from the neighboring
towns of Wilmot and New Chester (now Hill). The town area
includes the villages of Elmwood and South Danbury.

DORCHESTER

DORCHESTER was one of a number of New Hampshire towns
chartered in 1761 by Governor Benning Wentworth. Its name
is sometimes assumed to have been taken from Dorchester,
Massachusetts, founded in 1630 and named for the county seat
of Dorsetshire, England. The English Dorchester had its origins
as a fortified Roman camp in ancient Britain.

It is more likely, however, that our New Hampshire town
was given its name in honor of one of the prominent men who
held the Dorchester title in the English peerage. An ancestor
of Governor Wentworth's was Henry Pierrepont (1606-80),
first Marquess of Dorchester and Earl of Kingston, a partisan of
the King Charles I in the English Civil War, member of the
Privy Council, and in later life noted as a medical scholar and
fellow of the Royal Academy. A successor to the Dorchester title
was Evelyn Pierrepont (1711-1773), who was created Duke of
Kingston in 1726 and was a contemporary of Wentworth's. He
took part in King George's War, fought at Culloden, and attained the rank of general, but died without heirs. The Dorchester title was granted again, however, to General Sir Guy
Carleton, who fought with Wolfe at Quebec in the French and

Indian War. He became the widely respected Governor-General of Canada and was created Baron Dorchester in 1786.

Dorchester, New Hampshire's list of grantees included Captain John Thompson of Kittery, who was appointed the town's first moderator. His ancestor, David Thompson, was one of the earliest settlers of the colony, and the one for whom Thompson's Island in Boston harbor is named. Six other members of the Thompson family had original grants in Dorchester.

Because of the failure of a number of grantees to take up their claims, a part of the land was regranted to a new list in 1766, and again in 1772, each time retaining the name Dorchester.

ENFIELD

ENFIELD, first named by a group of pioneer settlers from Enfield, Connecticut, was later called Relhan, and after nearly two decades reverted to its original name. In 1761 Benning Wentworth granted the town as "Endfield", but his nephew John, who succeeded him as Governor in 1766, regranted it to commemorate one of England's most talked about physicians, Dr. Anthony Relhan.

Dr. Relhan, a graduate of Trinity College, Dublin, Ireland, who set up his practice in the English seaside town of Brighton, conceived the idea of sea-bathing as a definite curative value for all manner of human ills. This was a new and startling idea in eighteenth century England. As a result of his writings, then much opposed by orthodox medical opinion, Brighton became one of England's most fashionable resorts, visited and endorsed by royalty — and it remains so to this day. Although Dr. Relhan's son became one of England's most noted botanists, his name as that of a New Hampshire town was abandoned following the Revolution. In 1784 the town was renamed Enfield, leaving the great English physician to the oblivion of medical history books.

Enfield achieved fame in the early 1800's as the site of one

of New England's Shaker religious colonies. The Shakers' handsome and enduring stone buildings beside Lake Mascoma are
now owned and occupied by the La Salette Brotherhood of
Montreal, Canada. Lake Mascoma itself, four miles long and
nearly 800 feet above sea level, is said to take its name from the
Algonquin Indian words meaning fish and water.

GOSHEN

GOSHEN, incorporated in 1791 under the administration of Governor Josiah Bartlett, was first settled when it was a part of
Saville, now Sunapee, which was granted in 1768.

The names of only three of the first settlers can be traced
to Goshen. They were Benjamin Rand, his brother-in-law,
William Lang, and Daniel Grindall. The last named is of special interest because of his relationship with Edward Rawson,
secretary of state for Massachusetts, who was descended from a
sister of a famous Archbishop of Canterbury, Dr. Edmund Grindall of London, and whose son, Reverend Grindall Rawson,
Harvard 1728, was an early New England missionary to the Indians. The Grindalls in New England spelled their name variously, Grindall, Grindell, and Grindle.

Benjamin Rand, after whom Rand's Pond in Goshen is
named, appears to have been related to Governor John Wentworth and received a grant from him in Whitefield in 1774.
William Lang, who married Rand's sister Elizabeth, had a
grant in Lisbon, in 1763. The three settlers, however, occupied
their land in Goshen as a result of a sale, or gift, by Captain
Thomas Martyn of Portsmouth, who, in return for his services
as keeper of military stores under General Amherst in the
French war, received large grants in Sunapee, Ellsworth, Springfield, Lyme and Northumberland. All three of the early settlers
appear to have fought in the French war, and Daniel Grindall
was a captain in one of the forces personally commanded by
Washington in the Revolution.

Although the settlement of what is now Goshen had grown

to a considerable size, it was not made a town until 1791 when its territory was made up from parts of Newbury, Lempster, Unity, Newport and Sunapee. The name Goshen appears to have been suggested for the town by residents who had relatives in Goshen, Connecticut, and who had served in the Revolution in a regiment composed largely of soldiers from the Connecticut town.

GRAFTON

THE TOWN of Grafton takes its name, as does Grafton County, from an enthusiastic, pro-American member of the English government during pre-Revolutionary days, Augustus Henry Fitzroy, whose numerous titles were Duke of Grafton, Earl of Arlington and Euston, Viscount Thetford and Baron Sudbury.

The Duke of Grafton was a relative of Governor Benning Wentworth, who granted the town's charter in 1761. The name was further perpetuated in our history when the original five counties of Grafton, Rockingham, Cheshire, Hillsborough and Strafford were established by his successor, Governor John Wentworth in 1769. These names were all chosen in honor of parliamentarians who favored conciliation with the Colonies under the English Wentworth or Rockingham administration, in power at the time.

The Duke of Grafton was a grandson of one of the several illegitimate sons of King Charles II. His great-grandmother was the famous Barbara Villiers, sister of the renowned Duke of Buckingham from whom comes the name Buckingham Palace. Secretary of State under Pitt, he was active in demanding the abolition of all taxes against the colonies, particularly the Stamp Act, which was repealed during his term in office.

One of the Duke of Grafton's titles, Viscount Thetford, became the name of a New Hampshire town, now in Vermont.

Some of the grantees of the 1761 charter of the town of Grafton having failed to take up their claims, the town was regranted in 1769 to a new group of colonizers. Among them was John

Hancock, later to be a signer of the Declaration of Independence, and James Otis, his fellow-patriot in Boston. Another of the grants was made to John Hurd, afterward a New Hampshire Chief Justice.

GRANTHAM

THIS TOWN took its name from the English diplomat and politician, Thomas Robinson (1695-1770), first Baron Grantham. The town was granted by Governor Wentworth in 1761, the same year his friend Robinson received his peerage from the King as Lord Grantham. A graduate and fellow of Trinity College, Cambridge, he entered the diplomatic service as minister to Paris under Sir Robert Walpole.

He achieved considerable fame as a diplomat, having been ambassador to Vienna, and one of those present at the negotiations leading to the signing of the famous Treaty of Aix-la-Chapelle in 1748. Returning to England, he became a member of the House of Commons and was one of Great Britain's first postmaster-generals.

Among those securing land under the Grantham charter were the families of Howe, Dunbar, and Leavitt, all of whom have Grantham hills named after them. The Leavitts are said to have had at one time fifty children in attendance at the town's school, and over the years no fewer than seventeen teachers.

Other grantees included Captain Joseph and Deacon Mark Langdon, sons of Tobias Langdon who was grandfather of New Hampshire's early governor, John Langdon; Captain John Kathan who fought in the Crown Point expedition, with his four sons, one of whom was a colonel and another a major in the Colonial forces; and Jonathan Wallis, who was succeeded by five generations on the same Grantham farm.

Lord Grantham was active in his support of American independence, and was once quoted as saying that the Colonies would ultimately "have to fight for their own altars and firesides."

GROTON

GROTON was first named Cockermouth in 1761, after Charles Wyndham, whose titles were Baron Cockermouth, and Earl of Egremont. He served as lord lieutenant of Cumberland and, as a member of Parliament, sided with Fox and Pitt in their efforts at conciliating the Colonies. Lord Egremont succeeded Pitt as secretary of state.

At the time of the original grant but few of the grantees took up their claims, the land being thought to be "so remotely situated that it proved impracticable to comply with the conditions relating to its cultivation," and it had to be re-granted in 1776 when some of its acreage was set aside for Captain Samuel Hale of Portsmouth.

The largest early land-holder was John Nelson of Boston, a relative by marriage of Governor Benning Wentworth, who was prominent in Boston affairs at the time the governor attended Harvard. The Nelsons were engaged in the West Indies trade with the Lloyds, after whom Lloyd's Hills, now Bethlehem, is named; and the Temples, from whom the name of the town of Temple comes. John Nelson's mother was the sister of Lieutenant Governor John Wentworth, Benning's father.

Among the late grantees was Samuel Blood of Groton, Massachusetts, one of the petitioners, who succeeded in 1792 in re-naming the town Groton after "Old Groton," in compensation for territory lost to Massachusetts as a result of the adoption of a new boundary line between that colony and New Hampshire, in 1741.

The town of Groton still retains its Cockermouth River.

HANOVER

THIS TOWN, granted in 1761, does not, as might be assumed, take its name directly from King George III of the German house of Hanover, who was the ruling English monarch at the time, but instead, from a small parish called Hanover in eastern

Connecticut. This parish was originally part of the town of Lisbon, Connecticut, and was adjacent to Norwich, Mansfield, Lebanon, Coventry, and Hebron, all in that state.

Most of the grantees of Hanover in New Hampshire came from these Connecticut towns, whose names are all duplicated in our own state and in Vermont, once a part of New Hampshire. The names of Hanover, Connecticut, and its counterpart in Massachusetts, no doubt, derived from the house of Hanover, which came to the English throne in 1714.

The list of New Hampshire grantees included such old Connecticut names as Freeman, Strong, Hatch, Walcott, Curtis, Squire, Bissell, Walbridge, and Storrs. Jonathan Freeman, of Mansfield, who acted as agent for the New Hampshire proprietors in assembling the group, received a grant of 140 acres and another member of his family, of which there were seven in the list, was Edmund Freeman who served as moderator of the first town meeting.

Governor Benning Wentworth who made the grant, observed in one of his letters that "a more pleasant spot on the Connecticut River cannot be found" and endorsed this in his choice of Hanover as the site of Dartmouth College with Eleazar Wheelock, minister at Lebanon, Connecticut, as its first president. Wheelock's first project was the education of the Indians, to which he later added the education of "English youths in order to their being fitted for missionaries among the Indians."

One of Hanover's suburbs has inherited the name Etna, after the famed volcanic mountain in Sicily.

HILLSBOROUGH

HILLSBOROUGH is the name given both to New Hampshire's most populous county and to the substantial town in its northwest corner. The town was granted originally by Governor Jonathan Belcher of Massachusetts in 1735 and called "Number Seven", one of a line of nine towns, known only by number and intended as defense barriers against Indian attacks from the north.

After New Hampshire became a separate province in 1741 and its boundary line with Massachusetts was readjusted, these towns lost their numbers and were given new names. Most of them honored English parliamentary figures of the time, many of whom were friends or patrons of Governor Benning Wentworth. Thus in 1748 "Number Seven" became Hillsborough, in honor of Wills Hill, Earl of Hillsborough, a member of the Privy Council, and later to be appointed president of the Board of Trade and Plantations and Secretary of State for the Colonies.

While this origin of the town's name seems to have been an accepted fact at the time, it has since been suggested in occasional records that it may also have come from one of the original Massachusetts grantees, Colonel John Hill, who had received land in "Number Seven" from Governor Belcher. Hill was a prosperous Portsmouth merchant, owner of a considerable estate in Greenland, and a member of Governor Belcher's Council.

With the transfer of this land to the new province of New Hampshire, Colonel Hill's title to it became the subject of dispute. The matter appears to have been settled by Governor Wentworth, who compensated him with generous grants in New Boston, Peterborough, Rindge, Temple and Cornish — in exchange for his Hillsborough rights — and by inference left the Colonel to share with the English Earl any honor due from the naming of the town.

Hillsborough County, one of the original five counties of New Hampshire, was not created until 1769 by Governor John Wentworth.

Hillsborough is notable as the birthplace of Franklin Pierce, fourteenth President of the United States. The Pierce Homestead, a handsome house of the Federal period, is maintained as a museum by the state. It was built by the President's father, General Benjamin Pierce, who served two terms as Governor of the state, 1827-29. A soldier in the Revolution at Lexington and Saratoga, Pierce became a surveyor after the war, assisting

Colonel Sampson Stoddard who mapped out much of south-western New Hampshire, and as a result chose Hillsborough for his home.

Hillsborough was also the birthplace of such notable men as Benjamin Pierce Cheney, builder of the Atchison, Topeka and Santa Fe Railroad; General John McNeil, who fought in the War of 1812; and David H. Goodell, Governor of New Hampshire 1887-89.

LANGDON

LANGDON was incorporated in 1787 and named for John Langdon, New Hampshire's second governor, or "president," as he was then called.

Governor Langdon had a distinguished career. His native town of Portsmouth was one of America's leading shipping ports, and Langdon ranked as one of the largest ship-owners in the colony at the time of the American Revolution. During the war the ships *Raleigh, Ranger, America,* and *Portsmouth* were all built under his direction for the Continental Navy.

Taking an active part in the Revolution, Colonel Langdon commanded a detachment of troops, and supplied the funds to equip General John Stark's victory over the English at the Battle of Bennington. He was a delegate to the first Constitutional Convention at Philadelphia in 1775 and subsequent conventions, where he paid his own expenses and those of his fellow-delegate, and served on a committee with Benjamin Franklin and John Adams to secure military supplies for the American forces.

Governor Langdon also was elected a member of the State senate, speaker of the House of Representatives, and delegate to the New Hampshire convention which ratified the United States Constitution.

Appointed president pro-tem of the Senate in the first United States Congress, Mr. Langdon supervised the canvass of electoral votes to elect Washington as President, and personally submitted

the report to him. He became governor of the state in 1787, and
later in 1805, 1808 and 1810, serving, in all, eight terms, the
longest service of any New Hampshire governor except that of
Governor John Taylor Gilman, who served eleven terms.

Soon after the town of Langdon was erected out of the adjacent towns in 1787, to honor Governor Langdon, a proposal
was made to extend its borders to the Connecticut River. But
the town voted against expansion, one of the few such instances
in New Hampshire history.

LEBANON

THE UNITED STATES has at least eight towns named Lebanon,
but none with quite the same historical background as the Lebanon of New Hampshire.

All these towns, of course, derive their name from the same
biblical source, from which came the famous "cedars of ancient
Lebanon" and the nearby mountain in that country now so
much in the public eye. It takes its name from the Semitic word
meaning "white," referring to the perpetual snows on its summit.

The oldest and best known Lebanon is that in Connecticut,
but it has much in common with New Hampshire; it not only
was the first pastorate of our own Eleazar Wheelock, who
founded Dartmouth College (from it came many of the early
Connecticut settlers who established Lebanon in New Hampshire as a town in 1761) — but was actually the original home
of the "Indian Charity School" from which Dartmouth is descended. It is likewise significant that our Lebanon once came
very near to becoming the home of Dartmouth College, being
one of several nearby towns considered.

Other American towns named Lebanon are located in Indiana,
Kentucky, Missouri, Ohio, Pennsylvania and Tennessee. All
seem to have taken their names from the Lebanon of Bible
times, the historic home of the sea-trading Phoenicians from

whom the Greeks obtained our alphabet and whose city of Beirut became one of the great cultural centers of the world.

Lebanon, New Hampshire, was incorporated as a city in 1957, the thirteenth town in the state to have that honor.

Among its citizens who have achieved prominence in political life are Senator Norris Cotton and Governor Lane Dwinell.

LEMPSTER

LEMPSTER was originally granted as "Number Nine" of the nine numbered towns created by Governor Jonathan Belcher of Massachusetts in 1735, and was regranted by Governor Benning Wentworth in 1753 as a New Hampshire settlement. A group of some seventy or more individuals was given land there by the proprietors under the name Dupplin, after Sir Thomas Hay, Lord Dupplin of Dupplin Castle, Scotland.

Lord Dupplin was much interested in the colonization of New England, serving as Lord of Trade and Plantations, as Lord of the Treasury, and was in charge of the settlement of Nova Scotia. He also held the post of chancellor of the University of St. Andrew's in Scotland.

In the regranting of towns after the Peace of Paris in 1761, it was found that the terms under which many of the grants were made in Dupplin had not been carried out and were thus forfeited, so that the town was regranted as Lempster, named for Sir Thomas Fermor (or Farmer) of Lempster, a contraction of the name Leominster, in Northamptonshire, England. Sir Thomas owned the ancient manor at Easton-Neston with its extensive gardens, and here he assembled one of England's earliest art collections, the wings of his gallery having been designed by Sir Christopher Wren. His exhibits included many rare paintings, statues, and other art treasures.

Sir Thomas, later created Earl of Pomfret, was related to the Wentworth governors in New Hampshire through marriage with the Wodehouse family.

Among the early settlers in Lempster, New Hampshire were

the Binghams. A descendant was James H. Bingham, who was a classmate at Dartmouth of Daniel Webster, and with whom Mr. Webster conducted a correspondence which includes his earliest collected letters, a series continued for almost fifty years. It was also the home of Alonzo Ames Miner, who was president of Tufts College for twelve years and made a gift of $40,000 for its Divinity Hall in the Tufts Theological School.

Massachusetts has its Leominster, also named for the English Earl of the same name.

LYME

LYME's original charter is dated 1761, the same year in which many of the towns, especially in this part of the state, were granted by Governor Wentworth. Situated on the Connecticut River, it takes its name from Old Lyme which lies at the mouth of the same river and was named by Governor John Winthrop in 1664 from Lyme Regis in England, then prominent in English history.

Most of the grantees in Lyme, New Hampshire came from the Massachusetts towns of Palmer and Brimfield and included Captain John Thompson, who was its first moderator, together with three members of his family. Also given land were the Shaws, from the same section of Massachusetts, of whom there were six members, and the Lamont family, of whom there were three. A number of the grantees, including the McIlvains, McNitts, McClethens, Bells, Leys and Kennedys were Scotch colonists from Londonderry, Ireland, some of whom had earlier become settlers of Londonderry, New Hampshire in 1718.

Lyme's fine old Congregational Church on the village green was built in 1812. To the east of it stand the original horse sheds, a rare example of meeting-house outbuildings still surviving from the early days of the town.

NEWBURY

NEWBURY, at the south end of Lake Sunapee, has had no less than four names in its history. The town began its life in 1753 under the name of Dantzic, which was a variation in the spelling of the famous Baltic seaport, Danzig. It is significant that two other towns in the same section of the state which were named at the time also bore German names, Dresden, now Hanover, and Heidelberg, now New London — all three so called at the time to commemorate the state visit of King George II, then ruling monarch, to his lands in Germany. The King of England at that time was also ruler of the kingdom of Hanover. It is worth remembering too that Governor Wentworth, himself, had visited Germany in his youth and no doubt brought back associations with that country.

The first provincial grant in 1754, however, called the town Hereford, in honor of Edward Devereaux, Viscount Hereford. This grant was made to a group of Benning Wentworth's friends who had been at Harvard College with him — among them, Jeremiah Gridley, Peter Prescott and Stephen Minot.

A number of these grantees not having fulfilled the terms of their grants, the charter was renewed in 1772 by Governor John Wentworth, and the town was given the name Fishersfield, after his brother-in-law Captain John Fisher, royal naval officer at Portsmouth. It continued under this name until 1837 when it was incorporated during the administration of Governor Isaac Hill, taking the name Newbury at the proposal of a number of settlers who had originally come from Newbury in Massachusetts. The source of the name is, of course, English and comes from the market town of Newbury in the County of Berkshire.

Newbury's great scenic attraction is Mount Sunapee, and a part of Sunapee Lake lies within its boundaries, as does the town of Blodgett's Landing.

NEW LONDON

NEW LONDON, like its neighbor Newbury, had several changes of name in colonial times, and began its existence in the same year, 1753, with a German name. It was called Heidelberg in Benning Wentworth's original grant (spelled by the grantees "Heidlebourg" and "Hiddleburg"). The name was given in honor of George II's visit to his German possessions at that time, and the choice was also undoubtedly influenced by Governor Wentworth's own extensive European travels some years earlier.

The town was granted again in 1773 by the Governor's nephew and successor, John Wentworth, as Alexandria Addition — after one of the neighboring towns to the north. This name was short-lived, however, and in 1779, during the American Revolution, it was incorporated as New London, or New Londonderry — some of the early settlers having come from Londonderry, New Hampshire. The ending was soon dropped, perhaps to avoid duplication.

New London's attractive scenic location in the center of a group of rivers, lakes and mountains has been said to resemble that of the delightful German university town of Heidelberg, its original namesake. Early settlers of the town included the families of Colby, Messer, Gay, Hastings, Austin, Fisher, Clement, Shepard, Kezar, Fales, Slack, Sargent, Woodward, and Minot. Anthony Colby, one of its distinguished native sons, was Governor of New Hampshire in 1846-47. Colby College for Women, founded in 1837, was named for him. New London includes the village of Elkins on Pleasant Lake.

NEWPORT

ALTHOUGH there are many towns and cities of Newport in America and England, Newport in New Hampshire is probably not named for any of them. It appears to have been incorporated in 1761 and named in honor of a distinguished English soldier and statesman then much in the public eye, Henry Newport, Earl of Bradford.

Settled in 1753, Newport was first called Grenville, after George Grenville, friend of the colonies and brother-in-law of the great supporter of American rights, William Pitt. Grenville, who served as First Lord of the Admiralty and Lord Privy Seal under Prime Ministers Pitt and Newcastle, was a relative of the English family of which Governor Benning Wentworth was a member, and Henry Newport succeeded him as a member of Parliament.

In addition to grants given to Massachusetts and New Hampshire settlers, Newport land was also granted to a considerable group from the town of Killingworth in western Connecticut. Among these early settlers was Gordon Buell, keeper of the Rising Sun Tavern in Newport, who was the father of one of the first woman editors in America. Sarah Josepha Buell Hale, his daughter, widow of David Hale of Newport, became the editor of the Ladies' Magazine, with costume pages in color, and later famous as *Godey's Ladies' Book*. She edited several books, among them *Poems for Children* which included *Mary Had A Little Lamb* which would become world famous as a nursery rhyme written by John Roulston, a Harvard student. Mrs. Hale's greatest claim to celebrity is probably her successful appeal to President Lincoln in the closing years of the Civil War for a national holiday to be known as Thanksgiving Day. In her lifetime she also campaigned strenuously to encourage the nursing profession and to improve health and sanitation. She died in 1879, and today is commemorated by the Sarah Josepha Hale Award given each year at Newport.

Newport has been the county seat of Sullivan County since 1827 when it was created, the new county comprising fifteen towns that had formerly been part of Cheshire County.

Newport's fame is associated with that of Edmund Burke, early New Hampshire editor and statesman, and Austin Corbin, founder of the Long Island Railroad, who once established a 26,000 acre game preserve at nearby Cornish, at a cost of more than a million dollars. Newport includes the villages of Kellyville, Guild, and Wendell.

ORANGE

ORANGE originally bore the name of Cardigan, so granted in 1769 by Governor John Wentworth in honor of his English friend, George Brudenell, fourth Earl of Cardigan, who was "warden of the King's forests, parks, chases and warrens," and who was related by marriage to the governor's cousin, the Earl of Dartmouth.

At one time Lord Cardigan was High Constable of Windsor Castle. One of his successors, the seventh Earl of Cardigan, James Brudenell, was in command of the famous "Charge of the Light Brigade," immortalized by the poet Tennyson. This disastrous action at Balaclava in 1854 in the Crimean war resulted in the death of all but 150 of its entire force of 600 men.

The town's original name is retained in Mount Cardigan, 3121 feet, and in Cardigan State Park. Cardigan had the distinction of having among its grantees four ministers of the church, the Reverends Abial Leonard, Samuel Drowne, Jonathan Fuller, and Alexander Miller.

During and after the American Revolution several attempts were made by the voters to change its name: first to Bradford, in 1779, then to Middletown in 1783, to Liscomb in 1789, and by the last and successful attempt to Orange, in 1790, which name appears to have been chosen because of the large deposits of orange-yellow ochre found in Mount Cardigan, which lies within its borders.

ORFORD

THIS TOWN, granted a charter in 1761, was named for the Earl of Orford, better known in the history books as Robert Walpole, England's first Prime Minister.

Walpole came from one of England's oldest families. He served as Secretary of War and Treasurer of the Navy and had great influence with the important figures of his time, including Lord Chesterfield and the Duke of Marlborough. He became

Prime Minister in 1721, remaining in that office for two decades, longer than any other man. His unsuccessful opposition to England's war with Spain in 1739, when he insisted that the country could remain prosperous without war, caused his resignation in 1742.

Orford, New Hampshire, first called No. 7 in the line of Connecticut River "fort-towns," numbered among its grantees ten members of the Moulton family and five Marstons. Another was General Israel Morey, whose son Samuel achieved national fame when, in experimenting with hydrogen gas, he discovered a way to separate it from the oxygen in water and applied it to the operation of America's first marine steam engine.

His "steamboat," first tried out on the river at Orford, was later exhibited in 1793 on the Hudson, and its operation explained by Morey to Robert Fulton, whose improvements brought him what Morey considered undeserved credit, Fulton's boat not having been completed until 1803.

Most of the grantees and first settlers of Orford were from General Morey's town of Hebron, Connecticut, and the original charter was amended to allow the first six women settlers "to have one cow each," to be brought from Hebron. Another grantee, John Mann, was descended from Sir Horace Mann, friend of the Earl of Orford, and ancestor of America's Horace Mann who is said to have established the first normal school in the United States. Orford's share in New Hampshire scenery includes its 2911 foot Mount Cuba, now called Mount Cube, and its Yosemite Cliff.

PLAINFIELD

PLAINFIELD is one of sixteen towns granted by Governor Benning Wentworth in 1761 at the close of the French War and the beginning of the reign of King George III. It is also one of several whose settlers were all from one section of New England. The early settlers of Plainfield came from the southeastern part

of Connecticut in the vicinity of its Plainfield, after which the
one in New Hampshire was named.

Among the Plainfield grantees were the families of Stevens,
Wood, Cutler, Cady, Waterman, Clift, Shepard, Gallop, Howe
and Spaulding. The last named family included seven members,
the ancestors of two New Hampshire governors. The Cutlers
had a descendant, Manasseh, who with Rufus Putnam helped
to form the Ohio Company, which settled the Northwest Territory. The Woods were the ancestors of the Reverend Samuel
Wood who conducted a private school in Boscawen, where
Daniel Webster prepared for Dartmouth.

A part of Plainfield was known as Meriden Parish, named for
the Massachusetts "farm" of Governor Jonathan Belcher. It
became the site of Kimball Union Academy, founded by one
of the members of an early Plainfield family, the Kimballs of
Preston, Connecticut. Daniel Kimball possessed a considerable
estate, and, after assembling a large collection of books, gave it
to the town in 1797 for a library, along with $6,000 for a school,
to which his widow added $40,000, with which to build the
academy in 1813.

SALISBURY

SALISBURY received its first grant in 1736, before New Hampshire became a separate colony, by Governor Jonathan Belcher
of Massachusetts. It was then named Baker's Town in honor
of Captain Thomas Baker, a famous Indian scout and explorer
from whom also comes the name of Baker's River.

After New Hampshire had become a separate colony, Governor Benning Wentworth regranted it as Stevenstown in 1749
— after Major Ebenezer Stevens of Kingston, Massachusetts,
who had been employed by him as a surveyor. The town was
also known for a time as Gerrishtown, after an early settler, and
New Salisbury, and finally in 1768 was incorporated as Salisbury.
While the name goes back to the ancient cathedral city of Salisbury, England, the New Hampshire town takes its name directly

from Salisbury, Massachusetts, which in turn had been called after James Cecil, Earl of Salisbury.

Under the proprietorship of Major Stevens a group of residents of his native Kingston took up grants in New Hampshire's Salisbury, among them the Bartletts, Websters, Sanborns, Pettengills, Sawyers, Fifields, Meloons, Calls, Fellowses, Scribners, Blanchards, Greeleys and Bohanans. They were presided over by their first moderator, Captain John Webster, who, with his nephew, Ebenezer Webster, constructed a sawmill in his grant from which came the finished lumber of a group of houses of English design which were among the first of their type in northern New England.

One of these spacious well-built houses was Ebenezer Webster's own Salisbury home. Father of ten children of whom the famous Daniel Webster was next to the youngest, he had been brought up as a boy in the family of Major Stevens in Kingston, served in the French war, and under General Washington as a captain in the War of the Revolution, enlisting for his company in the latter more than half the able-bodied men of Salisbury.

The town's area was originally one of the largest tracts in the state, including a good part of Mount Kearsarge, now partitioned among the neighboring communities.

SPRINGFIELD

GRANTED in 1769 by Governor John Wentworth, Springfield was one of several towns established by him in the last years of his term, which ended with the Revolution.

It has the distinction of being one of the few in this state in which an entire area was allotted to settlers from one town, this being the governor's native Portsmouth. The grantees were selected under the jurisdiction of Captain John Fisher, the governor's brother-in-law, a Royal Navy officer who was engaged in the West Indies trade. He named as grantholders a total of sixty leading families, among them the Sherburnes, Yeatons, Towles, Martins, Trefethens, Warners, Stoodleys and Jacksons.

Captain Fisher also received grants from Governor Wentworth in the adjacent towns of Newbury (once named Fishersfield), Bradford, Cornish, Alexandria, Sutton and Washington.

The new town, in 1769, was called Protectworth, possibly signifying its position as a "protection" for the other Fisher grants.

At the time of the Revolution, Captain Fisher chose to side with Governor Wentworth in his loyalty to his native England, and after his property had been confiscated by the colonies, returned to London, where he became secretary to Lord Sackville, who had been secretary to the colonies.

The town deprived itself of the unique and distinctive name "Protectworth" when, upon its incorporation in 1794, it adopted the name Springfield, one that is common to several notable American towns and cities.

SUNAPEE

DURING the two hundred years of its history, this town, like a number of others, has had four names. It was originally granted a charter in 1768 as Saville, out of respect for an illustrious English friend of the colonies, George Savile.

Sir George Savile was Secretary of War and an influential member of Parliament. After the repeal of the Stamp Act his followers energetically urged negotiations between England and America, but were not powerful enough to prevent the war which followed. There was included in the grant the name of Oliver Corey, a soldier in the French wars and later in the Revolution, whose settlement in the area was known as Corey's Town.

Oliver Corey's fellow-grantees included his sons Samuel and Oliver Jr., John Sullivan and Matthew Thornton (both to be famous as Revolutionary soldiers), and a number of prominent Portsmouth citizens, among them Nathaniel Treadwell, Foster Trefethen, William Yeaton, and John Wendell. The town was regranted in 1772 as Wendell, after the last named who was one of the Masonian proprietors.

The name Sunapee was substituted for Wendell by the Legislature in 1850 and the town incorporated by Governor Samuel Dinsmoor Jr. The town and the nearby mountain taking their names from its lake, once poetically described as being a "thing of tamed beauty, surrounded by a girdle of happy homes." The name Sunapee is thought to have been that used by the Algonquin Indians whose word "suna" means goose and "apee" lake, — Goose Lake, probably so called because it was once the favorite home of large flocks of wild geese. The town of Sunapee at one time contained more than 23,000 acres, but parts of it have been taken away in the past to form adjacent units of population. Sunapee today includes the territory occupied by George's Mills and Burke Haven. Wendell remains as the name of a village on the Sunapee-Newport boundary.

SUTTON

This town, first settled in 1748, comes by its name in a roundabout way, through Sutton, Massachusetts.

It was originally called Perrystown, granted to an Obadiah Perry, who applied to Governor Wentworth for land for some of his neighbors in Haverhill, Massachusetts. In that year Perrystown was Indian country and, as in those other north country settlements, many of the grantees dared not take up their grants for fear of being attacked. The land was adjacent to Mount Kearsarge and not highly desirable; and it is not surprising that all but a small percentage of the land owners forfeited their claims.

Thus after much litigation, following the Revolution, the six-mile tract was finally regranted in 1784 to a new group of citizens so that an entirely new town was incorporated under the name Sutton. The name was proposed by certain New Hampshire settlers who had come from Sutton, Massachusetts.

The name Sutton originated there through the then governor of Massachusetts, Joseph Dudley, son of Thomas Dudley of Dudley Castle in Northampton, England. The governor was descended from Sir John Sutton, Baron Dudley, and named the town in his honor. Governor Dudley was provincial governor of New Hampshire under Massachusetts for two years in the 1680's, so that the New Hampshire name of Sutton is properly derived from its English origin.

Sutton, New Hampshire, has the distinction of having a record of seventeen hills in its topography, and it also was the home of the Osgoodites, a religious sect. It provided two American governors, Matthew Harvey of New Hampshire and John S. Pillsbury of Minnesota.

UNITY

BUCKINGHAM was the name given this town by Governor Benning Wentworth when he first granted it in 1753. It was probably named in honor of John Hobart, lord lieutenant of County Norfolk, England, who was created first Earl of Buckinghamshire in 1746. His sister, Henrietta, Countess of Suffolk, was the mistress of George II, then King of England. The origin of this early town name has sometimes mistakenly been ascribed to the second George Grenville, Marquess of Buckingham, but he did not receive that title until 1784, over thirty years after Governor Wentworth's grant.

The original grantees of Buckingham included a number of Connecticut families, five of whom bore the name Stiles, and were related to the Reverend Ezra Stiles, president of Yale College. Other Stiles relatives were Timothy Goodwin who married Bethea Stiles, William Symes (Simms), and the Connecticut Bissells and Leavitts.

The name Unity was chosen to replace Buckingham for the town in 1764 because of a dispute between the Connecticut grantees and residents of Hampstead and Kingston, who claimed prior rights from the early Massachusetts government. "Unity," the legal name for a friendly settlement, was finally arrived at.

Unity once had the honor of having as the principal of its "Scientific and Military Academy" Reverend Alonzo Miner, who

later became, in 1862, president of Tufts College and who left
the college the sum of $40,000 to erect its "Divinity Hall."
Mount Miner in Rockingham County is named for him.

WARNER

THIS TOWN, granted as Number 1 in 1735 by Governor Belcher,
having been variously called New Amesbury, Jennesstown,
Waterloo and Ryetown, after coast-town colonizers, got its incorporated name of Warner in 1774, taking it from Jonathan
Warner, a leading citizen of Portsmouth and a relative of Governor John Wentworth. It was one of the last towns to be
established under English province rule, prior to the American
War of Independence.

Jonathan Warner occupied what is thought to have been the
oldest brick house in New Hampshire, built with great care in
the early 1700's by Captain Archibald Macpheadris, a prosperous
trader in furs, timber, wool and iron, whose large surrounding
farm acreage is said to have provided land for a thousand sheep
and twenty cattle. Upon the death of Captain Macpheadris his
property was inherited by his widow, the former Sarah Wentworth, who became the wife of Mr. Warner.

The "Warner House," as it is called, remains one of the most
frequently visited and admired of Portsmouth's many distinguished homes, containing fireplaces built with tiles imported
from Holland and walls papered with elaborately painted scenic
designs. It is said to have been from the tall roof of this house
that Benjamin Franklin made one of the first tests of his his-
torically famous lightning rod.

The early settlers of Warner included such New Hampshire
families as the Davises, Cloughs, Colbys, Sawyers, Pearsons,
Hoyts, Ordways, and Bartletts. One of its imposing homesteads
is that in the Davisville section built by Francis Davis, father of
General Aquila Davis and containing a spacious dance hall
with a "spring floor."

Warner has given New Hampshire two governors, Ezekiel

A. Straw and Walter Harriman, and its Nehemiah G. Ordway was governor of Dakota Territory. For many years Warner was the country home of United States Senator William E. Chandler.

Warner also includes settlements of Roby, Dimond, Bagley and Davisville.

WASHINGTON

WASHINGTON is one of the smallest of the many towns and cities in the United States named after General George Washington, but was undoubtedly one of the first to be so named. In December 1776 the town was incorporated by one of the first acts of Congress of the newly established American revolutionary government. Meshech Weare, New Hampshire's first "president" as the governor was called, made the recommendation.

Washington was known by other names, however, prior to the Revolution. It was first granted in 1735 by Governor Jonathan Belcher of Massachusetts as one of the numbered towns whose purpose was to form a protective barrier for the colony from Indian attacks in the north. Designated as "Monadnock Number Eight" in a line of towns, not surprisingly it failed to attract more than a few hardy settlers. But in 1752 it was renamed by Governor Benning Wentworth and called New Concord after Concord, Massachusetts, from which a group of Bay Colony grantees came to establish homes there. This group included the families of Farnsworth, Lowell, Brockway, Severance, Copeland, Safford, and Burbank.

Following the accession of John Wentworth as Governor of New Hampshire in 1767, the town was again regranted the next year as Camden, bearing the name of his friend, Charles Pratt, (1714-94) then Baron Camden, later to become the first Earl Camden. He was a distinguished jurist, a champion of constitutional liberties, and staunch defender of the rights of the American colonists. Camden served as England's Lord Chancellor and Chief Justice; the present towns of Camden in Maine, New Jersey and South Carolina are named for him.

WEBSTER

WEBSTER was originally a part of Boscawen. It was incorporated in 1860 and named in honor of Daniel Webster, the great American lawyer and statesman, who had died eight years previously.

Webster practiced law in Boscawen for two years, having earlier attended the private school at the north end of the town conducted by Reverend Samuel Wood, where he prepared for Dartmouth College. The site of the school is now marked by a bronze tablet.

In addition to having a town named for him, Webster, who served as Secretary of State during the administrations of Presidents Harrison, Tyler and Fillmore, also has named in his honor a mountain, Mount Webster (formerly Notch Mountain) and a lake, Webster Lake. An imposing bronze statute of Daniel Webster graces the entrance to the State Capitol.

Mr. Webster's father, Captain Ebenezer Webster of Kingston, was the owner of a large tract of land in what is now Franklin and Salisbury. Here he erected a sawmill and a house, now standing on state land, in which his son Daniel was born in 1782.

WENTWORTH

THIS TOWN obtained a charter in 1766, for a tract of land which it appears had been reserved by Governor Benning Wentworth for his own private estate. Finally regranted by John Wentworth, who upon his uncle's retirement succeeded him as governor, to a group of settlers, and named Wentworth in honor of Benning Wentworth. It was the first grant made by the new governor.

The list of grantees of Wentworth as a new town included for the most part families from Salisbury, Massachusetts, among them Major John Page who served as moderator, his five sons, and the families of Maxfield, Ames, Gove, Davis, Lunn, Pillsbury and Savage. Its location at the foot of Carr Mountain in the Baker River valley has long been pronounced one of New Hampshire's finest scenic areas.

The two Wentworth governors whose name it bears are credited with having issued in their more than thirty years of service no fewer than 152 charters establishing new towns in New Hampshire and 128 more in what is now Vermont, thus providing homes and farms in the hitherto undivided and unpopulated two million acres in northern New England for more than thirty thousand families.

To many of these towns they gave their present names, often those of English parliamentarians who were in sympathy with the desire to see American independence take place. To the foresight of these two governors may also go the credit for having, in a critical period in American history, established a two-state "barrier" colony, as Franklin called it, to ward off possible invasion on its northern and western borders. The naming by them of a town called Wentworth thus honors a family of great significance in New Hampshire history.

WILMOT

ORIGINALLY a part of New London, Wilmot was not established until the early days of the American Republic. The town was carved out of the "gore" of Mount Kearsarge in 1807, long after most of our town names were issued. Wilmot took its name in honor of an Englishman — not from a member of the titled nobility as many other towns did — but from a scholar and clergyman. Dr. James Wilmot was a fellow of Trinity College, Oxford, and rector of the church at Barton-on-Heath in Warwickshire, England.

Dr. Wilmot never came to America, but he belonged to a group of London "radicals" in pre-Revolutionary days who protested vigorously against the treatment of the New England colonies by the English crown. This group was led by William Pitt, Earl of Chatham, Edmund Burke, and the Marquess of Rockingham, a cousin of our Wentworth governors. They came into prominence through the circulation of the "Junius" letters, promoting freedom of the press and the rights of the colonies, in the late eighteenth centurty.

Dr. Wilmot was rumored to have been the author of these letters. He denied their authorship — although agreeing with their contents — and the author was later found to be Sir Philip Francis. Among the group was Herne Tooke, a friend of Voltaire, who promoted a fund to "pay the relatives of Americans murdered at Lexington and Concord by the King's troops," and William Bosville of Gunthwaite, who gave the famous "four o'clock" dinners to the group.

The naming of Wilmot in 1807, the year of Dr. Wilmot's death, probably came about through the friendship of Eliphalet Gay, one of the first settlers of the town, with Bosville, with whom he had fought together in Canada. General Gay was a tavern-keeper at Wilmot, represented the town in the legislature, and served as its first selectman. He is commemorated in one of America's rarest books, a copy of which is in the State Library. This is a poem by Ernest Vinton Brown, called *Eighteen Hundred and Froze to Death,* relating how, in the "coldest ever known" winter of 1816, when "the cellars were empty and the bins were bare," General Gay refused to sell his corn and hay to speculators and gave it freely to his neighbors. General Gay commanded the 30th New Hampshire Regiment in the Revolution.

WINDSOR

ONE OF New Hampshire's smallest towns, Windsor was originally known as Campbell's Gore and appears to have taken its name from Windsor, Connecticut, the home of James Campbell and his son, James Campbell, Jr.

The Campbells, whose name appears in the early records as Cammell, were among those who received grants in the new town of Thornton in 1768, and later migrated to the Hillsborough section, bringing with them a group of Connecticut settlers, which included the families of Chapman, Jones, Dresser, Lovejoy, Knowlton, McCintock and Atwood.

The town was incorporated as Windsor in 1798. Although it appears to have prospered in its early days through the establishment of several mills, one of the first annual town reports stated that it had "no church, no minister, no doctor, no store, no post office, no hotel, no voice in the legislature, no paupers, no drunkards, and no troubles, with no prospect of having any."

Although one of New Hampshire's smallest towns, Windsor has shown a growth of twenty per cent in the past decade.

II

Lakes Region

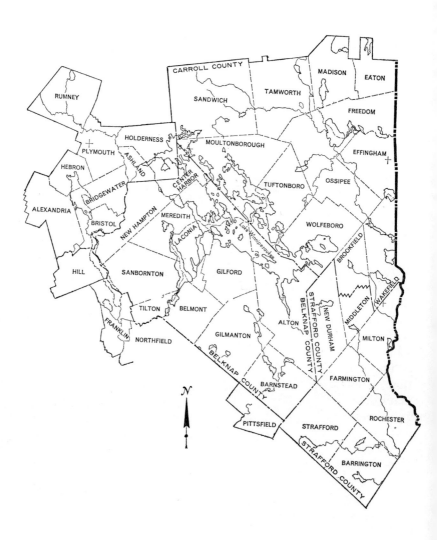

ALEXANDRIA

GRANTED in 1753 by Governor Benning Wentworth, the derivation of this pleasant-sounding town name has long eluded research and guesswork. It comes not from Alexander the Great or Alexandria, Egypt, as might be supposed, but from America's own Alexandria, Virginia. The Virginian town was the scene of an event much publicized in the mid-1700's that was to anticipate the eventual federation of the colonies.

The choice of the name was a significant one, for in the same year, five colonial governors met at Alexandria, Virginia for the first joint conference of governors ever held in America. Present were Governors Shirley of Massachusetts, Morris of Pennsylvania, Delancey of New Jersey, Sharpe of Maryland, and Dinwiddie of Virginia. Each of them was assigned the task of protecting his own territories. Such protection was declared to be sorely needed since the French government, then at war with England, had established a string of forts or trading posts which almost completely surrounded the American colonies.

Thus the Alexandria conference became in effect a declaration of war, an event which the naming of Alexandria in New Hampshire commemorates. English history calls this the Seven Years War, while in America it has become known as the French and Indian War.

New Hampshire, then closely allied with Massachusetts, whose Governor Shirley was an English relative of our Governor Wentworth and who with the help of our troops had captured Louisbourg a few years earlier, supplied both arms and soldiers in this war. It began in Pennsylvania with Braddock's defeat at Fort Duquesne, and ended with the conquest of Canada by General Wolfe at Quebec in 1759.

Alexandria in Virginia, originally Belhaven, was named for his daughter by John Alexander, who helped to resettle it in 1731. Alexandria in New Hampshire became famous as having been the birthplace of Luther C. Ladd, the first enlisted soldier to lose his life in the Civil War. One of the town's scenic attractions is Mount Mowglis, commemorating the hero of *The Jungle Books* by Rudyard Kipling.

ALTON

FRONTING on Alton Bay in Lake Winnipesaukee and bordering on New Durham. Alton was originally called New Durham Gore, a name indicated by its rocky terrain carved into Mount Major.

The early settlers, coming first from Roxbury in Massachusetts to Roxbury in Connecticut (later called Woodstock), and from there to the "Gore," included many long-established New England families, bearing the names of Hurd, Chamberlain, Bond, Meader, Allard, Lyon, Child, Alton and Bugbee.

In this group were Revolutionary soldiers who had fought in the north country under General St. Clair and who received grants from him after he was made governor of Northwest Territory under the Ordinance of 1787, for the new "bounty land" in Illinois administered by the fiscal agent and explorer, Manasseh Cutler, born in Connecticut's Killingly, near Woodstock.

In 1796, following the Revolution, the New Durham Gore settlers applied to the state of New Hampshire for incorporation, and asked to have their town named for their home town of Roxbury. As there were already two New England Roxburys, a compromise appears to have been arrived at, and the incorporation made under the name Alton, that of one of the prominent Roxbury families among the new settlers. John, David, and Captain Joseph Alton were land owners in the town at the time.

The western migration from Alton in New Hampshire appears to have resulted in the naming of Alton, Illinois, and there is also a town near it named Merrimack. Alton in New Hampshire was one of the earliest camp meeting sites in the state.

ASHLAND

ASHLAND originally formed the southwest section of Holderness and was not separately incorporated as a town until 1868. It is one of several towns in the United States bearing the name, the earliest probably being Ashland, Hanover County, Virginia, birthplace of Henry Clay, the nineteenth-century statesman, Secretary of State, and Senator from Kentucky. Clay adopted the name Ashland for his country estate in Kentucky, and it was in his honor that Ashland, New Hampshire was named.

Senator Clay came to New England in the 1830's during one of his campaigns as Whig candidate for President of the United States. He was given a reception at Brighton, Massachusetts, where he also exhibited some of his prize Durham and Hereford cattle at the annual livestock fair. As a result of this visit, James Jackson, a prominent mill owner from Unionville, Massachusetts, suggested renaming that town Ashland in honor of Clay's Kentucky home.

Another admirer and political follower of the Kentucky statesman was Colonel Thomas P. Cheney of Holderness, New Hampshire. As a young man he had been assistant sergeant-at-arms in Congress during Clay's service in Washington, and in the 1850's after Clay's death he was active in the formation of the Republican Party (successors to the Whigs) in New Hampshire. Cheney took part in the Civil War, and in 1868 was a delegate to the Republican National Convention which nominated General Grant for President. In that year, when the new town was being formed from part of Holderness, Colonial Cheney proposed the name Ashland in memory of his late friend and political mentor.

Members of the Cheney family were among the early settlers of the Ashland section of Holderness, as were those with the names Livermore, Cox, Ames, Rollins, Scribner, Peaslee, and Dustin. One of their descendants, Person C. Cheney, was elected governor of the state in 1875.

BARNSTEAD

GRANTED in 1727 by Lieutenant-Governor John Wentworth, Barnstead was one of a dozen or more towns established by Massachusetts in the early eighteenth century, when New Hampshire was under the jurisdiction of that province, to take care of its rapidly expanding population.

The Reverend Joseph Adams of Newington was entrusted with the task of finding new settlers, and he enlisted many grantees in the older towns along the New England coast. Some of them came from Barnstable on Cape Cod and others from Hampstead, Long Island — then settled by Connecticut colonists. It was from the first and last syllables respectively of those two town names that Barnstead, New Hampshire was named.

Mr. Adams, who graduated from Harvard College in 1710, was an uncle of President John Adams, who visited him often and described his sermons as "preached in a powerful and musical voice, quoting texts and chapters of Scripture without notes." While he owned some land in Barnstead, Joseph Adams's parish was in Newington, where he was minister for sixty-eight years until his death in 1783 at the age of ninety-four.

Among the early settlers given grants in the new town were the families of Emerson, Tasker, Bunker, Chesley, Lord, Jenness, Lougee, Nutter, and Garland. Barnstead was one of the first New Hampshire towns to have its "parade" or central highway on the famous "province road." A century or more later, in 1840, part of Alton was annexed to the town.

Barnstead today contains three villages within its boundaries, South Barnstead, Center Barnstead, and Barnstead itself. The town has no less than nine lakes and ponds, of which the Suncook Ponds are the largest. Another important natural feature is the Belknap Mountain Range.

BARRINGTON

ONCE the third most populous town in the state — ranking only after Portsmouth and Gilmanton — Barrington bears a family name of the English governor of Massachusetts and New Hampshire, Samuel Shute of Barrington Hall. The governor's elder brother was John Shute, Viscount Barrington, who was a lawyer and leader of the Presbyterian dissenters in the reign of Queen Anne.

Governor Samuel Shute had fought with Marlborough at Blenheim, and upon coming to the colonies had negotiated one of the first treaties with the Indians. At the same time he gave official encouragement to the new settlers from Scotland who came here in 1718.

Governor Shute was probably the first chief magistrate to promote new industries in this state. He set aside what was known as the "two-mile strip" in the vicinity of Dover, which would be a part of the town he named Barrington in 1722, for the purpose of securing and smelting iron ore on the Lamprey River.

Among the grantees was Captain Archibald Macpheadris who had charge of the project. Captain Macpheadris, an enterprising trader and merchant in Portsmouth, with ships going to Cork, Belfast and Dublin, also sought new colonists from abroad, to each of whom he offered a hundred acres of land in the "two-mile strip" for twelve pence an acre. In one of his advertisements he referred to the "grait iron mines upon the river" and he "wants men that understand ye making of iron, wch might be brought to grait fashion." He married a daughter of Lieutenant-Governor John Wentworth and built the famous Warner House which is still standing in Portsmouth.

Governor Shute also made efforts to encourage the production of earthen ware, tar and turpentine, and flax for linen, by the settlers of Barrington, and induced the English government to remove the tax on lumber exports.

BELMONT

THIS TOWN was not named, as has sometimes been assumed, after the Earl of Bellomont, governor in 1701 of Massachusetts of which this state was then a part, but as now established, for August Belmont, the famous New York financier in Civil War days.

The town of Belmont was originally a part of Gilmanton which was first chartered in 1727 to a group of settlers from Exeter, and included twenty-four members of the Gilman family, all of whom received grants and after whom it was named. Like most early towns, Gilmanton became separated into parishes, among them Upper and Lower Gilmanton, Gilford, Gunstock, and Gilmanton Iron Works. Up to 1859 Belmont was known as Upper Gilmanton, and so incorporated in that year.

Following the Civil War, with the extension of postal facilities, there being several post offices called Gilmanton, the voters in what is now Belmont met and came to the conclusion that the similarity of the name Upper Gilmanton to those of neighboring parishes was confusing and undesirable. They petitioned the legislature to rename their town Belmont, "after August Belmont of New York."

So far as is known Mr. Belmont was unaware of this petition. His only relation to New Hampshire was the remote one of having been appointed by the state's former governor, afterward President Franklin Pierce, to be ambassador to The Netherlands. Nevertheless, perhaps because of his wealth and prominence, the fifty-eight voters who attended the town meeting in Upper Gilmanton in 1869 not only adopted his name for their town but voted to notify him that the name "had been chosen as a mark of honor to him" and "to invite him to make a donation to the town as a token that he appreciates this action."

The records of Belmont do not indicate that such a donation was ever made by Mr. Belmont or that he ever even took the trouble to acknowledge the act. In extenuation of his lack of interest it should be pointed out that Belmont died in 1869. August Belmont married a daughter of Commodore Matthew

Perry who concluded the first treaty with Japan, and to whom he erected a statue at Newport, Rhode Island.

Among the many famous citizens who have lived in what is now Belmont was William Badger who, in 1834, was elected to office by one of the largest majorities ever given a New Hampshire governor. Belmont borders on Winnisquam Lake and also includes the town of Winnisquam.

BRIDGEWATER

AMONG the first towns to be granted following the war of the Revolution, Bridgewater received its charter in 1788.

It was then a part of the town of New Chester, which later became Hill, and the Bridgewater incorporation papers were signed by John Sullivan, New Hampshire's "president," afterward called "governor."

The then town of New Chester was one of the largest ever granted, and the new town of Bridgewater was one of four carved out of it, the others being Bristol, and parts of Danbury and Wilmot. It included a considerable part of Newfound Lake. Among the first families to settle in that section were the Fletchers, Dolloffs, Heaths, Woodmans, and Mitchells, the last of whom included four members of that name, all from Bridgewater, Massachusetts, who appear to have chosen the new town name.

Bridgewater, Massachusetts, made a town in 1656, was the first to be established in the interior of that province. It appears to have been named in honor of John Egerton, first Earl of Bridgewater in England, who was prominent during the reign of King Charles I, and was a friend of the poet Milton. He died in 1649. His great-grandson, Francis Egerton, third Duke of Bridgewater (1736-1803) constructed many canals and was the originator of inland navigation in Britain.

The Egertons' title appears to have been taken from the town of Bridgewater (without the "e"), situated in the west country of England. Bridgwater Bay is part of the Bristol Channel.

BRISTOL

EVERY New England state has a town by this name, most of them probably taken directly from the busy English seaport, except for Bristol, Vermont which was named in 1762 for George Hervey, Earl of Bristol, a privy councillor under George III.

New Hampshire's Bristol, however, seems to have taken its name only indirectly from the English city. In the early days it was discovered that the terrain of the New Hampshire town produced a type of alluvial deposit of fine sand or clay which had the same characteristics as that used in Bristol, England to make its famous china, earthenware and pottery. It thus became known in America as "Bristol sand." A product of the land adjoining Newfound River, Bristol Mountain, and Newfound Lake, New Hampshire's "Bristol sand" was used to make a superior quality of brick which was marketed as "Bristol brick," and in considerable demand in the early 1800s.

Bristol enterprises seem to have outnumbered those of many early New England towns, and included the manufacture of paper, leather, woolen goods, flannel, strawboard, flour, croquet sets, crutches, piano stools, bed-steads, and wooden pillboxes.

The town was originally a part of Hill and Bridgewater, and was incorporated in 1819. Much of its land was first owned by Captain Jonas Minot, whose service in the French wars was rewarded by grants in Alexandria, Sutton, Bridgewater and New London. Other early settlers included the Tolford, Sleeper, Flanders, Clough, Ingalls, Dearborn, and Colby families.

BROOKFIELD

THE NAME of this town was originally intended to be Coleraine, and it was settled under Massachusetts in 1726 by Scotch-Irish immigrants from the Irish town of that name. Most of these, however, finally found new homes in our Londonderry. Later

Brookfield, as now named, had become a part of Middleton, from which it was separated as an independent town in 1794.

Brookfield's unusually fertile area at once attracted purchases by would-be farmers, and by 1796 a survey of cattle-owners in the town indicated a total of no fewer than ninety-six individuals. Most of the early settlers were from Massachusetts, and included the families of Chamberlain, Hanson, Lyford, Toscan, and Whitehouse. The growth of the town was so rapid that in 1826 the New Hampshire General Court voted to ignore the usual restrictions and give it full representation.

Brookfield is surrounded by mountains, two of which have picturesque names — one of them "Tumble-down-Dick" which recalls a local Indian legend about a blind horse which couldn't "make the grade," and the other "Copple-crown," its shape suggested a crested bird's head.

Colrain in Massachusetts had one of the two earliest "Scotch-Irish" settlements in that state, its colonists arriving in 1718. The Massachusetts' Brookfield, from which the Brookfield of this state appears to have derived its name, was established in the same year.

CENTER HARBOR

THIS TOWN shares the credit for its name with the two best known harbors of Lake Winnipesaukee, Meredith Harbor and Moultonborough Harbor, of which it was long considered to be the "center," and with the famous Senter (or Center) family which at one time owned considerable property there.

The question of the true origin of the name, whether that of location or family, first arose at the time the town was incorporated in 1797 after its having been separated from New Hampton. Prior to that time application was made to have the new town called Watertown, but it was felt that this name might also be said to apply to other towns on the lake. So a compromise name was chosen, and it was called Center Harbor (spelled Centre), pleasing all parties including the Senter family. The town later became one of New Hampshire's most important summer resorts, being a landing place for the lake steamers and a stagecoach terminus for tourist passengers.

John Senter, founder of the Senter family, was a proprietor of Londonderry in 1719. His son Joseph who had been captured by the Indians and taken to Canada, escaped and with his brother Samuel settled on grants given to their father in Albany, Chatham, and Eaton. The Senter House at Center Harbor, of which they were proprietors, was long known as one of the most popular hotels in the Lakes region.

The incorporators of Center Harbor included Senters, Adamses, Moultons, Greeleys, and Parkers, all of whom were related, the Senters spelling their name variously as Senter, Scenter, and Center. Center Harbor was once the favorite summer resort of the poet John Greenleaf Whittier. It was also the home of Dudley Leavitt, who first issued his famous *Farmer's Almanac* in 1797.

EATON

EATON bears the name of one of New England's best loved and longest-serving governors, Theophilus Eaton of Connecticut.

Governor Eaton had been a "prosperous and fashionable" merchant in London, and had contributed generously to the funds needed to settle Massachusetts in 1630. Later he came to America to "explore" the coast, and founded a colony which he financed, at New Haven, Connecticut. He was accompanied by John Davenport, his school classmate, and David Yale, great-grandfather of Elihu Yale, founder of Yale College, purchasing the land from the Pequot Indians.

Eaton was elected governor of the colony for nineteen successive years until his death in 1658, having laid out the town in squares, in a design said to have been the best ever carried out in early American times.

The naming of Eaton, New Hampshire resulted indirectly through Governor Eaton's marriage with Anne Lloyd, daughter of the English Bishop of Chester, and that of his daughter Mary Eaton, with Valentine Hill of Boston. Governor Benning Wentworth was long-time friend of the Lloyd family in Boston and of the Hills, who at one time owned a considerable estate in Greenland, which town Valentine Hill represented in the General Court in 1655.

Valentine Hill's grandson, Valentine, was appointed by Governor Wentworth a lieutenant in the Seven Years War with France, and received grants in Dover, Canterbury, and New Durham in New Hampshire.

Governor Wentworth granted Eaton in 1760. The original town grant contained 23,000 acres, and the grantees included Walter Bryant, who surveyed most of the towns in eastern New Hampshire, and a considerable number of soldiers who had fought in the French wars. Eaton was the home of "Squire" Thomas Randall, early New Hampshire poet.

SNOWVILLE, the picturesque name of a part of the town of Eaton, is not, as might be supposed, that of a popular winter ski center. The Snows, from whom the name comes, were an old New England family descended from Nicholas Snow, a Massachusetts Bay Colony pioneer. In 1825 Joseph Snow came to New Hampshire by way of Maine "with an axe and a gun and a bag of corn." He built a sawmill at Snowville and turned out the wide boards needed to provide homes for his family and their neighbors for many years. By 1853 they were making furniture at the mill; a few years later coffins; in 1860 clippers and bobbin machinery; and in 1881 carriages and sleighs, while the coming of the 1890's found the original "factory" listed again, as it had been in the first town records, as a sawmill, still owned by the Snows. Snowville, as a busy part of Eaton, had its own post office in 1883, and is still listed in the *U. S. Postal Guide*.

EFFINGHAM

EFFINGHAM was granted in 1749 by Governor Benning Wentworth, and its name was taken from the Howard family of England, who were the Earls of Effingham and were related to the Wentworths by marriage. Francis Howard of Effingham, a distinguished soldier, was created first Earl in 1731, and his son and grandson, who succeeded him, were deputy earl marshals of England. They were descended from Lord Howard of Effingham, admiral and political figure of Tudor times, and uncle of Catherine Howard, fifth wife of Henry VIII.

The first settlers of Effingham were the Leavitts of Hampton, led by Captain John Leavitt, a soldier, who fought the French and Indians at the battle of Lake George, and whose father, Moses Leavitt, was a prosperous Hampton tavern keeper. From them the settlement first took the name Leavittstown.

One of Captain Leavitt's cousins, Benjamin Marston of Salem, nephew of Governor Leverett and a classmate of Governor Benning Wentworth at Harvard, became interested in the new town, renamed Effingham by the governor, and together they induced no less than twelve other Marstons to take grants there, along with fifty others sharing in its thousand acres of north country wilderness.

Captain Marston, like Governor Wentworth, was a ship owner and trader, dealing in molasses and sugar from the West Indies, and importing the fine wines as well as the salt so much needed by the New England fisheries from Spain and Portugal. In the year 1719 one of Captain Marston's ships, the brig *Essex*, returned from a Spanish voyage by way of Ireland, bringing back to America one of the first shiploads of "Scotch-Irish" passengers to settle in New Hampshire. Captain Marston owned a considerable estate on what is now Summer Street in Boston, where he was a member of the Massachusetts House of Representatives and a high sheriff.

Effingham was not officially incorporated until 1778, after the Revolution had begun. Outstanding features of the town are Green Mountain on the north side of Province Lake, and the fine old church on Lord's Hill, built in 1798.

FARMINGTON

FARMINGTON was originally known as "Farmington Dock," so named because of its location on the Cocheco River, where the land adjacent to the river at that point was used to store logs waiting to be sawed into lumber. It was then the "West Parish" of Rochester, which included the large farms of Aaron Wingate and others, all of which were separated from Rochester in 1798, to become Farmington. Although there are towns by the same name in Maine and Connecticut, Farmington, New Hampshire appears to have been named for its farms and fertile land.

The area is interrupted only by the Blue Mountain Range, one of its peaks being called "The Blue Job" after Job Allard, an early settler. Other pioneers included the Portsmouth and Dover families of Waldron, Canney, Drowne, Berry, Varney and Runnells.

Like many New England towns, Farmington's first industry was a sawmill on its river. This was soon expanded into a shoe-making factory operated by Elijah Badger of Natick, Massachusetts, who, with other plants owned by Hayes, Herring, Edgerly, Cloutman, and Nute, replaced hand shoemaking with improved machinery, thus creating one of the first "automation centers" in America. Most of the shoes so made were shipped to the marketing town of Natick.

One of the many who entered the shoe trade at the time was the self-educated Jeremiah J. Colbath of Farmington, who became known as the "Natick Cobbler." Colbath officially changed his name to Henry Wilson, and was elected Vice-President of the United States during the term of U. S. Grant. He had previously been chosen senator from Massachusetts, and while Lincoln was President was chairman of the Senate Military Committee and one of the great anti-slavery leaders of his time.

Wilson began his political career as a Whig, but became a Republican after he was elected to the Senate in 1855. He received the nomination as Grant's running mate at the Republican National Convention of 1872, but Wilson did not live to serve out his term as Vice-President. He died in office in 1875, aged sixty-three.

FRANKLIN

THE CITY of Franklin was originally known as Pemigewasset Village, located at the junction of the Pemigewasset and Winnipesaukee Rivers where they meet to form the Merrimack. It is one of the largest "new towns" in the state ever to be carved out of other surrounding towns.

Incorporated in 1828 during the administration of Governor Benjamin Pierce, Franklin was set up to comprise parts of Salisbury, Andover, Sanbornton and Northfield. The largest section was known as "Salisbury Lower Village," at one time the location of the "Call Farm," later owned by Colonel Ebenezer Eastman and afterward by Captain Ebenezer Webster, father of Daniel Webster who spent his boyhood days there. The homestead, located on Route 127 in Franklin where Webster was born on January 18, 1782, attracts many thousands of visitors every year. Webster Lake nearby is named in honor of the statesman.

The name Franklin, in commemoration of Benjamin Franklin, was first adopted in New Hampshire in 1820 when one of the mountains in the Presidential Range was named in his honor. The town of Franklin, which became a city in 1895, came into national prominence through its machine-made hosiery mill, operated under the process developed by the New Hampshire Shakers in the 1870's.

FREEDOM

THIS distinguished town name is not associated with American independence, as sometimes assumed, but came about instead through the same simple process as has frequently occurred in this state, the separation of a section or parish of an established town from its parent. In this case the parent town was Effingham, and the one which gained its "freedom" in 1831 was North Effingham, which a year later became Freedom.

The separation, however, was more than the result of some

of its people desiring a town of their own. It was caused, in great part, by the influx of a considerable colony which crossed the border from neighboring towns in Maine, attracted by the fertile North Effingham farm and mill-stream lands on the Ossipee River. The settlers from these Maine border towns, among them Porter and Parsonsfield, while not unwelcome, brought with them some of their own native customs, often at odds with those of the New Hampshire coast towns from which the earlier Effingham grantees had come. Religion was one cause of dispute. Before separation, feelings ran high between what was known as the "new church" and "old church" party, the "liberals" represented by the new settlers and the "conservatives" by the old.

With the incorporation of North Effingham and the resulting change of the town name to Freedom, the entire problem seems to have been amicably settled. Among the names of Maine families involved, many of which are still to be found in Freedom, are those of Towle, Danforth, Shaw, Dwight, Huntress, Thurston, Kenison, Taylor, Foss, Marston, Milliken, Andrews, Harmon, McDaniel, Lougee, Hodgdon, and Wedgewood. One of Freedom's highways is named Scarborough Road after the town of that name in Maine, and Freedom has its Thurston and Durgin Hills, its Towle Ridge, and its Shawtown, all named for the Maine settlers who ultimately mingled happily with those of Effingham, but retained these reminders of their origin.

GILFORD

GILFORD appears to be the only town in the state taking its name from a Revolutionary battlefield, that of Guilford Court House in North Carolina. The North Carolina Guilford, named in 1770 for Frederick Lord North, English prime minister and Earl of Guilford, first spelled its name Guildford, and that of New Hampshire in a later transition became Gilford.

The Battle of Guilford Court House in 1781 was one of the decisive conflicts of the war, fought between the British forces with their crack English regiments under Lord Cornwallis and the Americans under General Nathaniel Greene of Rhode Island. The American side did not immediately win this battle but succeeded in so depleting the ranks of Cornwallis's army that it was forced to make the retreat which led to his surrender to Washington at Yorktown, thus ending the war.

One of the officers serving under General Greene at Guilford Court House was Lieutenant, then Sergeant, Lemuel B. Mason, who had enlisted from Newington, New Hampshire under General George Reid's command. At the close of the war he retired to Gilmanton, where in 1812 he successfully proposed changing the name of its Gunstock Parish to that of a new town to be called Gilford, after the battleground on which he had so valiantly fought in North Carolina. Gunstock Parish took its name from nearby Gunstock Mountain, so named by a party of hunters, one of whom is said to have broken the stock of his gun there.

North Carolina resembles New Hampshire in the naming of many of its towns and counties after English notables in pre-Revolutionary years, among them being Rockingham, Chatham, Hillsborough, Surrey, Cumberland, Salisbury, and Charlotte. Its town name, Guilford Court House, has long since been changed to Martinsville.

GILMANTON

GILMANTON was originally called Gilmantown. It was granted in 1727 by Lieutenant-Governor John Wentworth of Massachusetts, one of eleven towns granted by him in his brief jurisdiction over New Hampshire. It bears the distinction of having the largest number of members of a single family, the Gilmans, in any town ever granted in New Hampshire.

The Gilmans came mostly from Massachusetts, and there were twenty-four of them who received grants. Dr. Josiah Gilman was clerk of the proprietors; Captain John Gilman was moderator and a member of the Board of Selectmen; Colonel

Antipas Gilman surveyed the land and became an inn-holder in the early town.

Gilmanton was at one time New Hampshire's second most populous town, ranking only after Portsmouth. It was nearly triple its present land area in the Colonial period, before Belmont and Gilford (Gunstock Parish) were formed from it. Among its other villages and parishes were Hurricane, Tioga, Factory Village, and Lakeport. Another of the parishes of Gilmanton was first known as Averytown. It was the scene of an iron-mining enterprise carried on by Archibald Macpheadris of Portsmouth, who conducted extensive operations twenty feet below water in what was known as Gilmanton Iron Works, a project ultimately abandoned as unprofitable. The name Gilmanton Iron Works still persists as a part of Gilmanton.

The Gilmans became the ancestors of many notable members of the family: Colonel Nicholas Gilman, an officer on Washington's staff at Yorktown; Nathaniel Gilman, who served as New Hampshire state treasurer, and Governor John Taylor Gilman, who was elected for eleven terms, the longest tenure of office for any United States governor, before or since. Among other Gilman descendants were Bartholomew Thing, founder of Thingstown, now Chelmsford, Massachusetts; Trueworthy Gilman, who took his name from James Treworzie, an early Maine settler; Meshech Weare, president of New Hampshire under its temporary constitution in 1776, and Dudley Leavitt, celebrated almanac author.

HEBRON

HEBRON was originally a part of Cockermouth, which in 1792 was renamed Groton. Part of its territory was stripped away in the same year to become Hebron, a name suggested by one of its early settlers, Samuel Phelps, in memory of his native town of Hebron, Connecticut.

The Phelps family, of whom Colonel Alexander Phelps, a graduate of Yale in 1744, was a prominent member in pre-

Revolutionary days and who played an important part in the
establishment of Dartmouth College by Dr. Eleazar Wheelock,
whose daughter he married, had grants in several new towns
in the section, including Franconia, Gilsum and Lempster. The
town of Thetford, Vermont, then a part of New Hampshire,
contained land given to no fewer than twelve Phelpses, all from
Connecticut.

Among the settlers of Hebron was General Israel Morey, also
of Hebron, Connecticut, who later moved to Orford, where his
famous steamboat won him lasting respect as an early American
inventor. Samuel Phelps of Hebron, New Hampshire, married
his daughter, Lydia.

Other Connecticut family names in the list of Hebron pioneers were those of Cummings, Morse, Bartlett, Hazelton, Kendall, Gould, Crosby, Breckinridge, and McClure, for whom
McClure's Corners is named.

HILL

HILL was first named New Chester when it was granted in 1753
to a group of colonizers from the old town of Chester, New
Hampshire.

The group included a number of Scotch families who had
come to America in 1718 and established homes in the Londonderry district on the Merrimack River. Among those who
moved to New Chester were the McMurphys, McClures, Shirlas,
McPhersons, Craigs, Huses, and their first moderator, Elisha
Tolford. Dr. Matthew Thornton, later a signer of the Declaration of Independence, also was a grantee in the colony.

Like a number of other towns, New Chester gave up its English name following the Revolution and adopted, in 1837, that
of one of the state's most popular and politically prominent governors, Isaac Hill. A Democrat, Hill's influence as editor of the
Concord Patriot was said to have been "so great that he carried
New Hampshire in his pants pocket." President Buchanan, in
whose administration he served as senator, said of him that he

had "never known a man with a wider range of information on American affairs."

In 1941 the entire village of Hill was transplanted to its present site on higher ground and rebuilt, thus allowing the use of its original land for a Merrimack River flood control project.

HOLDERNESS

EARL OF HOLDERNESS was a title held in the eighteenth century by the English family of Darcy, and before that by a member of the Royal Family. Prince Rupert, grandson of James I, was granted the title by his uncle, Charles I, in 1644. Rupert, who was much beloved by the English, fought in several military campaigns and commanded a fleet of ships in the war with the Dutch in 1662. He was later governor of the Hudson's Bay Company and achieved fame as a chemist, having several discoveries to his credit in the field of metallurgy. The town of Rupert, Vermont is named for him.

After Prince Rupert's death in 1682, the Holderness title was granted by the king to the Darcy family. It was Robert Darcy (1718-1778), fourth Earl of Holderness, for whom Holderness, New Hampshire was named in 1751. Darcy was ambassador to Venice and minister at the Hague under King George III, but as secretary of state actively opposed his policy toward the colonies. He joined with the English Rockingham or Wentworth administration of which William Pitt was one of the leaders, and became a close friend of New Hampshire's Governor Wentworth in an effort to promote friendly trade relations abroad.

At the close of the Indian wars in 1761, the Holderness charter was regranted to a group of some sixty or more New England families, among them that of Samuel Livermore of Londonderry, who had served as counsel to the governor and had received land grants in seven other north country towns. A staunch adherent of the English church, Mr. Livermore determined to establish at Holderness a pretentious estate comprising over 40,000 acres, on which there would be a mansion, gardens, grain fields, a grist mill, school, and church, all developed in the English countryside fashion of the times.

At the beginning of the revolutionary years Mr. Livermore, who by this time had acquired large portions of Holderness, Compton (now Campton) and Plymouth, transferred his loyalty to America and became not only New Hampshire's first Attorney General, but Chief Justice of the Superior (Supreme) Court. He married a daughter of the Reverend Arthur Browne, early Episcopal minister of Portsmouth, who had one of the Holderness grants.

LACONIA

LACONIA, first made a town in 1855 and a city in 1893, was originially a part of Meredith and Gilford, and known for many years as Meredith Bridge.

The name Laconia, which it finally adopted, comes from a region of ancient Greece. Classical names were popular in the mid-nineteenth century, as witness such American towns as Troy, New York, Athens, Georgia, Euclid, Ohio, and many others. In New Hampshire, however, Laconia was first used in the 1620's when the Masonian records described the lands in the Plymouth Council's charter as "extending back to the great lakes and rivers of Canada," most of which they had never seen, but which were supposed to be there according to Indian legends. The explorers of these lands hoped to follow the Piscataqua River northward from the coast to Lake Champlain, then called the Iroquois, and were known as the "Laconia Adventurers," holding what they described as the "Laconia Patent."

The present City of Laconia as now constituted includes what was formerly Lake Village (Lakeport) and The Weirs, the latter name being that of the primitive fishing devices discovered at the outlet of Lake Winnipesaukee. Laconia is the county seat of Belknap County, which was established by the legislature in 1840 and named for Dr. Jeremy Belknap, the famous minister and author of the *History of New Hampshire.* Before that the area had been part of Strafford County.

Charles A. Busiel, who became Laconia's first mayor following its incorporation as a city, an occasion for which he was largely responsible, was elected governor of New Hampshire in 1894. Also elected from Laconia were Governor Henry B. Quimby, who served from 1909 to 1911, and Senator Thomas McIntyre, elected in 1962.

MADISON

ORIGINALLY a part of Eaton and Albany, Madison was one of the first towns to set aside land grants to New Hampshire soldiers who had survived the Seven Years War against France which brought Canada under English rule, in 1763.

Among those soldiers who received land in 1765 were Alexander Blair, Daniel McNeil, Samuel Stark and John Caldwell of Derryfield; Josiah and Joshua Martin of Goffstown; and Nathaniel Martin of Weare.

Long afterward, in 1852, the section covered by these grants was incorporated and called Madison, after President James Madison who was born a hundred years earlier and died in 1836. He is famous for having supported the Jefferson "embargo" which culminated in the War of 1812, and which was vigorously opposed by Daniel Webster whose Federalist Party sought to protect New England prosperity which depended largely on English trade.

The War of 1812 was referred to by the Webster Federalists as "Mr. Madison's War." The Capitol at Washington was captured and burned by the British, but the war was won by victories at Baltimore, Plattsburgh, Fort Erie, and New Orleans. New Hampshire has its Mount Madison in the Presidential Range of the White Mountains.

MEREDITH

MEREDITH was first known as Palmer's Town, named so from Samuel Palmer of Hampton, who, as a teacher of surveying and navigation, had laid out much of the land surrounding Lake Winnipesaukee, and appears to have been an early settler.

It was one of the first towns to have a charter granted by the proprietors, in 1748, and, as most of the lots went to prospective colonizers from Salem, Massachusetts it was called New Salem. Not all of them fulfilled the terms of the charter, however, and in 1768 it was regranted to those who had not settled, and renamed Meredith, after Sir William Meredith, a prominent member of the English Parliament.

Sir William, a friend of Governor Wentworth through his allegiance to the colonies and allied with William Pitt, Lord Grenville, the Earl of Dartmouth, and Lord Rockingham, was out-spoken in his opposition to taxes on America. In 1764 he spoke in Parliament, saying, "If I were an American, I would not submit to them."

He was a graduate of Oxford, Lord of the Admiralty and controller of the Household and privy councillor under King George III. He was a brother-in-law of Barlow Trecothick, after whom the New Hampshire town of Trecothick, now Ellsworth, was named.

MIDDLETON

ALMOST every state in the Union has a Middleton, or Middletown, most of them so named because they happened to be half-way, or in-between, places on a highway or turnpike. The Middleton in New Hampshire is one of the few, perhaps the only one, which didn't get its name that way.

Our Middleton appears to have come from Sir Charles Middleton, later Lord Barham, who was born in 1726 and spent most of his life in the British Navy. His connection with New Hampshire came about through his naval operations in Barbados in the West Indies, a long-established shipping point in the 1700's for Portsmouth exports and imports. During the French war, our trade there in molasses, sugar and rum, and other "West India" goods was considerably harassed by French privateers. Middleton, who fought them successfully as captain of the *Arundel,* was given charge of the British convoy service and later made a vice admiral under the direction of William Pitt, Earl of Chatham. In appreciation of his record in the navy the government of Barbados gave him a gold-hilted sword, and in England he was chosen controller of the Navy in 1781.

Middleton, New Hampshire, was granted in 1749. The town got into the state records during the administration of Governor John Wentworth when he complained about the neglect of what was then known as the Middleton or "Province" Road, on which Wolfeboro, his summer home, was located. The complaint, which asserted that he had "more than once had his life endangered" on the road, was addressed to the proprietors who made the grant, and the bill for repairs sent to them listed, among the items charged by the sixty-one citizens who worked on it, "one-half quintal of fish, replacing a grindstone worn out and spoiled, and a gallon of rum, gave to the people on His Excellency's orders."

New Hampshire had another town named Middle Monadnock, or Middletown, prior to 1773, when it was renamed Jaffrey.

MILTON

MILTON was originally a part of Rochester and for many years was known as "Three Ponds," or Milton Mills. The ponds were Town House, Middleton, and March. The "Mills," of which there were several — all located on the Salmon Falls River which forms the Maine border — were the scene of much early New Hampshire manufacturing. The name was shortened to Milton in 1802 when the town was incorporated. The name may have originated from the town's early mills. It has also been suggested that the settlement of Milton Mills took its name from one of the numerous English relatives of the Wentworth governors. A cousin of the colonial governors was William Fitzwilliam, fourth Earl of Fitzwilliam and Viscount Milton, for whom the town of Fitzwilliam was also named. The town of Milton, Vermont, originally a New Hampshire grant, was named for him in 1763. The older town of Milton, Massachusetts, founded in 1662, probably took its name from Milton Abbey, Dorset, England.

One of Milton's chief attractions has been for many years Mount Teneriffe, described as a "bold and rocky elevation," which got its name from the famous extinct volcano, Mount Teneriffe, in the Canary Islands off the coast of Spain. The Spanish Teneriffe is over 12,000 feet high, while the Milton mountain is only 1,100, so that the resemblance is not a matter of size.

Mount Teneriffe in Spain takes its name from the Canary Islands dialect's "tener" meaning snow, and "iffe" meaning hill. It is Spain's highest mountain and the island on which it is located, Cape Teneriffe, is said to be its largest in extent, wealth and fertility.

Mount Teneriffe in Milton is among New Hampshire's earliest to be named, appearing on Holland's map in 1784.

MOULTONBOROUGH

Like other New England towns whose early settlers included many of the same family, New Hampshire's Moultonborough took its name from a group of its grantees with one name, Moulton. The list of these shows no fewer than sixteen Moultons, of which there were Jonathan and Josiah, with their sons and grandsons, and ten others. There were, however, forty-five additional grantees not of the name Moulton, among them the Sanborns, Toppans, Garlands, Marstons, and Lampreys.

Most of the Moultonborough Moultons came from Hampton under the leadership of Colonel Jonathan Moulton, who got his title through having fought in the Indian wars. He was descended from the first English de Moulton of Brimfield in

Wales, and the Henry Moulton who married Sobriety, daughter of Edward Hilton, a proprietor of Dover.

In addition to his land in Moultonborough, Colonel Moulton also received grants in Cornish, Tamworth, Eaton, Campton, Gunthwaite (now Lisbon), Chatham, Burton, Orford and Piermont, as well as Huntington and Lunenburg in what is now Vermont. He is also said to have had the entire area of what is now New Hampton deeded to him as "Moultonborough Addition" by Governor Wentworth in return for his present to the governor of a "fine fat ox."

At the beginning of the Revolution Colonel Moulton was considered to be one of the richest men in the province, with an estate totaling more than 80,000 acres. In 1785 he inserted an advertisement in a newspaper in Ireland, offering some of his acres to "any gentleman or company" interested in settling, "with everything needed to be supplied on reasonable terms."

Colonel Moulton joined the protest against England's taxation of the colonies in 1775, and was colonel of the third regiment of militia which fought at Ticonderoga. Toward the end of his life he was affectionately known as "General Moulton."

Moultonborough got its charter in 1763. The document was signed in the famous Stoodley's Tavern in Portsmouth, and declared to be "for the encouragement and promoting of the settlement of the country," the entire area being described as "near Winnepisseoky Pond."

NEW DURHAM

THE ORIGINAL settlers of this New Hampshire town came almost entirely from its parent town of Durham which got its name earlier from Durham, England. New Durham was granted in 1749 as Cocheco Township and incorporated under its present name in 1762.

The leading citizen of the new village was Colonel Thomas Tash, whose Scotch ancestors under the name of McIntosh had come to America from Belfast, Ireland. He had fought in

England's Seven Years War against France, and the land he received at New Durham, along with that given to other veterans of this war, was in reward for this service, Colonel Tash having been made proprietors' clerk.

The early New Durham families bore such New Hampshire names as Chesley, Drew, Edgerly, Torr, Durgin, Meader, Burnham, Reynolds, Boody, Willey and Bickford. Colonel Tash later commanded a regiment in the American Revolution, in which his Negro servant Oxford Tash also served and, though wounded, refused to apply for a pension.

One of New Durham's first ministers was Reverend Benjamin Randall. He had worked in the section as an itinerant tailor, and became a devoted admirer of George Whitefield who toured New England in the 1770's. From Whitefield's preaching came Mr. Randall's inspiration to found a new and vigorous religious denomination which he called the "Free-Will Baptists," afterward known as the "Free Baptists."

Like Whitefield, Mr. Randall sought to incorporate what he thought to be needed reforms in the prevailing methods of worship. The enduring popularity, which he acquired through having travelled on foot over more than a thousand miles of New England countryside yearly in response to demands for his preaching, is said to have resulted in the building of more than a hundred new churches.

NEW HAMPTON

NEW HAMPTON granted in 1765, was first named "Moultonborough Addition," after Colonel Jonathan Moulton of Hampton, who had several other grants as reward for his services in the Indian wars. He was moderator of the "Addition," which in 1777 was renamed New Hampton, after Hampton, his native town, which in turn had taken its name from Hampton, England, the home of his ancestors. The New Hampton grant was among the last to be parcelled out by Governor Benning Wentworth, and probably the largest ever granted by him.

The Moultons, of whom there were no fewer than twelve in the original Moultonboro Addition settlement, brought with them a colony of their neighbors in Hampton, who established what was one of the most prosperous towns in the province. Colonel Moulton's "mansion," a costly edifice, burned in 1769 with a loss to him of valuable furniture, an extensive library, and a large sum in gold and securities.

New Hampton was at one time the scene of a severe earthquake. Its first meeting house was built in 1798, and the New Hampton Literary Institution, now the New Hampton School for Boys, was established in 1821.

NORTHFIELD

NORTHFIELD granted in 1780, was one of the first towns created in the years following the Revolution. It appears to have been incorporated during the term of the then temporary "president" of the state, Governor Matthew Thornton, signer of the Declaration and delegate to the first Continental Congress. Prior to this it had been known as North Hill and Factory Village.

Formerly a part of Canterbury, Northfield attracted settlers from that and other nearby towns, including the families of Heath, Blanchard, Whicher, Glidden, Perkins, Forrest, Cross, and Williams, some of whom took advantage of the waterpower available in the Winnepesaukee Valley, surrounded by North, Oak, Bay and Bean Hills, to establish what later became prosperous woolen and paper mills.

Northfield has the honor of having organized one of New Hampshire's first "local" libraries called the "Northfield Improving Society for the Promotion of Useful Knowledge." The title was the same as that applied in 1743 to the American Philosophical Society in Philadelphia, by Benjamin Franklin, its founder.

The Northfield library, which was also a "parliamentary drill and debating club," was chartered by the state in 1718, and began operating with a supply of 24 books loaned against a membership fee of $5 annually collected to insure against "loss of books by damage or failure to return." The library continued in existence under its original name until 1842.

OSSIPEE

New Hampshire has many a mountain, lake, and river named for its native Indians. Only four of its towns, however, of which Ossipee is one, are so named. Originally known as New Garden and prior to that, Wigwam Village, it was what the settlers called "Indian country," and in 1785, the year in which our Constitution was first written, was named for the Ossipee Indians, of which few remained in the section. The Ossipees were among the twelve Algonquin tribes in New Hampshire listed by William Little, the Indian authority, as the Nashuas, Souhegans, Amoskeags, Penacooks, Squamscots, Newichwannocks, Pascataquacs, Pequaukets, Winnipesaukees, Ameriscoggins and Cossucks. Probably no state in the union was the home of a greater number of Indian tribes, who spoke more than forty separate languages.

Most of these tribes were peaceful Indians, not given to warfare unless molested. While sorry to see their hunting and fishing grounds invaded, their plantations overrun by the new "civilization," and their right to trade with each other ignored by a new kind of "barter" which made trinkets and beads more desirable than furs and skins, they accepted it as their fate.

The name Ossipee was a derivation taken from the names of two of these tribes, the Cossucks, or Cowass, now called Coos, meaning pine tree, and "sippee" meaning river. Thus Ossipee, with the first syllable omitted in the combination, became "river of the pines" in translation. Its main stream still remains Pine River.

Here the Ossipee Indians erected what was among the very first stockade forts in New England, designed to protect themselves from the Mohawks in the west. Their village was destroyed in 1725 by Captain John Lovewell, who built a new fort enclosing an acre of ground, said to have been, with its corner turrets, the most formidable of all the many timber-enclosed palisades in New Hampshire, only equalled by that at Fort Dummer on the Connecticut River in Massachusetts.

The Ossipee region included the famous Bear Camp valley, famous for its painters and poets in the late 1800's, among them John Greenleaf Whitter. Near the shores of Ossipee Lake is located the Indian "burial mound," twenty-three feet high, much advertised in the 1870's as containing several thousand fossilized Indian bodies. Recent archaeological explorations have indicated that none seem any longer to be in evidence.

Ossipee is the county seat of Carroll County which was set aside from Strafford County in 1840 and today includes seventeen towns. The present court house at Ossipee was built in 1916.

PITTSFIELD

LIKE the Pittsfield in Massachusetts and the Pittsfields and Pittsburgs in other states, this town was named in honor of William Pitt, Prime Minister of England, who was probably the best English friend the colonies ever had in their great time of need in pre-Revolution years.

Our own Pittsfield, however, has one further distinction. It was named in the years nearest Pitt's death in 1778 when a great wave of admiration swept the country following the last of his many eloquent speeches in the House of Lords extolling America and when he was mourned in this section as "the idol of all parties in New England."

For several decades prior to its incorporation in 1782 Pittsfield existed as an unnamed parish in Chichester. Its settlers, led by Colonel John Cram, known as "Good Old John," came for the most part in a single group from Hampton. John Cram had several other grants in New Hampshire, but chose this one because of its possible mill site on the Suncook River, and most of the early homes on and around Catamount Mountain, built in the 1700's, secured their timber from Cram's Mill.

Among the Hampton families which grew up in this settlement were the Drakes, Leavitts, Dows, Sanborns, Gilmans, Hooks, Tiltons, Garlands and Rollinses. Nathaniel Gookin of Hampton became Pittsfield's first moderator.

In the century following its incorporation Pittsfield became a thriving industrial center. Hiram Americanus Tuttle, born in Barnstead, made his home in Pittsfield most of his life. He was elected governor of New Hampshire in 1891.

PLYMOUTH

As MIGHT be expected, this town takes its name from Plymouth, Massachusetts, the first point of English colonization in New England. It was named by the early colonists in honor of the English seaport and their financial sponsors, "The Council Established at Plymouth in the County of Devon for the Planting, Ruling and Governing of New England in America."

Granted in 1763 by Governor Benning Wentworth, the New Hampshire town was first named New Plymouth, and was a part of a large plot of undivided land in the Pemigewassett Valley. It had remained unoccupied in the northern colonization movement which followed the Treaty of Paris, ending the English war with the French in 1763.

Much of this desirable land was in demand from soldiers in the long Seven Years' War. The Plymouth grant went to a group of thirty-five prospective settlers from Hollis who bore the titles of ensign, lieutenant, captain or colonel, and who had employed their own surveyors, Colonel Joseph Blanchard and Matthew Patten, to lay out home lots under the terms of a new charter.

Among the Hollis families given grants were those with the names of Blood, Hobart (Hubbard), Parker, Brown, Powers, Webster, Worcester, Willoughby and Cummings, all originally from Massachusetts, and several from Plymouth, Massachusetts. Joseph Blanchard was the first moderator.

One of the grantees was Meshech Weare, who afterward became the first president (governor) of New Hampshire.

Plymouth is the site of Plymouth State College, now part of the State University.

ROCHESTER

ROCHESTER was one of four towns granted by Massachusetts during the brief term of its English governor, Samuel Shute, the others being Barrington, Chester and Nottingham. It took its name from Laurence Hyde, Earl of Rochester, a close friend of Governor Shute.

Rochester, brother-in-law to King James II, was the son of the Earl of Clarendon, and during the strenuous times in English history following the restoration of the monarchy, served as member of Parliament, ambassador to Poland and Danzig, Lord Lieutenant of Ireland, and Lord High Treasurer of England. He is considered to have been "a statesman of great eminence." Lawrence Hyde adopted his title from the ancient city of Rochester in Kent. The English Rochester was settled by the Romans, who gave to their fortified camp or *castra* the name *Durobrivae*. In English, the word *castra* became "chester"; thus Rochester has the same roots as our towns of Chester and Dorchester.

The town of Rochester became a city in 1891. It includes the town of Gonic, named for the Indian Squamanagona meaning day and water. It has given the state three of its best known governors, Samuel D. Felker, Rolland H. Spaulding and Huntley N. Spaulding. The last named came by his middle name, Nowell, from his ancestor, the famous Reverend Increase Nowell, early Boston minister whose widow, Mrs. Parnell Nowell, and her son, Samuel, were given a grant from the Massachusetts government upon the death of her husband in 1672. This comprised 2,000 acres of farm land in the area which is now Rochester. Because of the Indian wars, however, the Nowells do not appear to have ever occupied the land, and it was regranted when Rochester became a town, in 1722.

RUMNEY

THE NAME of this town, which was spelled in England as both Rumney and Romney, comes from Robert Marsham, second Baron Romney, who succeeded to the title in 1724 and died in 1793. Lord Romney was a fellow of the Royal Society, president of the Society for the Encouragement of Arts, Manufactures and Commerce, and a doctor of civil law. His family took their title from the ancient Kentish seaport of Romney on the southeast coast of England.

Granted by Governor Benning Wentworth in 1761, Rumney, New Hampshire was chartered to a group of "colonizers" from the Connecticut River towns of East Haddam and Colchester. The leader of the group was Daniel Brainerd, who was descended from a Huguenot family which originated in Braine, France and settled in Braintree (Brainterre), England before coming to America.

This group of early grantees included twenty-two members of the same family, among them eight Brainerds, and members of the related Connecticut families of Spencer, Gates, Olmstead, Preston, Warner, and Hungerford. One of the contemporary Brainerds was David, who, under the direction of the Society of Christian Knowledge of Scotland, and Jonathan Edwards, famous as a preacher to the Indians and translator of the Bible into their language, had helped to form the first Indian mission school at Stockbridge, Massachusetts, thus providing the model which served Eleazar Wheelock in his founding of the Indian school which later became Dartmouth College.

Not all the grantees under the 1761 charter of Rumney took up their claims in the time allotted them, and the town was regranted in 1767 to a new group of settlers replacing those who had not complied with the terms of the charter.

Rumney includes the village of Quincy, named for Josiah Quincy of Massachusetts, and located in the southeastern section of town are the famous Polar Caves.

SANBORNTON

THIS TOWN was originally named Sanborntown, after John Sanborn, a close friend of New Hampshire's first provincial Governor Benning Wentworth. Granted in 1748, it was one of the first four towns to be given a charter following the purchase of the colonial lands from the Mason claim by the Portsmouth proprietors in that year.

Out of the sixty individuals who were given land under this grant, twelve were Sanborns, all descended from William Sambueren or Sambourne, whose family came to America from England towns with such picturesque names as Timsbury, Nunney, Maidens Newton and Turner's Puddle. The first Samborn, who settled in Hampton, married Ann, daughter of the Reverend Stephen Bachiler, famous in New Hampshire history.

The early settlers of Sanbornton included the Danforths, Copps, Foggs, Fifields, Shepards, Dustins and Rowans, the entire settlement coming from the towns of Hampton, Exeter, Stratham, and Chester. At the time of the French wars a fort was built at "Union" Bridge, now Sanbornton Bridge, where the colonial army under Colonel Theodore Atkinson was stationed in "Winter Quarters" for the duration of the "Canada Expedition" in 1746. The town was officially incorporated by Governor John Wentworth in 1770.

Midway between Sanbornton and North Sanbornton is the community of Gaza, named for the biblical land much in the news today.

SANDWICH

SANDWICH was chartered in 1763 by Governor Benning Wentworth and incorporated in 1770. The grantees were members of several prominent Exeter families, among them eight Gilmans, including a future governor of New Hampshire, and the families of Folsom, Coffin, and Rundlett. Sandwich, as first laid out, was found to contain so many "inaccessible mountains and shelves of rock" that much of it was thought to be uninhabitable and the grant was enlarged to 64,000 acres. It remains one of the state's largest townships.

The town is famous for its mountain climbing centers in the Sandwich range. Among the town's seventeen listed peaks is "Sandwich Dome" the highest mountain in Carroll County. Another of its mountains, called Israel, is one of the few in the state bearing a biblical name. Sandwich includes the settlement of Whiteface, named for the mountain which is located to the north in Waterville.

The town was named by Wentworth in honor of John Montagu (1718-1792), fourth Earl of Sandwich. Lord Sandwich was descended from a famous English seaman and admiral (the first Earl) and inherited his title at the age of eleven. Educated at Eton and Cambridge, he went on to hold many high government posts under George II and George III, and it was undoubtedly because of his influence that Governor Wentworth named the town in his honor. Afterwards, however, the Earl's popularity and reputation declined owing largely to his conduct as First Lord of the Admiralty, 1771-1782. One historian wrote: "For corruption and incapacity, Sandwich's administration is unique in the history of the British navy. Offices were bought, stores were stolen, and ships were sent into battle unseaworthy and inadequately equipped."

Notwithstanding, the Earl's name today is associated with a more pleasant institution. His chief claim to fame was his "invention" of the sandwich, a thin slab of meat placed between two slices of bread, which he chose as his diet for an entire day while intent upon the gaming table.

Captain Cook named the Sandwich Islands (now Hawaii) after him during his voyage around the world.

STRAFFORD

STRAFFORD, which was settled before the Revolution but not incorporated until 1820, takes its name from the county in which it is located. Strafford County was one of the five original counties established in 1769 by Governor John Wentworth, the others being Rockingham, Hillsborough, Cheshire, and Grafton.

Earl of Strafford was a title borne by the Wentworth family in England. The most illustrious of them, and an ancestor of the governor's, was the first Earl, Thomas Wentworth (1593-1641) who was a friend and chief adviser to King Charles I. A member of Parliament, and later Lord-Deputy of Ireland, he originated many reforms in the Irish government and introduced the cultivation of flax to that country, resulting in the production of Irish linen. Strafford was a strong upholder of the king in his struggle with Parliament; he was beheaded in 1641 for allegedly intending to use Irish soldiers to quell the Parliamentary forces.

William Wentworth, the fourth Earl of Strafford, (1722-1791) was a cousin and contemporary of Governor John Wentworth. Strafford, Vermont, once part of New Hampshire, was also named for this family.

The name Strafford also has historical significance through having been adopted in 1822 by a state militia company in Dover, known as the Strafford Guards. In 1824 the company acted as escort to the Marquis de Lafayette on the occasion of his visit to America, and saw service in the Civil War at Fort Constitution in New Castle. It afterward became a part of the New Hampshire National Guard.

The town of Strafford, New Hampshire includes the settlements of Bow Lake, a popular vacation area, and Crown Point, where the first settlement of the town was made.

TAMWORTH

TAMWORTH in the picturesque foothills of the White Mountains, surrounded by Mounts Chocorua, Paugus and Passaconaway, was granted in 1766. It appears to have been named in honor of Washington Shirley, Viscount Tamworth, a vice-admiral in the British navy in the Seven Year's War with France and Spain, 1756-1763.

Admiral Shirley was one of several navy officers who were close friends of Benning Wentworth, who had engaged in shipping at Portsmouth before he became first provincial governor of New Hampshire.

Admiral Shirley joined the English navy at the age of sixteen. He was in command of one of the ships taking part in the blockade of Brest, in 1759, after which he was made a vice admiral and a fellow of the Royal Society. Shirley succeeded to the title of Viscount Tamworth in 1745; in 1760 he became the fifth Earl Ferrers, upon the death of his brother Lawrence, who was hanged at Tyburn for the murder of his steward. Admiral Shirley died in 1778.

The naming of Tamworth in Admiral Shirley's honor has special significance in New Hampshire history because of the fact that his daughter, Selina Shirley, who became Lady Huntingdon and was known as "Lady Bountiful," was at the center of a chain of circumstances which resulted in the founding of Dartmouth College.

When death took from Selina Shirley her four sons and her husband, the Earl of Huntingdon, in the 1760s, she sought and found consolation in religion and devoted her entire fortune to the great revivalist movement which swept through England at the time. To her chapel, in which the famous open-air evangelist, George Whitefield, served as chaplain, came John and Charles Wesley, the composers Handel and Isaac Watts, and the hymnodists Augustus Toplady, who wrote *Rock of Ages,* and Philip Doddridge, author of *Awake My Soul.*

Here also came the Earl of Dartmouth, first lord of trade and secretary of state, known as the "Psalm Singer," friend of the colonists and of Governor Wentworth. Here too the plans were developed to promote the establishment of Eleazar Wheelock's "Indian Charity School," later Dartmouth, with the Earl as its English treasurer and Whitefield its "missionary" to America.

Tamworth comprises the villages of Chocorua, named for the famous Indian sachem, and Wonalancet. The last was originally called Birch Intervale, but changed in 1893 to Wonalancet in honor of the nearby mountain and the Indian chief for whom it was named. Chief Wonalancet was the son of Passaconaway. Wonalancet was the site of the famous Chinook Kennels, founded by Arthur T. Walden. Another famous summertime resident of Tamworth was President Grover Cleveland, for whom New Hampshire's Mount Cleveland is named.

The settlement of Whittier in Tamworth takes its name from the poet, John Greenleaf Whittier, who spent many summers in the region. His name is also commemorated by Mount Whittier in neighboring Ossipee, so named in 1893.

TILTON

PRIOR TO its official separation from Sanbornton in 1869, Tilton bore the names Sanbornton Bridge and Bridge Village. It was given the name Tilton at the suggestion of its then most prominent citizen, Charles E. Tilton, in honor of his grandfather, Nathaniel Tilton, who had come from Stratham to settle there before the Revolution. He established the famous Sanbornton iron foundry at "tin corner," which was long known as the "trip-hammer shop," and built the first hotel, the Dexter House.

Charles Tilton "went west" to engage in shipping and South American prospecting in the 1849 gold rush era, and accumulated a considerable fortune. Coming back to his home town in 1869, he made it a gift of costly statues he had collected abroad. These he stationed at various points in the town, at the center of which he erected the famous Tilton Arch, a replica of the Arch of Titus in Rome. Among his sculptures were life-size figures of legendary Indians, and other classic marble figures he had purchased on his travels.

Thanks to Charles Tilton's generosity, Tilton not only became an architectural center, but a show-place for the sculptor's art, said to be "the most European thing upon this continent."

Mr. Tilton built for himself a thirty-five-room mansion or

"pagoda" on an elaborately landscaped eight-acre estate, which is now a part of the Tilton School.

Tilton includes the town of Lochmere, its name taken from the Scottish word "loch" (lake) and "mere," an old English word for sea.

TUFTONBORO

TUFTONBORO has the distinction of being the only town once having been owned entirely by one man, John Tufton Mason, after whom it was named in 1750. The town was incorporated in 1795.

Mason, a native of Boston, was the great-grandson of Captain John Mason. His wife, Anne Tufton, was descended from William Tufton, or Toketon, from whom also was descended Christopher Tufton, Earl of Thanet and governor of Barbados. The Tuftons, of whom there are said to be more than fifty buried in the churchyard of Tufton Chapel at their English home in Rynham, Kent, were related to the Wentworth Governors by marriage.

John Tufton Mason inherited the claim to the undivided lands of northern New Hampshire assumed to be held by Captain John Mason, selling it in 1746 for one thousand five hundred pounds to a group of Portsmouth merchants who disposed of it under grants made to prospective settlers in the years preceding the American Revolution. The town of Tuftonboro, bordering on Lake Winnepesaukee, was laid out to be six miles square, containing approximately 23,000 acres.

Tuftonboro includes the villages of Melvin Corner, Melvin Village, and Mirror Lake. The name Melvin is that of David and Eleazer Melvin, who fought in the French and Indian War. Mirror Lake was the site of one of the earliest summer residences in New Hampshire, a house built in 1765 by Peter Levius, a friend of Governor Benning Wentworth.

WAKEFIELD

THIS TOWN originally bore three successive names: Ham's-town, East-town, and Watertown. It was finally named Wakefield in 1774 by Governor John Wentworth after the home of his English ancestors who lived for many years in Wentworth Castle, or "Wentworth-Wodehouse," in Wakefield, Yorkshire. The name of the town has also been ascribed, probably incorrectly, to John Ker, third Duke of Roxburghe, a Scottish noble, who also held the title of Baron Ker of Wakefield. He inherited his titles in 1755 and died in 1804.

Most of the early settlers of Wakefield in New Hampshire came from Dover and Somersworth, among them members of the Ham, Gilman, Copp, Weeks, Hutchins, Hussey and Downs families.

Wakefield is especially famous through having been the birthplace of a descendant of the Wentworth family, Professor Albert C. Wentworth, a distinguished authority on mathematics. After graduating from Harvard, he was for many years head of the mathematics department at Phillips Exeter Academy, and was the author of more than fifty textbooks on arithmetic, algebra, geometry and allied subjects.

The town of Wakefield includes the villages of Sanbornville and Union.

WOLFEBORO

THIS TOWN dates back to 1759 when it was granted to four young men of Portsmouth who asked the proprietors of New Hampshire for "some of your waste land." These applicants were William Treadwell, Dr. Ammi Ruhama Cutter and David Sewall, all of Portsmouth, and Henry Apthorp of Boston. Dr. Cutter was Mr. Treadwell's brother-in-law and a leading Portsmouth physician, who got his picturesque name from two biblical characters in the Book of Hosea, much discussed at the time because of their matrimonial difficulties. He later became a president of the New Hampshire Medical Society, and personal physician to Governor John Wentworth.

Both Treadwell and Sewall married daughters of Judge William Parker, whose mother was Zeruiah Stanley, sometimes incorrectly publicized as the daughter of Lord Stanley, the Earl of Derby, but who was actually the daughter of Matthew Stanley of Topsfield, Massachusetts. The Parkers were directly related to the Portsmouth Hales, among whom were the ancestors of John Parker Hale whose portrait and statue are familiar to visitors to the Capitol.

Henry Apthorp was one of the several sons of Charles Apthorp, Eton scholar and merchant who, in the early 1700's had come to Boston from England as crown officer and paymaster to the Royal Navy and was a close friend of both Wentworth governors. His memory is also perpetuated as having been the early name of our towns of Littleton and Dalton.

The 1759 charter named the town Wolfeboro after General James Wolfe, under whom the enlisted New Hampshire patriots fought at Louisbourg in 1758 and who won his great victory at Quebec in 1759. The town then consisted of 547 acres, sixty reserved for the governor. In 1763 the proprietors added approximately 2,300 acres to the estate of the new governor, John Wentworth, to be known as "Kingswood," also deeding to him 1500 additional acres in Brookfield and New Durham. Smith's Pond, about which the Wolfeboro land lay, has been renamed Lake Wentworth.

Governor Wentworth established what is considered the first summer country estate in northern New England. His extensive house, stables and gardens were in charge of Matthew Stanley Parker, relative of the early grantees; and another of the first owners, Dr. Cutter, often visited him as his physician. The house burned in 1820, but the land, first requested as "waste", later described as "good soil but rocky and broken", turned out to be among the most valued areas in New Hampshire.

III

Merrimack Valley Region

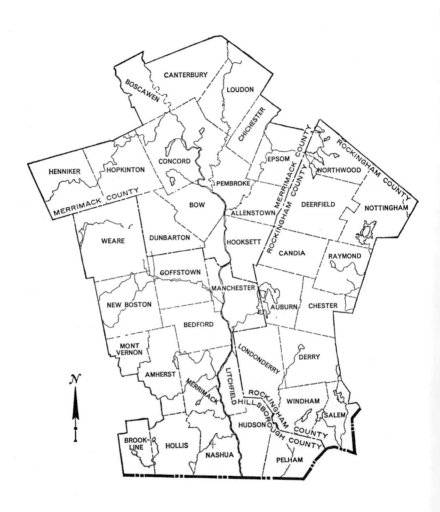

ALLENSTOWN

ALLENSTOWN was first granted in 1721 by Governor Shute of Massachusetts, and named in honor of his predecessor, Samuel Allen, who had been governor of the province for one year in the late 1600's while it was under the jurisdiction of Massachusetts.

Governor Allen does not seem ever to have visited this section of New Hampshire. His brief term as governor resulted from his having invested in land here to the extent of five hundred pounds while a prominent merchant in London. But he returned to England after presenting his claim in Massachusetts and it was disallowed by the courts.

Samuel Allen is described in the records as having been "fair and upright, mild, obliging and charitable in character and of a pacific and condescending disposition." The New Hampshire lands, after long litigation, passed in 1746 into the hands of the "proprietors" who paid 1,500 pounds for 200,000 acres of them. Allenstown was one of the first new grants made by Governor Benning Wentworth under the new ownership.

In the proprietors' map the thirty or more lots awarded to settlers (which included the families of Cochran, Packer, Buntin, and Gay), were designated as "exceeding good," "very good," "middling good" and "good," contrasting with "bad," "middling bad" and "very bad." The "good" lots outnumbered the "bad" ones. The new settlers were required to build a bridge over the Suncook River within one year and to build homes for themselves within two years or forfeit their land.

The Allenstown region was originally known as excellent "bear country" as well as good hunting ground for wild geese and ducks. Its Bear Brook, now the center of one of the state's most attractive recreation spots, was once bordered with prosperous mill-sites, long since outdated in usefulness. The records indicate that Allenstown lay on the favorite travel route to the southeast from the "North Country," as it still does, and that it was the overnight stopping-place for Ebenezer Webster on his three-day horseback journey to Exeter where he took his son Daniel in 1796, to be educated at Phillips Academy.

In 1815 part of Bow was annexed, and in 1853 part of Hooksett. Allenstown was incorporated in 1831.

AMHERST

AMERICA'S first adventure in international warfare really began in 1758 when, as English colonies, we took part in what was known as the "Expedition against the French in North America" under the direction of Lord Jeffrey Amherst as commander-in-chief. A great college song, one of the most popular ever written, commemorates his name; but long before then New Hampshire, in 1760, named one of our towns in his honor.

General Amherst spent most of his life in uniform. He fought under King George II's son, the Duke of Cumberland, in the wars in Europe, and when at last the great statesman, William Pitt, convinced the English parliament that England's real problem was to subdue the French in Canada, he sent Amherst here to do it.

The capture of Crown Point, Ticonderoga, Quebec and Montreal were all Amherst's victories, even though they would probably never have occurred without the help of New Hampshire and other English colonies. General Amherst himself would have been the first to concede the aid given by New Hampshire's Pepperell, Stark, Rogers, and the men who served with them.

Our town of Amherst was originally granted in 1728 by Governor William Burnet as Narragansett No. 3, and was populated by the families of pensioned soldiers who had fought at Narragansett, Rhode Island, in King Philip's War with the Indians. It was also known as Salem Narragansett and Souhegan West.

Amherst was for a brief time county seat of Hillsborough County.

Besides the noted college town in Massachusetts, there is a town in Burma named for General Amherst, and another in Nova Scotia. New Hampshire archives contain a letter from Governor Benning Wentworth expressing his pride in having named a town for his friend, "Lord Jeffrey Amherst."

Within the town of Amherst lies one of New Hampshire's many Indian named lakes, Baboosic, comprising some 350 acres.

Amherst was the birthplace of one of New Hampshire's greatest native sons, Horace Greeley (1811-1872). Greeley founded the *New York Tribune* in 1841 and became one of the most influential Americans of his time. His assistant at the *Tribune* was Charles A. Dana, who became a famous journalist himself and was also a New Hampshire native. Greeley, famed for his phrase "Go West, young man, go West," was a founder of the Republican party and nominee for the presidency in 1872. President Franklin Pierce was married to Jane Appleton Means at Amherst in 1834.

AUBURN

THIS TOWN is one of five carved out of the large township of Chester, the others being Candia, Derryfield, Hooksett and Raymond.

Prior to its incorporation in 1845 during the administration of Governor John H. Steele, it had several names: first, Chester Woods, later Chester West Parish and Long Meadow, and finally Auburn. Settlers of the town came to live in what they called the "Chestnut Country" because of its many chestnut trees. The name Auburn appears in English literature in Goldsmith's lines, "Sweet Auburn, loveliest village of the plain," and in the early and middle years of the last century place names in this country were often taken from literary and mythological sources. Other Auburns in nearby states were named in this same period: Auburn, New York (1805); Auburn, Massachusetts (1837); Auburn, Maine (1842). There is also a village of the same name in County Westmeath, Ireland; and a village called "Aubourn", near Lincoln, England.

The town of Auburn includes a considerable portion of Lake Massabesic, which was acquired to provide Manchester with its water supply, because of the purity of its waters. This lake, with its drainage area of more than 28,000 acres, was at one time one of New Hampshire's most popular pleasure resorts with fashionable hotels, boat houses, and lake steamers. Its name is of Indian origin, "Mass" or "Massab," meaning much, and "sok" or "suc" meaning place, or place of much water.

BEDFORD

BEDFORD came into existence in 1730 when it was known as Narragansett No. 5, one of a group of settlements established by Massachusetts for the benefit of dependents of soldiers who fought against the Narragansett Indians in Rhode Island in the early Indian wars.

Great care was exercised in compiling the lists of possible new homesteaders in this district but, since few restrictions were made by Governor Jonathan Belcher of Massachusetts as to its development, much of the land fell into the hands of speculators and little was done with it until twenty years later. It was then regranted, first as Souhegan East, after the Souhegan River, and then, in 1750, by Governor Benning Wentworth of New Hampshire, as Bedford.

Bedford was named for Lord John Russell, who became fourth Duke of Bedford in 1732. His first wife was Diana Spencer, cousin of the famous Duke of Marlborough. Beginning his diplomatic career as Lord of the Admiralty, Russell became Secretary of State under King George II, and later was ambassador to France and Lord Lieutenant of Ireland. One of his activities was to carry on a vigorous campaign against the hiring by England of German soldiers, and during his years in Parliament the wars with France and Spain were terminated. He was a close friend of the New Hampshire governor, who had spent considerable time in London prior to his appointment here.

The incorporation of Bedford in 1750 was put into effect by Major John Goffe of Londonderry, its first moderator. Goffe came to Bedford accompanied by a group of Scotch settlers who helped to found the new town. Among them were the families of Walker, Orr, McQuaid, Barron, Gilmore, McAllister, Moore, Patten, Kennedy, Kidder, Bill, Morehead, and Woodbury.

BOSCAWEN

BOSCAWEN, now over two centuries old, got its name in 1760 from a famous English admiral who fought under General Amherst in the conquest of Canada in 1758. He was much beloved by the English people and bore the nickname of "Old Dreadnought" given him by his sailors.

The town of Boscawen was originally granted in 1732 as Contoocook, the Indian name of the river which joins the Merrimack just below it. It was a thriving mill town in 1760, the year marking the end of New Hampshire's long series of clashes with the Indian tribes who made the settlement of the north country a dangerous adventure. The town of Boscawen includes North Boscawen, now Gerrish, the home of the Merrimack County Farm and the State Forestry Nursery.

Admiral Edward Boscawen's mother was related to the Duke of Marlborough. His father, Viscount Falmouth, was a relative of Admiral Vernon, under whom he enlisted at the age of twenty-eight to begin a lifetime career in the navy, with promotions from commander of a ship to rear admiral and finally vice admiral of a squadron. His crowning achievement was the capture of the fortress of Louisbourg, a menace to New England fishing expeditions during England's wars with France and Spain. He died in 1761, the year following the naming of the town in his honor.

Boscawen is one of the few New Hampshire places to erect tablets in memory of its sons, among them General John A. Dix,

of Civil War fame, William Pitt Fessenden, Secretary of the
Treasury, and Reverend Samuel Wood, principal of the private
school which prepared Daniel Webster for Dartmouth. The
town also has a tablet to commemorate the Contoocook Fort
on the Merrimack, built in 1739, and one of the first of the
many log enclosures in New Hampshire used for protection
against the Indians. The early records of the town show a charge
of fourteen shillings for a "bowl of punch" used at the opening
of court presided over by its first Justice of the Peace, George
Jackman. Boscawen is also the birthplace of Moody Currier,
governor of New Hampshire 1885-87, and donor of the Currier
Art Museum in Manchester.

BOW

GRANTED in 1727, Bow was one of several towns established in
the lower Merrimack Valley as a part of an early provincial
colonization plan, extending northward into New Hampshire
and intended to relieve the population congestion in New England coast settlements. These towns included Bow, Chichester,
Epsom, Allenstown, Canterbury, Pembroke and Litchfield, and
the expansion project was conceived and executed by Lieutenant-Governor John Wentworth, who bore the title of governor
of the province of New Hampshire which was then a part of
Massachusetts.

In selecting grantees for land in these proposed towns Governor Wentworth chose members of almost every prominent
family in the Portsmouth area, among them those with the
names Wiggin, Atkinson, Gilman, Jaffrey, Hunking, Odiorne,
Sheafe, Waldron, Plaisted, Downing, and Blanchard. These
names were often duplicated in the entire seven towns, and
their presence on the charters there aroused considerable appre-
hension among "natives" of Rumford (now Concord) to the
north, who had earlier claims and objected to being "hemmed
in" at the south.

The result was a legal action on the part of these individuals, protesting to the English crown any extension of such colonization farther north than Bow, against which town it was directed specifically, by a committee led by the Reverend Timothy Walker, a Concord minister. A decision establishing a satisfactory boundary line between Bow and the town of Rumford was finally reached.

Bow appears to have taken its name partly because of a "bend" in the Merrimack River within its borders, and partly because the group of towns of which it was one formed a "curve" on the surveyors' maps. There is, however, an English village called Bow, near Exeter in the county of Devon, and the name may have come from that source. Bow originally measured a total of eighty-one square miles, but a portion of its territory was later ceded to neighboring towns.

Bow is internationally known as the birthplace of Mary Baker Eddy (1821-1910), founder of Christian Science. Mrs. Eddy was the daughter of Mark Baker, a prominent man locally, who later moved his family to Tilton. Remarkably gifted, even as a child, Mary Baker Eddy was admitted to membership in the Bow Congregational Church at the age of twelve, and at that time was so well educated that she could dispute a point of theology in applying for admission.

BROOKLINE

THIS TOWN, originally part of Dunstable and settled as West Hollis, was granted in 1769 by Governor John Wentworth as Raby. He named it in honor of one of the English peerages held by the Wentworth family. His cousin, William Wentworth (1722-91), was fourth Earl of Strafford and Baron of Raby Castle. The castle is located in County Durham, England. After a distinguished career as commander of a regiment of British dragoons, the Earl served as an aide to the king, ambassador to Germany, and member of Parliament. Raby was one of several names associated with the Wentworth family in England, which was applied by Governor Wentworth to his New Hampshire grants.

Brookline retained the name Raby until 1798, when by act of the New Hampshire legislature, it was reincorporated as Brookline. It appears to have been so named at the suggestion of one of the town's leading citizens, Benjamin Shattuck, who came from Brookline, Massachusetts, and was the owner of considerable property in the town.

Many of the early Brookline settlers were from Nashua (then called Dunstable) and from the Massachusetts towns of Groton, Townsend, Pepperell, and Lunenburg, several of these places having been affected by the re-establishment in 1741 of the frontier boundary line between New Hampshire and that province.

CANDIA

ORIGINALLY called Charmingfare, probably because of its many bridlepaths, or "parades" through pleasant scenery, Candia came by its present name in 1763, given it by Governor Benning Wentworth possibly in memory of his sea-going travels as a Portsmouth trader following his graduation from Harvard in 1715. The name is the same as the principal city and former capital of Crete, largest of the Greek islands.

The territory covered by Candia, New Hampshire was once a part of Chester, one of the state's earliest settlements in the 1700s. Many Chester families secured grants in Candia, among them the McClures, Calefs, Moores, Dearborns, Carrs and Fittses, and the town bordered on the 500-acre "farm" allotted by Massachusetts to its then lieutenant governor, John Wentworth, grandfather of Benning.

Among Candia's later families were the Fosses, descended from John Foss, or Vos (Scandinavian name for "fox") who were first in Boston, then in Dover and Cornish. A descendant was Sam Walter Foss, born in 1859, who became a world-famous poet.

Graduating from Brown University in 1882 where he was class poet, Sam Walter Foss, who preferred the name "Sam" to Samuel, worked on New York and Boston newspapers, became an editor of the *Boston Globe,* and finally served as librarian of the Somerville, Massachusetts, Library.

He wrote and published many poems, best known among them *The House By the Side of the Road.* In this poem he adopted from Homer's *Iliad* the phrase "Fast by the road an ever-opened door obliged the wealthy, relieved the poor." Foss's lines read:

> Let me live in my house by the side of the road
>   Where the race of men go by;
> They are good, they are bad, they are weak, they are strong,
>   Wise, foolish—so am I
> Then why should I sit in the scorner's seat,
>   Or hurl the cynic's ban?
> Let me live in my house by the side of the road
>   And be a friend of man.

Foss himself was a founder of the Candia Club which attained prominence for its much talked of literary meetings in Candia and Boston in the early 1900's, and he helped to establish the Fitts Museum, one of the first such town institutions in New Hampshire.

CANTERBURY

ONE OF SEVERAL towns granted in 1727 under the authority of Lieutenant-Governor John Wentworth of Massachusetts, Canterbury appears to have taken its name from William Wake who was Archbishop of Canterbury at the time, and who achieved fame for his efforts to unite the state churches of England and France. The English Canterbury, the county borough of Kent, is renowned for its ancient cathedral and as the center of Christianity in England dating from 597 A.D.

Previous to its granting, Canterbury, New Hampshire had been an important "fort" or Indian "trading post" where the peaceful Penacook Indians frequently came to exchange skins and furs for American-made proprietary articles. Among its early settlers were the Massachusetts families of Ames, Clough, Gibson, Foster, Blanchard, Morrill, Emery and Kimball. The town was incorporated in 1741.

Canterbury was the home of one of the several colonies of Shakers who, originating in England as revivalists at the time of Whitefield and Wesley, brought to America in 1792 the dance ritual through which they "atoned their sins" by means of music and prayer. Their creed did not forbid marriage, nor require the separation of man and wife, but held that "one of the secrets of man's sin" was the premature and self-indulgent use of the sexual union" which, they thought, "led to crimes of all degrees, war and suffering" instead of high spiritual development.

The Shakers who, upon joining the movement, gave up their property, but who could take it back if they decided not to stay (though none ever did), engaged in blacksmithing, shoemaking, silk raising, weaving and general farming. They are thought to have originated the washing machine, knitting machine, and "Shaker" furniture. One of their inventions, sarsaparilla, made from roots and herbs, appears to have successfully brought to an end much of the rum drinking habit which prevailed in many parts of America in the eighteen hundreds.

CHESTER

THIS ANCIENT TOWN apparently took its name from a forgotten section of Kingstown, Massachusetts, called Cheshire, from which Captain Samuel Ingalls (Ingolds), a blacksmith, had emigrated to New Hampshire in 1721. The names Cheshire and Chester both come from England, Chester being the county seat of Cheshire, from which our Cheshire County is derived. Earl of Chester is one of the hereditary titles always held by the Prince of Wales.

Chester, New Hampshire, was at first called the "chestnut country," and seems to have been the first of the grants by Massachusetts, under Governor Shute in 1722, to propose the terms under which settlements could be made. The land was to be planted, houses built, roads laid out, and a church and schoolhouse constructed, else the land be forfeited.

Chester was apparently selected as a "test town" for the expansion of the New Hampshire coastal area, granting land to such populations as those of Hampton, Newbury, Kingston, and Portsmouth, which had outgrown their boundaries.

As Chester increased in size, it became also an area for the settlement of expanding populations of nearby Londonderry and other adjacent sections which included the Scotch colonizers who came to New Hampshire from northern Ireland in the years following 1722. The towns of Auburn, Candia, Derryfield, Hooksett and Raymond were later formed from Chester.

Chester in England was known to the early Romans as "camp of the legions." It surrendered to William the Conqueror in 1070. The New Hampshire provincial government in 1761, also gave the name Chester to a grant of land in Vermont, then a part of this state.

CHICHESTER

CHICHESTER was one of seven towns granted in New Hampshire in 1727 while Lieutenant Governor John Wentworth administered the affairs of the province, then a part of Massachusetts. It was one of several places in the state named in honor of Thomas Pelham Holles, Duke of Newcastle and Earl of Chichester, one of the most influential English politicians of the mid-eighteenth century. As Secretary of State during the years following 1724, he assumed charge of the colonial policy and had much to do with relations between the American colonies and England. The Earl's title was taken from the ancient town of Chichester in County Sussex, England, built on the site of a Roman camp — or *castra* in Latin, which evolved into English as "chester." In 895 A.D. it became the capital of the Saxon king, Chissa, Chichester being a combination of the two names.

The granting of Chichester, New Hampshire and the other towns chartered by Lieutenant-Governor Wentworth was the result of the outgrowth of several Massachusetts towns whose sections, or "parishes" asked for additional land to be populated by new settlers, most of them adjacent to land already settled. Chichester became a new town because of this movement.

Among those receiving Chichester grants were the Gilmans of Exeter, Peter, Nicholas and Captain John; William Pepperell, Jr.; Captain Thomas Westbrook; Captain Paul Gerrish, and many others who had participated in the English wars against the French in Canada.

The original charter of Chichester served as a pattern for future charters for the undivided portions of New Hampshire, providing for the planting and cultivation of land, the building of dwelling houses, roads, and a schoolhouse and church, with a time limit of three to five years. The charge to settlers was one ear of corn per grantee per year.

CONCORD

NEW HAMPSHIRE'S capital city, like other cities and towns of the same name scattered throughout the United States, was so named because of a coming to agreement concerning a boundary dispute, peacefully settled at last, and the Latin word for "peace" chosen.

Concord in this state is thus not named for any other Concord, as is sometimes assumed, but was taken after a long and bitter protest over the boundary line to be drawn between what was then called Rumford and the territory to the south now called Bow. It took a decision on the part of the English government to decide the matter and the appearance before it by the town's lawyer-minister, the Reverend Timothy Walker, who won his case almost single-handed.

What is now Concord was a part of the original town of Penacook, named in 1659 for the Penacook Indian colony at the junction of the Merrimack and Contoocook Rivers. Many of its early settlers were from the Massachusetts town of Haverhill and had come from Essex in England. The name Romford, afterwards changed to Rumford, was given in their grant of 1725 and the town was incorporated in 1733. The name is perpetuated by the Maine town of Rumford Falls, which Concord people helped to settle, and also by its adoption by one of Concord's distinguished citizens, Benjamin Thompson (1753-1814) who, for his rehabilitation efforts in Germany following the European wars in the late 1700's, was rewarded with the name Count Rumford by the Holy Roman Emperor. Count Rumford was also knighted by King George III for his endeavors as a diplomat, scientist and philanthropist.

At the time the town of Rumford adopted the name Concord in 1765, there was already another Concord in the province, which then became Gunthwaite and is now Lisbon. Concord became the seat of the New Hampshire government in 1800, when the capital was moved from Portsmouth.

PENACOOK, which is now part of Concord, is the name of New Hampshire's best known Indian tribe, a name afterwards given to the village on the Merrimack. The early colonists spelled the name as they understood it from the Indians, "Pannukog." The Penacooks were thought to have been originally allied with the Pawtuckets who inhabited Eastern Massachusetts. The name "Pannukog" meant "crooked place" or bend in the river; but as there were several such bends in the vicinity where Penacook now is, it is difficult to locate the camps of this tribe exactly.

It is established that there was, however, a formidable Penacook Indian "fort" on what is now known as "Sugar Ball" bluff in East Concord, and that in the early 1600's, the period when Penacook was first settled, there was a vigorously fought battle there in which the Penacooks successfully defended themselves against their Western enemies, the Mohawks.

It is also established that after this battle the Penacooks became openly friendly with the white settlers, hoping to secure arms and ammunition from them in case the Mohawks attacked again, which apparently they did not.

The Penacook tribe had a succession of chiefs or "sachems," the first, as recorded in history, being the famous Passaconaway, who in his farewell speech warned his fellow-Indians not to quarrel with their English neighbors lest it prove the means of their own destruction. His words were said to have been heeded by his son and successor, Wonalancet, and his grandson, Kanca-magus, who became anglicized to the extent of calling himself John Hawkins, or Hodgkins.

A part of the village of Penacook was for many years known as "the Fort" and the settlement itself dates from 1659 when it was granted by Massachusetts, of which New Hampshire was then a part. The name also remains as that of Penacook Lake, or Long Pond, and some of the early Penacook settlers founded a town in Maine, also called Penacook.

DEERFIELD

DEERFIELD, originally a parish in Nottingham, was incorporated as a separate town in 1766. It appears to have been named for Deerfield, Massachusetts, from which some of its early settlers came.

Deerfield in New Hampshire, like that in Massachusetts, once suffered severely from Indian attacks, and its famous Longfellow Garrison House was one of the best known New England stockades. Also famous were its "Deerfield Parade" and its "Coffee-town" with its experimental coffee plantation, finally given up as unsuccessful.

Deerfield's early families included the Dearborns, Batchelders, Marstons, Robinsons, Trues, Crams, Winslows, Freeses and Simpsons. The last named included John Simpson who was a member of the company of Revolutionary soldiers enlisted by Dr. Henry Dearborn, afterward Colonel Dearborn, who fought at Bunker Hill.

John Simpson achieved lasting fame by so disobeying the

instructions of his commanding officer, Colonel William Prescott, who had ordered his men not to fire at the British soldiers "until you can see the whites of their eyes," that he discharged his gun prematurely, killing one of them, thus making history as having fired the "first shot" in the war. Private Simpson was court-martialed and reprimanded, but afterwards was made a lieutenant and cited for bravery. At the close of the war he would accept no pay and refused to apply for a pension, saying that "my country is too poor to pay."

Captain Dearborn later became famous as an American general, ranking among Deerfield's native sons along with General Benjamin Butler, one-time governor of Massachusetts, and Thomas Cogswell Upham, pioneer professor of philosophy at Bowdoin College.

Because of its location on the highway from Portsmouth to Concord, Deerfield was once proposed as a possible site for the state capital. Located in Deerfield is the fieldstone enclosed private cemetery built in honor of John D. Philbrick, former United States commissioner of education and a large contributor to Deerfield Academy.

DERRY

DERRY received its charter in 1827 during the administration of Governor Benjamin Pierce. Prior to that date, Derry had been a part of the important New Hampshire town of Londonderry, which included what are now Londonderry, Windham and parts of Salem, Hudson and Manchester. At one time it was the second largest town in the state. Londonderry was first granted by Massachusetts Governor Samuel Shute in 1722 to a colony of Scotch settlers who were born on Irish soil granted them by the English government.

Derry takes its name from the Isle of Derry in Ireland, from the Gaelic word "Doire," meaning "Oak woods." The first settlers came here about 1719, and among the early families were the Aikens, Mitchells, MacMurpheys, Nesmiths, Greggs, and McKeans. The first gristmill was operated by Captain James Gregg in 1722.

Derry, New Hampshire, was the home of Joseph McKean, first president of Bowdoin College; Aaron F. Stevens, Congressman and Civil War general; Charles M. Floyd, who was governor of New Hampshire from 1907 to 1909; and more recently, Alan Shepard, the astronaut. Also born here was General John Stark, hero of the Battle of Bennington, and another Revolutionary War general, George Reid.

Derry was at one time among the leading shoe manufacturing towns in America, and the home of two of America's oldest private schools, Pinkerton Academy, founded in 1814, and the Adams Female Seminary. Robert Frost, the famous poet, taught at Pinkerton from 1900 until 1911, and some of his finest early poems were composed at his farm in Derry.

DUNBARTON

THIS TOWN NAME is from Dumbartonshire in Scotland, on the River Clyde. It is the site of the famous Dunbar Castle, once perched on the top of the tall cliff known to North Sea sailors as the "Gibraltar of Scotland."

Dunbar Castle had a long history, dating from the days when King Edward II was welcomed there by Patrick Dunbar and it was successfully held by "Black Agnes," Countess of March, against a three-year siege by the English. Later it was owned by the ill-fated Mary, Queen of Scots, who was captured near there by the Earl of Bothwell and his men. Mary was kept prisoner in the castle for eleven days, resulting in her marriage to Bothwell, her third husband. The marriage was later annulled by the Pope.

Dunbarton in New Hampshire was first granted in 1735 by Governor Jonathan Belcher as Gorham's-town to surviving soldiers and their heirs in return for service in the "Canada Expedition" under Sir William Phipps and Captain John Gorham. It was regranted in 1748 as Starkstown to "Scotch-Irish" settlers who had left Scotland and, after a brief sojourn in Northern Ireland, arrived in Massachusetts, New Jersey and Maine and in 1718 found their way to New Hampshire.

Their leader, Archibald Stark, for whom the town was then named, brought with him the families of McGregor, Stinson, Putney, Todd, Cochrane, Gregg, Jameson and others. Archibald Stark's son was General John Stark, the patriot of Bunker Hill and Bennington and his grandson was Caleb Stark, also famous as an industrialist who set up the early textile mills on the Merrimack at Manchester.

The grant was confirmed by the "proprietors" in 1752 under a new charter and called Dunbarton in memory of Archibald Stark's native county of Dumbartonshire. Dunbarton was incorporated in 1765.

The Starks and their neighbors brought to English New Hampshire "a new system of agriculture before unknown" and, with their manufacture of flax and wool, helped to make possible the great commercial enterprises which were the foundations of New Hampshire's long-enduring river industry.

Dunbarton was the birthplace of Ernest Martin Hopkins, president of Dartmouth College from 1916 to 1945.

EPSOM

THIS TOWN NAME is one of the earliest in New Hampshire history. The town was one of seven granted by the Massachusetts authorities under whose jurisdiction it then was, in 1727, by Lieutenant Governor John Wentworth.

The name chosen probably came from Epsom, England, a famous horse-racing center since the days of King James I. At the time our town in New Hampshire was granted, William Stanley, the Earl of Derby, had established his racing stables there, and Epsom become famous for its "Derby" at Epsom Downs.

The English Epsom takes its place in history as a favorite watering place on the outskirts of London, where its fashionable mineral springs, of a curative value, have their parallel in our Saratoga with its springs and race-track. Epsom salts are known throughout the world, not only for their medicinal value, but for their use in the weighing and sizing of cotton cloth, made in English cotton mills. Analysis has shown that to some extent their contents correspond to those of sea water.

Among the grantees of New Hampshire's Epsom were Thomas Blake, its surveyor, Captain Thomas Weeks of Greenland, who built the famous "Brick House" in that town in 1710, and Charles McCoy, whose wife was taken prisoner in 1747 by the Indians. Mrs. McCoy left records of her experiences at Montreal where she was taken and held for ransom. When it was finally paid, and she was released, she reported that she had enjoyed her treatment by the French there as "so comfortable, and her husband being a man of rather rough and violent temper, she would never have thought of attempting the journey back home had it not been for the sake of her children."

One of Mrs. McCoy's children, Nat McCoy, achieved fame by getting lost in one of the mountains near Epsom, which bears the name "Nat's Mountain." Epsom also has its "Nat's Village" and Gossville.

GOFFSTOWN

PRIOR TO the establishment of the provincial government in New Hampshire, this town was a part of Massachusetts and had been known as Narragansett No. 4 and Piscataquog village. It comprised land awarded by Massachusetts to soldiers in the Narragansett Indian War, among them Edward Shove, who called it Shovestown. The failure of many of the early grantees to comply with the terms of the Massachusetts charter resulted in a new grant, issued in 1748 by the New Hampshire provincial government, to another group of settlers headed by Colonel John Goffe, whose farm at Goffe's Falls and Goffe's Ferry was one of its first settlements, and from whom the town officially was named.

Colonel Goffe appears to have been well qualified for leadership. Serving with the colonial troops in the French and Indian Wars, he fought at Ticonderoga, Crown Point and Montreal. At the close of the war he worked for Governor Wentworth as a surveyor, and the governor incorporated Goffstown in 1761 as a town, with Colonel Goffe as moderator. As such he served for many years, being known as "Squire" Goffe, and was judge of probate of Hillsborough County, which post he occupied until his death in 1786.

Colonel Goffe received many grants of land in addition to that in Goffstown, among them Grasmere and parts of Bedford, Gilsum (Boyle), Mason, Piermont, Jefferson, Thornton, Weare, Woodstock, Warner and Claremont in New Hampshire, and Hartland, Lunenburg, Manchester, Sudbury, and Wilmington now in Vermont, but originally a part of New Hampshire.

GRASMERE, which is a part of Goffstown, takes its name from the lake and the village in the Lakes District of England which was the home of the great poet William Wordsworth. The poets Coleridge and De Quincey also lived in the village of Grasmere, England.

Goffe's Mill in Bedford, so widely publicized in recent years, was built and owned by Colonel Goffe's son, Major John Goffe. Goffstown is the location of St. Anselm's College.

HENNIKER

SIR JOHN HENNIKER, a prosperous London merchant, was a member of a group of traders doing business with Colonial shipping interests in Boston and Portsmouth in pre-Revolutionary days. Henniker, New Hampshire, was named in his honor by Governor Wentworth in 1768.

Sir John, who also was one of the first to carry on trade relations between England and Russia, was associated with John Thomlinson, Charles Apthorp, Barlow Trecothick and Samuel Gray, all of whom dealt as London agents in English and West Indies goods, which they sent here in exchange for New England exports of fish, furs, lumber, sperm oil, turpentine, barrel staves and potash. Sir John Henniker married Anne Major, sister of Elizabeth Major, wife of Henry Brydges, Duke of Chandos, a famous English patron of the arts.

Henniker in New Hampshire was first known as "No. 6" in the line of towns running between the Merrimack and Connecticut Rivers. Later it was settled by families from Marlborough, Massachusetts, and called New Marlborough. In 1752 land was granted there to Andrew Todd, who called it Todd's-town, the new settlers having come from Londonderry, Hopkinton, Chester and Bedford.

Henniker is the site of the historic Ocean Born Mary House and of New England College.

HOLLIS

This town takes its name from one of the oldest families in England. It was incorporated in 1746 by Governor Benning Wentworth whose ancestor, Thomas Wentworth, the first Earl of Strafford, married Arabella Holles, daughter of John Holles. The names "Holles" and "Hollis" are interchangeable.

John Holles, Earl of Clare, was said to have been the "richest and most powerful man in England" in his day, and his grandson, Thomas Pelham Holles, Duke of Newcastle, became Secretary of State in 1724 and First Lord of the Treasury in 1754.

The English Wentworths had as their relatives not only the Holles family, but the Pelhams, Straffords, Cavendishes, Graftons, and Monsons, all of whom had New Hampshire-granted towns named for them, while Claremont takes its name indirectly from John Holles, the Earl of Clare.

Hollis, New Hampshire, was originally called West Dunstable or Nittisset, a part of Massachusetts which at one time included portions of Groton, Massachusetts, and what is now Nashua. Among the early settlers was the Reverend Francis Worcester, father of sixteen children, four of whom—Noah,

Leonard, Thomas, and Samuel—were ministers, all distinguished for their various publications and literary attainments. Noah Worcester was a founder of the American Peace Society. Another early settler was the Reverend Peter Powers, author, historian, and missionary to the North Country in the late 1770's.

HOOKSETT

THIS TOWN, which consisted of a rocky ledge surrounded by clay soil, flanking the Merrimack River above Manchester, was not officially named "Hooksett" until 1822, although it had borne this name for almost fifty years prior to that time. Before that it was called Chester Woods and Rowe's Corner.

Hooksett's geological formation appears to have suggested its name, because of its having been an island in the Merrimack in the shape of a hook, just as the geographically located town to the north took the name Bow because of its site at a curve of the river. The name Hooksett is also said to have been given to it by early fishermen whose baited hooks helped to bring in a plentiful supply of salmon, sturgeon, and shad below Hooksett Falls, and who sometimes referred to it as "Hookline Falls."

The name Hooksett has been variously elaborated with the prefixes "ana," "hannah," "onna," and "ama." Existing records refer to one of its rock formations as Hooksett Pinnacle, and it has been given the French name of "Isle au Hooksett." At one time it was the location of a cross-river ferry, of which there were several in that section, connecting with settlements to the east. The "Pinnacle" is nearly five hundred feet above the river level, and the water power created by the falls led to the establishment of early lumber mills. These were later superseded by a prosperous brick-making establishment, and in 1794 by the lottery-built Hooksett Canal which became a part of the transportation facilities of the Amoskeag cotton mills at Manchester.

Prominent in the early settlement of Hooksett was Colonel James Head who fought with the victorious General John Stark at Bennington, and was killed there. His descendant, Natt Head, served as adjutant general of New Hampshire, and was the author of a series of reports giving biographical information regarding every New Hampshire soldier from 1623 to the close of the Civil War. He became governor of the state in 1878.

HOPKINTON

ORIGINALLY known as New Hampshire No. 5, this town was granted in 1735 by Massachusetts, of which it was then a part, to settlers from Hopkinton in that state, to be known as New Hopkinton.

The original Hopkinton in Massachusetts, incorporated in 1715, got its name from Edward Hopkins, a prosperous merchant of London, England. Hopkins married a daughter of Theophilus Eaton, governor of the New Haven colony in Connecticut, and followed him to America, to become Connecticut's governor in 1640, serving for six terms. Returning to England, he became a member of Parliament and upon his death bequeathed a considerable sum to purchase American land from the Indians, a part of which became the town of Hopkinton, Massachusetts.

This town may be said to have set the pattern for the establishment of New England towns, as it provided that its sixty settlers should build homes for themselves within seven years, fence in their acreage, plant it with English grass, and provide a home for "a learned orthodox minister."

Many of the grantees of New Hopkinton in New Hampshire found it impossible, because of the French wars, to fulfill the terms of their charter, and took up a new grant in 1762. Among them were the Jones, Kimball, Mellen, Haven, and Morris families. Hopkinton's charming main street is lined with many stately old houses of colonial style. The town is noted as the birthplace of Commodore George Hamilton Perkins, Civil War naval officer, whose statue is located on the State House grounds in Concord, and whose ancestor, Bimsley Perkins, was a popular tavern keeper in Hopkinton in the early days of its settlement.

CONTOOCOOK village, long a part of Hopkinton which at one time it exceeded in population and commercial resources, takes its name from one of the tribes of Penacook Indians inhabiting the fertile valley through which flows the Contoocook River.

At one time the abundant water power in this river attracted a cluster of local Contoocook businesses which included a lumber mill, a grist mill, a silk mill, and a paper box mill, all dependent upon it for their existence. The early records also list two general stores, a drug store, millinery store, tin shop, shoe store, meat market, a printing office, two churches, and a thriving academy.

On the village's Putney Hill, now dignified by the title of "Mount Putney," was located a prosperous tavern, surrounded by stately homes, one of which was that of Reverend Elijah Fletcher, whose daughter married Daniel Webster.

HUDSON

ONCE known as Nottingham West, Hudson first came into existence when, in 1741, it was separated by order of Governor Benning Wentworth in the first year of his governorship, from the old town of Nottingham, Massachusetts which in turn had originally been a part of Dunstable in that state.

The name Nottingham, selected in 1722, was that of Daniel Finch, (1647-1730), second Earl of Nottingham, Secretary of State, during the reign of William and Mary, president of the King's Council, and related to the Rockingham family, of which the Wentworth governors were members.

Hudson remained as Nottingham West until 1830 when, because of its confusion with the town of Nottingham to the north, the voters petitioned to have it renamed. The choice of the name Hudson was made during the term of Governor Matthew Harvey, who at one time was president of the New Hampshire Historical Society and a close student of New Hampshire history.

He appears to have proposed calling the town Hudson because of its location near the point at which the Merrimack River, once supposed to flow east from the Hudson River for its full length, thus establishing a boundary line between New Hampshire and Massachusetts, was found instead to have come from the north.

The fertility of much of the intervale land adjacent to Hudson attracted the settlement in the early days of several large "estates," known as the Brattle Farm, after Captain Thomas Brattle, Brenton's Farm, (now Litchfield), after Governor William Brenton of Rhode Island, and the Hills Farm after Colonel William Hills who owned considerable land in Hillsborough.

Hudson is today one of the state's fastest growing towns.

LITCHFIELD

This town of fertile fields on the east bank of the Merrimack River, bore its early Indian name, Naticook, until 1729 when it was granted by Lieutenant-Governor John Wentworth as Brenton's Farm.

William Brenton, who owned a considerable section of what is now Litchfield, had come to Boston from London, received a large grant in Rhode Island and had married a daughter of Governor Cranston, later succeeding him as governor of that province. The Brentons were a prominent English family, of which Sir Jahleel Brenton, Vice Admiral of the British Navy, was a member. Brenton's Reef and Brenton's Point in Rhode Island are both named for him.

William Brenton had been a close friend of "King Philip," and Brenton's Farm is said to have been purchased by him of the Naticook Indians, of which tribe Passaconaway was a chief. Brenton occupied it until his death. The land was then granted to new settlers in 1749 and named in honor of George Henry Lee, Earl of Litchfield, a relative of Governor Benning Wentworth, and Chancellor of Oxford University in England. The Earl became a privy councilor to the King and is remembered as having founded the first clinical professorship at Oxford.

One of the early settlers of Litchfield was Wyseman Claggett, a West Indian trader who had come to Portsmouth from Antigua to become attorney general in Governor Wentworth's cabinet. Another colonist was Edward Goldstone Lutwyche (Lutwich) of Boston, who owned a farm in the town of Merrimack and established a ferry, later to become Thornton's Ferry, across the river to Litchfield.

LONDONDERRY

THIS TOWN was named in 1722 from Londonderry in northern Ireland, where a colony of Scotch people had settled, prior to emigrating to America in 1718. Its Irish name was originally Derry Calgach, derived from Calgach, meaning "fierce warrior" and Derry, meaning "oak woods." Because of its heavily wooded area, Londonderry in New Hampshire was first called Nutfield.

The Scotch settlers were encouraged to come to America by Governor Samuel Shute of Massachusetts, of which New Hampshire was then a part, and they brought with them the art of raising, spinning, and weaving flax for the linen trade, and the cultivation of the potato. The settlement included as members Reverend James McGregor, its first minister, and the families of Cargill, Morison, Weare, Holmes, McKeen, Bell, and many others whose more than a hundred names are perpetuated in this state.

The early Londonderry Scotch extended their settlement into several surrounding villages which took their names from towns in Scotland and Ireland, among them being our Antrim, Dunbarton, Derry, and Windham, as well as Coleraine and Blandford in Massachusetts. Londonderry was in early Colonial times the second largest town in New Hampshire, and the present towns of Derry and Windham were formed from it. Matthew Thornton (1714-1803), signer of the Declaration of Independence and first "president" of New Hampshire, was brought to

Londonderry by his parents at the age of four from his birth place in Londonderry, Ireland.

LOUDON

LOUDON was part of the town of Canterbury until 1773, when it was chartered by Governor John Wentworth. The new town took its name from John Campbell (1705-1782) fourth Earl of Loudoun, a Scottish soldier. The name Loudoun, which has been shortened in American usage, is similar to a French town Louduin, scene of a treaty following the religious wars of 1616.

John Campbell, Lord Loudoun, raised a regiment and fought with the English army as aide-de-camp to the king in the Seven Years' War which ended in 1763 with the conquest of Canada. In 1756 he was sent to America by William Pitt to assemble and organize the forces for that conquest, toward which the English government contributed not only men and ships but more than four million pounds to meet the expenses in the colonies.

In his capacity as a provincial commander-in-chief Loudoun was criticized because of his policy of quartering troops in private houses. He was highly praised, however, in Boston, where, at a dinner in his honor, he was toasted for "the warm affection he has displayed for his countrymen here and the signal service he has rendered to this province." It was under Lord Loudoun's orders that Major Robert Rogers organized his famous frontier fighters, "Rogers' Rangers." Succeeded in the campaign by General Amherst in 1758, the Earl returned to England where he was made second in command of the army.

The name Loudoun is also known because of John Loudoun McAdam who served here as an aide to the Earl. McAdam, remembered as "the father of American road building," was the inventor in 1810 of the "McAdamizing" process which revolutionized road-surfacing throughout the world. He served here for several years as a consultant, refusing to take any remuneration or patent rights for his invention.

MANCHESTER

MANY A New Hampshire town was once thought to have derived its name from an English town, only to be revealed as the namesake of some English notable. Manchester, however, was unquestionably named for the industrial city of Manchester, England.

Long before this occurred, however, the town was granted as Derryfield by Governor Benning Wentworth in 1751, taking its name from its neighbor Londonderry. Before that it had been called Harrytown and Tyng's Town.

Samuel Blodgett, who first thought of changing the name of New Hampshire's quiet countryside Scotch town of Derryfield to Manchester, was born in 1724. His father was a popular Haverhill, Massachusetts innkeeper who operated a busy stage coach to Boston. The name Blodgett was orginally the Huguenot "Bloetgoet," or Bloodgood and although the name has at least twenty-four New England pronunciations, the nearest the Haverhill people could come to it was Blodgett.

Young Sam fought in the French wars and later in the Revolution. Then he went to the English coast as a deep-sea diver in search of Spanish gold — without getting any. He did, however, visit London and Manchester, with its canals around the falls filled with barges. Returning home he set up a lumber and potash business. When the Amoskeag falls on the Merrimack impeded his shipping, he at once thought of the canals at Manchester, England and he made up his mind to build one here.

Bad luck beset his progress at first. No sooner was his canal finished than a spring flood washed it away. His funds exhausted, he asked the legislature for the right to run a lottery, which he got and it netted him $9,000. Later he needed more and raised another $12,000. Finally with additional funds from Massachusetts, he completed his canal, safe and sound, and it was opened in May of the year 1807.

Sam Blodgett was now eighty-three and had in the meantime become prosperous from his duck, linen and white sail mills in Manchester. But he lived on only until September of that year, never to reap the harvest from his great canal project. This undertaking was to become the basis for making his town into a great city, and as a result of his suggestion the town was re-named Manchester. It was incorporated as a city in 1846. In 1887, the world-famous Manchester ship canal in England was opened to allow traffic from this inland port to the sea, a fitting event to tie the two Manchesters together.

MERRIMACK

THIS TOWN, of all those on the Merrimack River which might have been so named, received this honor in 1746, when it was separated from Nashua, then Dunstable. Before that, Merri-mack and Litchfield, its neighboring town across the river, were called Naticook — after the Indian tribe occupying the region. The first log cabin here is said to have been built by John Cromwell in 1665, but real settlement did not begin until 1722. Merrimack was also the site of what is probably the first "public utility" in New Hampshire, Lutwyche's Ferry.

Merrimack's first settlement was encouraged by the fact that it lay opposite a plot of land on the Merrimack known as Bren-ton's Farm, now Litchfield, the estate of a governor of Rhode Island upon whose death the fertile area was divided into lots which had a ready sale, and some of which were directly across the river at Merrimack.

This caused the need of a ferry, plans for which were con-ceived by Edward Lutwyche (or Lutwich) who obtained a charter for what became known at Lutwyche's Ferry. Mr. Lut-wyche was a Boston tavern keeper, the son of Lawrence Lut-wyche of the family of Sir Edward Lutwyche of London, and a close friend of Governor Benning Wentworth, who granted Edward Lutwyche of Merrimack the right to "transport men, horses, carriages and other things" and no other ferry was to be allowed two miles north or south of his concession.

Lutwyche's right to collect fees on this ferry was subject to considerable litigation prior to the Revolution. Finally he retired to England in 1774, and the ferry rights were bought by Dr. Matthew Thornton of Merrimack, who operated the crossing during his declining years and for whom the present settlement of Thornton's Ferry is named. Dr. Thornton, the Revolutionary War patriot, is buried in Merrimack.

MONT VERNON

To THE average American this name suggests the majestic homestead of George Washington, visited by thousands of tourists each year. To commuters on the New Haven Railroad it means the first station north of New York, and there are Mount Vernons in Illinois, Indiana, Ohio and Washington, to name only a few.

New Hampshire got its Mont Vernon in 1803, probably the earliest in the United States when the town was formed from the northwestern part of Amherst.

The original name in Virginia was the outgrowth of a chain of circumstances resulting from the illness of Lawrence Washington, half-brother of the first President, who had taken a sea trip for his health to the West Indies in the 1700's. There he had met the great English admiral, Edward Vernon, who was in charge of the fleet blockading the Spanish ports of Cartagena and Portobello.

Admiral Vernon (1684-1757) was the idol of the British, who have a statue of him erected in London, and he was much endeared to his men, because of his famous grogram (grosgrain) coat which he wore on duty, and which earned him the nickname of "Old Grog." When the admiral issued orders to his ships, designed to stop over-drinking by requiring the rations of rum and whiskey to be mixed with water, the men transferred the admiral's nickname to their daily supply. Thus did "grog" come into the dictionaries for all time.

When Lawrence Washington recovered, he served on one of the admiral's ships as an officer, and returning home, named his estate Mount Vernon after the admiral. It became George Washington's property on Lawrence Washington's death in 1752.

While the naming of New Hampshire's Mont Vernon occurred in 1803, four years after George Washington's death, and only one year after the death of his Martha, the name of Admiral Vernon is directly connected with New Hampshire history. Probably entirely without the knowledge of those who chose the town name in 1803, the fact remains that the English Vernons or Venables, were directly related to the Wentworth governors, and our Governor Wentworth was a close friend of Admiral Vernon.

NASHUA

THIS OLD New Hampshire town, long since a city, was originally a part of a 128,000-acre land grant measuring 200 square miles. It was made in the late 1600's by Governor Richard Bellingham of Massachusetts to Edward Tyng, formerly of Dunstable, England who named the settlement which followed after his native English town, where he owned a considerable estate.

Tyng and his family held this grant of valuable river land, of which Tyngsboro in Massachusetts was then a part, for more than sixty years. An early name for Manchester, New Hampshire, was Tyng's Town. But in 1741 the English courts set the new boundary line between Massachusetts and New Hampshire, dividing the grant almost in half. The northern part, retaining the name Dunstable (derived from the English "dun" meaning "hilly place" and "staple" meaning "trading place"), was then again partitioned over the years to form several New Hampshire border towns. In 1836 what had been Dunstable took the name Nashua, from the Nashua River, home of the famous tribe of Nashaway Indians, whose name translated into English would mean "beautiful river with a pebbly bottom."

Nashua which contained several rivers and brooks, also had its sections called Nashville, Indian Head and Dram Cup Hill. It ultimately became one of New Hampshire's most prosperous manufacturing centers, whose water power was increased by the building of the famous Middlesex Canal connecting the Merrimack River to Boston. It was incorporated as a city in 1853, during the administration of Governor Noah Martin. Nashua is the county seat of Hillsborough County and the city's population is now close to 50,000.

NEW BOSTON

NEW BOSTON got its name, as might properly be supposed, from Boston in Massachusetts. First settled in 1736, when New Hampshire affairs were administered by the Bay Colony, Governor Jonathan Belcher made grants here to prominent Boston families bearing the names of Peabody, Bridge, Lane, Bullfinch, Dodge, Simpson, Dudley and others, for a town six square miles in size, to be called Lanestown or Piscataquog Township.

Not all these grants were taken up and ten years later when the "proprietors" purchased the New Hampshire claim from the English heirs of Captain John Mason, the state's founder, the town was regranted and opened to an entirely new group of "colonizers." The newcomers were Scotch-Irish from Ulster, Northern Ireland, and came by way of Londonderry, New Hampshire.

Thus a long list of Scotch names found its way into the New Boston town records. Among them were those of Cochrane, McNeil, Moor, Kelso, Beard, Wason, Blair, Cristy, Willson, Crombie and Clark, so that soon, with their large families, New Boston became one of New Hampshire's leading Scotch-Irish towns. A commentary on its growth is to be found in a remark by a member of the Beard and Burns families in New Boston in the early days to the effect that she had "twin brothers and a twin sister, twin children, twin grandchildren, twin greatgrandchildren, twin nieces, twin grandnieces, twin grandnephews, a twin brother-in-law, a twin son-in-law, and am a twin myself."

The name New Boston, long used, was finally officially adopted at the incorporation of the town by Governor Benning Wentworth in 1763.

NORTHWOOD

NORTHWOOD, first settled in 1763, was separated from its parent-town of Nottingham ten years later, under a grant by Governor John Wentworth. It had been known for some time as North Woods and Northwood Narrows, a name still retained within its borders.

Among Northwood's early settlers were some of the original Boston families which had come north by way of Hampton, Exeter, and Durham. They included the Batchelders, Bickfords, Johnsons, Knowltons, Hoyts and De Merritts. At one time the town had as many as twelve sawmills and, as it grew more prosperous, some of these were replaced by shoe factories, of which the town once had five, employing almost one-third of its population.

In recent years Northwood has been known as the "town of lakes" (ten in all), among them Suncook, Pleasant, Harvey, Bow, Little Bow, Morison and North River, all providing attractive vacation spots for visitors.

NOTTINGHAM

DANIEL FINCH, second Earl of Nottingham, had a distinguished career in the English government during which he enjoyed a close friendship with colonial governors, Joseph Dudley and Samuel Shute, at the time when New Hampshire was under the jurisdiction of Massachusetts. Thus did our town of Nottingham come to bear his name in 1722.

The son of Heneage Finch, the first Earl of Nottingham, Daniel served as Lord Commissioner of the Treasury, Controller of His Majesty's Household, First Lord of the Admiralty, and Lord Justice. He did much to establish extensive trade with the colonies, and through the Cavendish family he was related to the later Wentworth governors. His grandson was Charles Watson-Wentworth, Lord Rockingham.

Our Nottingham was granted as a result of petitions from residents of Portsmouth and Boston, who asked to have it named New Boston. This name, however, was reserved for later use, and the name Nottingham was suggested by Governor Shute and his lieutenant governor, John Wentworth. Among the grantees was Peregrine White of Boston, named for his ancestor Peregrine White of the Mayflower, the "first child of English parentage born in New England", the name Peregrine signifying "pilgrim in a strange land".

Deerfield was separated from Nottingham in 1766 and made a separate town. In the opening days of the Revolution Colonel Henry Dearborn trained his militia regiment in Nottingham before marching to the Battle of Lexington. Dearborn later became a general, member of Congress, and Secretary of War under Jefferson.

PELHAM

THIS TOWN received its charter in 1746 from Benning Wentworth, the sixth to be so granted since his inauguration as governor of the new royal province in 1741.

Pelham takes its name from Henry Pelham, then Prime Minister of England, who was related to the governor through the English family of Cavendish, prominent in parliamentary affairs. Pelham had been a member of the House of Commons since 1717, and had been made Secretary of War in 1724. He succeeded Lord Wilmington as First Lord of the Treasury in 1721 and became Prime Minister in 1743, serving eleven years, so that the naming of the New Hampshire town in 1746 had special significance. Hollis, named for Henry Pelham's elder brother, Thomas Pelham Holles, was granted in the same year.

Governor Wentworth named several New Hampshire towns in honor of English prime ministers, among them Walpole for

Sir Robert Walpole, Grenville (now Newport) for George Grenville, and Chatham for William Pitt, Earl of Chatham.

Both Pelham and Hollis were originally a part of the area of New Hampshire once known as Old Dunstable, some of which remained as Nashua, and another section reverted to Massachusetts at the time of the change in the boundary line in 1741.

PEMBROKE

PEMBROKE, which comprises within its limits the much larger town of Suncook, was first granted in 1728 by Lieutenant Governor John Wentworth. It was called at the time Lovewell's Town after Captain John Lovewell, an early settler who was a noted hunter and Indian fighter. Lovewell was instrumental in building on Lake Ossipee the first stockade fort of the many erected in New Hampshire for protection against attacks by the Abenaki Indians from the north country. He led an expedition to subdue the Indians in 1725 and was killed at Fryeburg, Maine, in one of the very few Indian battles which occurred in northern New England. As was the custom at the time, the surviving soldiers of Captain Lovewell's company were given land grants by the provincial government.

The town, however, assumed the name SUNCOOK not long afterwards. Suncook was, and is, the Indian name of the New Hampshire river which flows through the area and joins the Merrimack where the present day municipality of Suncook is now located. For a time the town was also known by the name of "Buckstreet."

In 1759 the town was incorporated, and was given its present name by Governor Benning Wentworth. He named it in memory of Henry Herbert, ninth Earl of Pembroke (1689-1750) who, through marriage to a daughter of the Earl Fitzwilliam, was related to the Wentworth family. Lord Pembroke's career in the English army earned him the rank of Lieutenant General, and he was afterwards Lord Chief Justice. His home was the famous Wilton House (for which our town of Wilton is possibly named), and there he devoted much time to his favorite pursuit, the study of architecture. He was the designer of Westminster Bridge in London. His family took their title from historic Pembroke, the town and castle in southern Wales.

RAYMOND

THIS TOWN was named in 1764 after Captain William Raymond (or Rayment) of Beverly, Massachusetts, who raised a company of soldiers to fight in the war against Canada in the early 1700's, in an expedition to Quebec commanded by Sir William Phipps.

These soldiers were known as members of the "Canada Expedition" and were rewarded by grants in several Massachusetts and New Hampshire towns. The "Beverly-Canada" contingent, led by Captain Raymond, secured land in Raymond, and Captain Raymond himself had grants in Weare, first called Beverly-Canada, and in several other New Hampshire towns. He was probably descended from the early Raymonds who were sent to New Hampshire in 1631 in a group collected by Captain John Mason of Portsmouth, England, the founder of this colony. A later member of the English Raymond family was Sir Robert Raymond, Lord Chief Justice of England during the reign of King George II.

Raymond, New Hampshire, was originally a parish in Chester, known as Freetown, said to have been so named because it was exempted from the usual obligation of reserving its "tall pine trees" for masts in the royal English navy. It still has its "Freetown Pond" which competes with Lake Winona for scenic beauty.

Freetown was first settled by Stephen Dudley of Exeter, who claimed to have purchased the land from the Sagamore Indians. Other early families bore the names of Bailey, Blashfield, Byles, Ellingwood, Dodge, Pickett and Woodbury, all from either Beverly, Massachusetts, or Chester, then known as "Chester Woods."

SALEM

SALEM was originally known as early as 1736 as the "North Parish" of Methuen, Massachusetts, or "Methuen District." It had been named for Lord John Methuen of England who, as ambassador to Portugal, arranged to exchange English textiles for port and madeira wine which he helped to popularize in his native country in the early 1700's.

When the boundary lines between New Hampshire and Massachusetts were re-established in 1741, this section of Methuen fell to New Hampshire, and it was renamed Salem. The name was taken from nearby Massachusetts Salem which in the early days was one of the most important ports on the Eastern seaboard. Salem comes from the biblical word for "peace," and was chosen by the Reverend Francis Higginson of England after a friendly dispute between the early colonies of Roger Conant and Governor John Endicott.

Salem, New Hampshire was not officially incorporated until 1750. Among its grantees were the Duston, Wheeler, Bailey, Ayer, Merrill, Mussey and Sanders families. Canobie Lake is located in Salem, as is the Rockingham Park Race Track and the famous "Mystery Hill," site of a prehistoric settlement. Salem's population has more than doubled in the last decade, and is now over 20,000. The United States now has fourteen Salems, one of which is the capital of Oregon.

WEARE

WEARE has the distinction of having had five names during its long history, possibly more than any other town in the state. Its original land was included in a Massachusetts grant in 1735 to soldiers in the Canadian wars who came from Beverly, Massachusetts, and it was then called Beverly-Canada. Later it was called Halestown after Colonel Robert Hale, one of the soldiers, and in 1740 it was called Robiestown after an early settler, Ichabod Robie.

In 1748, after New Hampshire had become a separate province, a considerable part of the territory had still not been settled. As a result it was regranted to petitioners from Bedford, Hampton and other "boundary" towns, as Wearestown, after Colonel Meshech Weare who served as its first town clerk. In 1764 it was incorporated under its present name, Weare, in his honor.

The petitioners included the families of Dustin, Little, Atwood, Corliss, Quimby, Clement, and Jewell. Also among them was Colonel John Goffe of Bedford, and the Reverend Ebenezer Flagg who built the town's first sawmill, and who, in his petition, considered the new proprietors under the Wentworth government as "a good Providence, this," and hoped his land might be "as near Amoskeag as we could."

Colonel Weare, with his biblical name Meshech (meaning "merchant trader"), appears in the list of grantees with the title "Mr." — in those days a mark of respect. He served New Hampshire as a "farmer, lawyer, legislator, and patriot," and became its "president," a title afterward changed to "governor," in 1776, continuing in office until 1785. Before the Revolution Colonel Weare received grants from the Wentworth proprietors in Enfield, Lancaster, Orford, Piermont, Plymouth and Unity, and in eight towns then a part of New Hampshire but now in Vermont — Bridgewater, Cavendish, Dummerston, Halifax, Manchester, Norwich, Rupert, and Waterbury. His son, Richard died in the Revolution in 1777.

Weare has long been known as a "mineral" country of glacial origin, but its only products of commercial value seem to have been talc and soapstone. It has four mountains — Dearborn, Wallingford, William, and Misery, and includes the villages of Riverdale, Chase Village, Maplewood, and Clinton Grove.

WINDHAM

THIS TOWN gets its name from Sir Charles Wyndham (1710-1763) who in 1750 became Earl of Egremont and Baron Cockermouth. He served as a member of Parliament under two English kings and was Secretary of State during the period when the Rockingham government, led by Pitt and Fox, favored conciliation with the American colonies.

Sir Charles Wyndham (whose name was sometimes spelled Windham) appears to have been a close friend of Governor Benning Wentworth at the time he was made the governor of New Hampshire in 1741. Windham was the second town to be incorporated during his term. Its petition to be separated from its parent town of Londonderry was presented to the Governor on January 12 of that year, assented to by him on February 10; the act of incorporation by the legislature, dated two days later on February 12, indicating the promptness with which such transactions were carried on at that time. Later recognition of Charles Wyndham occurred in the naming of the town of Cockermouth (now Groton) and the Cockermouth River in New Hampshire.

Among Windham's earliest settlers was Reverend Thomas Cobbett, said to have been of the same English family as the famous William Cobbett, the journalist who, as "Peter Porcupine" occupied a leading place in English politics in the early 1800's. Cobbett's Pond in our Windham is named for him. Most of the other settlers who had occupied Windham land were from the Scottish families of Gregg, McCoy, Morison, Campbell, Cochran, McKeen, Dunlap, Jameson, Hemphill, Nesmith, and McMurphy, who had come to America from Ireland in 1718.

The exact line between Londonderry and Windham was not established until 1782. Windham was the birthplace of one of New Hampshire's best known governors, Samuel Dinsmoor (1766-1835).

IV

Monadnock Region

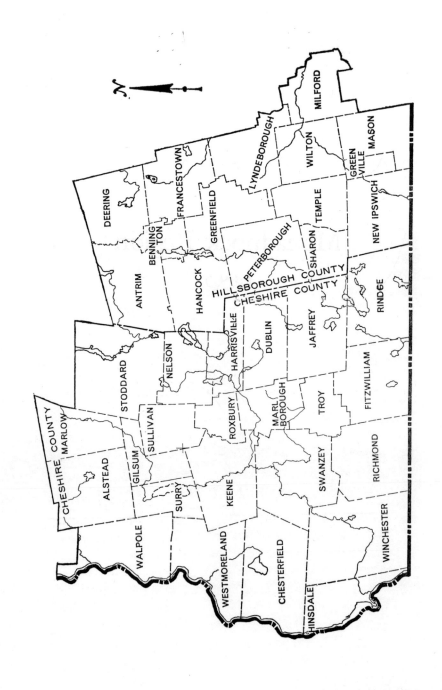

ALSTEAD

ALSTEAD, the northernmost town of Cheshire County and the Monadnock Region, was originally designated as Number Four, in a curved line of nine towns established by Massachusetts in 1735, beginning with Chesterfield (No. 1) and ending with Lempster (No. 9), all intended to protect the southwestern area of New Hampshire from Indian attacks.

When Benning Wentworth became governor of the province in 1741, he renamed some of these towns and gave Number 4 the name Newton, in 1752. However, as there already existed a Newton (or New Town) named earlier, it was decided to re-grant it, this time as Alsted (or Alstead), a name adopted in 1763.

The choice of the name Alstead for a town was a departure from the governor's usual custom of naming new towns after his English parliamentarian friends, as it was that of the compiler of an *Encyclopedia*, Johann Heinrich Alsted, whose books were among the most popular the governor had studied at Harvard. These text books, published in 1630, provided, for the first time in New England collegiate and church history, a complete lexicon of mathematical and astronomical knowledge and were considered by Cotton Mather to be a "Northwest Passage" to all the sciences, "treating of everything that can be learned about man in this life." They contained what is said to have been the first article ever published on "the use and abuse of tobacco," and rare copies are in the Harvard Library.

Alstead was once known as "Paper Village," the first paper mill in New Hampshire having been established on Cold River in 1793. Among the town's first grantees were sixteen members of the family of the pioneer settler, Aquila Chase, from whom was descended Bishop Philander C. Chase of Cornish, and Salmon P. Chase, Secretary of the Treasury under Abraham Lincoln, and Chief Justice of the United States.

ANTRIM

ANTRIM, situated on the northern edge of the Monadnock Region, forms part of the western boundary of Hillsborough County. Although a settlement prior to the American Revolution, the town did not get its incorporated name until 1777.

It was then a part of a large tract of land adjacent to Mount Monadnock, long known as Cumberland, or "Society Land". The name Cumberland was that of King George II's son William Augustus, Duke of Cumberland, who distinguished himself as commander of the English troops on the continent in the war with France. The name has been adopted by many sections of the eastern United States, among the best known being the Cumberland Mountains, situated between Kentucky and Virginia.

Antrim itself became by purchase the home of Philip Riley (or Roiley) of Sudbury, Massachusetts, who named it for his native County Antrim (the Gaelic *Endrimm*) in Ireland. Riley Mountain, near what was once his farm, is so called in his honor.

Antrim is but one of several Irish — or Scotch-Irish — town names brought to colonial New Hampshire by early settlers. Some of the others are Dublin, Kilkenny, Limerick, Londonderry, and Coleraine.

County Antrim in Ireland is famous for being the location of the Giant's Causeway, a basaltic formation much visited by tourists. Also in Antrim is the Shane's Castle, an ancient Irish round tower built in 1662. Antrim in Ireland was colonized from Scotland in the late 1600's, many of the settlers there migrating to New Hampshire in 1718.

In the last decade Antrim has become a college town with the establishment of Nathaniel Hawthorne College, a four year liberal arts institution, founded in 1960. The town of Antrim includes North Branch and Clinton Village.

BENNINGTON

Bennington, named in 1842, commemorates the Battle of Bennington, Vermont, fought on August 14-16, 1777, when General John Stark won one of the decisive victories of the Revolutionary War — against General Burgoyne's attempt to split the colonies along the Hudson River.

Bennington, Vermont, took its name from Governor Benning Wentworth who gave it its charter in 1749, when it was assumed to be a part of New Hampshire. The battle which bears its name actually took place on the opposite side of the Wallomsuc River, in New York State.

Bennington, New Hampshire, was originally a part of Hancock, and parts of it were also taken from Greenfield, Deering and Francestown. It was known as "Hancock Factory Village," deriving its name from its location at the Great Falls on the Contoocook River, where water power was abundant. Here the Putnams, cousins of General Israel Putnam of Revolutionary fame, had their mills, succeeded by the Monadnock Paper Mills and the Goodell Cutlery Works. Factory Village seceded from Hancock and became Bennington against the wishes of the people of Hancock, who protested the loss of taxes. Like Antrim, it was originally a part of Cumberland or "Society Land," set aside by the Portsmouth Proprietors to be their private estates modeled after the English countryside on the Contoocook River and centered about Mount Monadnock. It is one of the most recent New Hampshire towns to be incorporated.

Until it burned in 1965, the oldest covered railroad bridge in the United States stood near Monadnock Paper Mills, spanning the Contoocook River.

CHESTERFIELD

Chesterfield, on the westernmost edge of Cheshire County, was "No. 1" in a series of fort towns bordering on the Connecticut River. They were established in 1735 in the vicinity of what later became the famous Fort Dummer, as protective trading posts in the early Indian days. The others were Westmoreland (No. 2), Walpole (No. 3), and Charlestown (No. 4).

Some time after New Hampshire became an independent province with Benning Wentworth as its first governor, these towns were incorporated under new names, one of them, in 1752, being called Chesterfield after Philip Stanhope, fourth Earl of Chesterfield, England. Lord Chesterfield served as Secretary of State, and joined with William Pitt in opposing what both considered England's unfair treatment of the American colonies. In one of his speeches in the House of Lords he asserted that he "had never seen a forward child mended by whipping." Noted for his fashionable attire, he is said to have originated the famous Chesterfield overcoat, long popular in England and America.

The section in which the town of Chesterfield was located, while slow in being settled, played an important part in New England's history. The proposal of Massachusetts to build Fort Dummer was concurred in by Governor Wentworth but his Legislature failed to assist in providing a share of the needed funds. This share, amounting to more than ten thousand pounds, was raised and contributed by a group of colonizers, under the leadership of Colonel Josiah Willard. Associated with him were Colonel Joseph Blanchard and Colonel Benjamin Bellows. They were later reimbursed by Massachusetts.

Colonel Willard, who also had grants in Grafton, Stoddard, Keene, Jefferson, Westmoreland and Winchester, brought to Chesterfield no fewer than twelve members of his family. Among the other first settlers were the families of Lynde, Kendall, Wheelright, Stoodley, Field, and Chamberlain. Colonel Willard was afterward appointed commander of Fort Dummer.

Chesterfield has given the country a Chief Justice of the Supreme Court, Harlan Fiske Stone, born in the town in 1872. After a distinguished career as a professor of law, Stone was appointed to the Court in 1925, and became Chief Justice in 1941.

Chesterfield includes the town of SPOFFORD located on Spofford Lake, one of the largest bodies of water in the Monadnock region. It has been a popular summer resort area for many years. Spofford takes its name from John and Silas Spofford who were among the grantees. Spofford Lake was named as early as 1761.

DEERING

DEERING, in the northeast corner of the Monadnock Region, was the family name of the wife of John Wentworth, the last provincial New Hampshire governor, who named this town in her honor. The Deering family were allied with the Bennings, the name of Governor Benning Wentworth's mother, with the Wentworths, (Samuel, Benning Wentworth's brother, married Elizabeth Deering), and with the Atkinson family. Colonel Theodore Atkinson became one of the original proprietors, and his son, Theodore Atkinson, Jr., was the first husband of Frances Wentworth.

Henry Deering, the uncle of Frances Wentworth, was associated with a group consisting of Thomas Hancock, uncle of the "Signer," Daniel Henchman, and James Boies who organized what is said to have been the first paper mill in America at Milton, Massachusetts.

Lady Frances Wentworth, with her husband, the governor, left the country at the time of the Revolution for Nova Scotia, where he was made a baronet. They later resided in England, where she became a lady-in-waiting to Queen Charlotte, wife of George III.

The area which became Deering was originally adjacent to Cumberland, named for George II's son, the Duke of Cumberland, also known as "Society Land," reserved for the Masonian Proprietors.

In 1774 it was granted by Governor Wentworth as Deering, with William Clark of Boston as moderator, and the land was divided among twenty-one families.

DUBLIN

DUBLIN, one of the three highest villages in New Hampshire, takes its name from Dublin, Ireland. It was granted in 1749 as Monadnock and incorporated as Dublin in 1771 by Governor John Wentworth, whose English ancestor, Thomas Wentworth, Earl of Strafford, once served as Lord Lieutenant of Ireland. He had been associated with Sir Francis Bacon in the project of resettling portions of that country with Scotch colonists, many of whom later came to New Hampshire. Other Irish towns whose names were transplanted to this state or to Massachusetts were Antrim, Coleraine, Derry, Londonderry, Kilkenny and Limerick.

Dublin was originally known as North Monadnock, or No. 3, and was one of a group of eight towns in the Monadnock region all first designated by numbers, later to be given their present names. The entire section was settled by Scotch colonists, but Dublin appears to have had among its early inhabitants a number from Sherborn and other Massachusetts towns.

Among the grantees of Dublin following its incorporation were several who had taken leading parts in the English wars against the French, among them being Samuel Livermore, Captain Peter Powers, Colonel Benjamin Bellows and Dr. Matthew Thornton, together with the surveyors of the area, Colonel Joseph Blanchard and Sampson Stoddard.

Early family names in the town records of Dublin include those of Alexander, Scott, Strongman, Morse, Twitchell and Greenwood. Because of its high elevation in the picturesque Grand Monadnock region, Dublin has long been a favorite New England vacation resort, counting among its visitors and residents nationally known writers, such as Mark Twain, Emerson, Longfellow and Thoreau, and painters, such as George de Forest Brush, Abbott Thayer and Alexander James. *Yankee* magazine and the widely known *Old Farmer's Almanac* are published in Dublin.

FITZWILLIAM

FITZWILLIAM takes its name from William, fourth Earl Fitzwilliam of England, and was granted in 1773 by Governor Wentworth, who was the earl's American cousin. The town was originally settled as Monadnock No. 4, one of a series of Monadnock "towns" in the region. It was also at one time known as Stoddardstown after Samson Stoddard who surveyed the entire Contoocook valley and laid out its group of towns, one of which, Stoddard, bears his name today.

Lord Fitzwilliam, connected through his wife with the Rockingham and Wentworth families in England, was one of the wealthiest and most influential members of the House of Lords. He became a peer in 1756 and was politically allied with the group composed of Burke, Fox, Pitt, Conway, Dartmouth and Grafton, which favored negotiation with and conciliation of the American Colonies in the pre-Revolutionary years. He built the famous Wentworth House in the West Riding, Yorkshire, and served as Lord-Lieutenant of the county. Lord Fitzwilliam was appointed president of the council in Pitt's cabinet and later became Viceroy of Ireland. He died in 1833 at the advanced age of eighty-five years. His son, Charles, who succeeded him, hyphenated the family name to Wentworth-Fitzwilliam.

Samson Stoddard, one of the early grantees of Fitzwilliam, received several plots in the town for his services. Other owners were Roland and Josiah Cotton of Plymouth, Massachusetts, who did much to establish the Congregational Church in New England; General James Reed, one of New Hampshire's famous soldiers; Matthew Thornton, who signed the Declaration of Independence; and three members of the Treadwell family of Portsmouth who founded one of its leading shipping enterprises.-

Fitzwilliam was one of New Hampshire's earliest granite producing centers, and at one time had no fewer than six quarries in operation. Fitzwilliam today has many vacation visitors; there are ten lakes near it, and the Rhododendron State Park is famous for a large stand of native *Rhododendron Maximus*.

FRANCESTOWN

FRANCESTOWN, incorporated in 1772, like Deering, its neighbor to the north, takes its name from Frances Deering Wentworth, wife of Governor John Wentworth, who was "first lady" of New Hampshire at the time. She was a member of the Deering family of England and Boston, several of that name having intermarried with prominent New Hampshire families.

Frances Wentworth, who was only twenty-seven when Francestown was named, was one of the most beautiful women in America — as her portrait by Copley testifies. But three years after the naming of this town, she left New Hampshire forever, and with her husband and infant son fled to exile.

A part of Francestown itself was originally in the area known as "Society Land," or Cumberland, which was set aside as private estates for the use of the proprietors who had purchased the Mason claim. It was never so settled.

In 1800 the Second New Hampshire Turnpike, the only through route from Boston to Vermont, was completed through Francestown, bringing prosperity to the town for the next twenty-five years. The road was heavily travelled with coaches and wagons, for which the town collected tolls of one cent per mile. Francestown at this time had nearly 1600 inhabitants, eight taverns, two banks, and other businesses, among them a soapstone quarry, founded in 1800 by John Fuller, and said to be the best in the country. Soapstone was produced until the 1890's. The well-known Francestown Academy, founded in 1801, was attended by Franklin Pierce who later became our fourteenth president. Most of the beautiful old houses along Francestown's main street were built in this era.

It was at this time also that the town produced its most celebrated native son, Levi Woodbury (1789-1851). Woodbury was elected Governor of New Hampshire, and later served as Secretary of the Navy under President Jackson and Secretary of the Treasury under Martin Van Buren. He became a Justice of the Supreme Court. Also born in Francestown was James Bell, who was elected a United States Senator in the 1850's.

GILSUM

THIS TOWN with a name unlike any in America was originally called Boyle, after Richard Boyle, Earl of Burlington. He was one of England's most distinguished architects, designer of the famous Burlington House in Piccadilly, London, and author of several works on architecture in the 1700's. Granted by the New Hampshire proprietors in 1752 to a group of "colonizers," no claims were taken up in the town within the prescribed time because of the danger from Indian attacks. By 1763 a new charter was issued to Benjamin Sumner of Boston, who surveyed the area and established a settlement which included several of his relatives from Connecticut, among whom was Captain Samuel Gilbert, who became the first moderator, and whose daughter was Elizabeth, wife of Clement Sumner of Hebron, Connecticut.

With the consent of the proprietors the town adopted the name Gilsum, made up from the first syllables of the names of the two families. Other settlers in these families were Thomas, William, and Reuben Sumner, and Samuel Gilbert, Jr. Nearly all the grantees of Gilsum were from the Connecticut towns of Hebron, Lebanon, Bolton, Lyme and Andover. Its original area comprised some 23,000 acres. Reverend Clement Sumner, who graduated from Yale in 1758, became one of the early ministers at Keene, and Sylvester Gilbert served as a congressman from New Hampshire in 1818. Burlington, Vermont granted in 1763 as a part of New Hampshire, also takes its name from Richard Boyle, Earl of Burlington.

Gilsum's Lower Village is the site of the old Stone Arch Bridge over the Ashuelot River.

GREENFIELD

GREENFELD was originally a part of Lyndeborough and was known as Lyndeborough Addition. It was first settled in 1753 by the families of Captain David Lynde and Justice Benjamin

Lynde of the Massachusetts Supreme Court, who brought with them grantees from Andover, Londonderry and nearby Massachusetts towns.

Situated as it was in the Monadnock area, its people found themselves barred off from church and school by a mountainous district and in 1791, following the Revolution, they petitioned the Legislature for rights to a town of their own. Their petition was granted, and they appear to have chosen the name Greenfield, so designating their new location as being situated between hills on level and fertile ground. Greenfield's meeting house was begun in 1795.

Greenfield, when a part of Lyndeborough, was in a section of New Hampshire combined to be set aside for the proprietors for their own private estates, and called Cumberland, or "Society Land" and included in addition to Greenfield the present towns of Bennington, Deering and Francestown.

Crotched Mountain, a local landmark, is known for the Crotched Mountain Foundation, a rehabilitation center for handicapped children, and a ski area. The Greenfield State Park is at Otter Lake.

GREENVILLE

GREENVLLE, one of the newest and smallest towns, was incorporated in 1872 during the administration of Governor Ezekiel A. Straw, and was originally a part of Mason.

Located at what was known as the "High Falls" on the Souhegan River, it had been established more than a century earlier bearing the names "Slipton," "Mason Harbor" and "Mason Village." By 1872, it had become a prosperous New Hampshire community. Among its settlers were the families of Barrett, Taft, Dunster, Adams, Shattuck, Merriam and Davis, some of whom erected mills and became identified with New Hampshire's first industries.

Taking advantage of its copious water power, Greenville at one time had factories within its borders making cotton and woolen goods, furniture, shoes, twine, flour, lead pencils, and tinware. At least one of them, the Columbian Company, became world famous.

Jonas Chickering, pioneer piano manufacturer, and Benjamin Champney, famous American artist, were both natives of Greenville.

HANCOCK

HANCOCK, westernmost of the towns of Hillsborough county, took its name in the year 1779 from John Hancock, famous as the first governor of Massachusetts after the Revolution, president of the Continental Congress, and signer of the Declaration of Independence. Prior to this date the town had been an unidentified settlement in the "proprietors' reservation" on the Contoocook River, known as "Society land," embracing the neighboring towns of Antrim, Bennington, Francestown, Deering and Greenfield. Hancock was first settled in 1764, and its meeting house, a fine example of Colonial architecture, was built in 1788. Many fine old houses line its beautiful Main Street.

While John Hancock left no records to show that he was ever in Hancock, he not only owned considerable property there, but had important trade connections with the New Hampshire proprietors in the Portsmouth area which he visited frequently in his lifetime. Left an orphan at an early age, he was adopted and taken into partnership with his uncle, Thomas Hancock, who began as an obscure bookseller and amassed one of the largest fortunes in pre-Revolutionary Boston, trading for the most part with London, Spain, the West Indies and Nova Scotia.

John Hancock was in Harvard at the same time as Governor John Wentworth, and by his marriage with Dorothy Quincy, sister of the patriot Josiah Quincy, he became related to the Wentworth allied families of Jaffrey, Sheafe, Huske, Rindge, and Wallingford. Governor Hancock's firm equipped the famous Louisbourg expedition and helped to finance the Harvard College lotteries.

As distinguished visitors to Portsmouth to welcome Lafayette in 1782, the Hancocks arrived in an elaborate coach with six horses, accompanied by four servants, the governor being dressed in scarlet trimmed with lace. He had also been a delegate to London at the time of the passage of the Stamp Act, arguing for its repeal, which later took place.

The Hancock lands in what is now Hancock consisted of eighteen hundred acres; and he also had a grant in the town of Grafton. Mount Hancock in Lincoln is named in his honor. After John Hancock's death in 1793 his widow married James Scott, the captain of his ship the *Boston Packet,* and they at one time resided in Portsmouth.

HARRISVILLE

HARRISVILLE, one of the "youngest" towns in the state, in name dating back only to 1870, takes that name from one of its distinguished families, the Harrises.

Settled as early as 1760, when the town was an unidentified part of Hancock, Dublin, Roxbury, Nelson and Marlborough, it became a thriving mill center in its own right, beginning with the blacksmith shop of Jason Harris of Sherburne, Massachusetts. He was succeeded by Sergeant Erasmus Harris, his son Bethuel and his grandson Milan, a succession which built and operated one of the first woolen mills in New England.

The place was then known as Twitchellville, after Abel Twitchell, whose daughter Deborah married Bethuel Harris. The founders attracted a score of new settlers to work in the Harris mills: the Yardleys, Bakers, Willards, Bemises, Adamses and Hutchinsons, all of whom built homes and helped to establish the enterprise whose granite and brick buildings still stand as sturdy as in the 1800's.

The Harris mills having been renamed the Cheshire mills, the town retained the Harris name at the suggestion of Milan

Harris, and it was incorporated as Harrisville. The town of Milan in Coos County is also named for Milan Harris.

Today it is a favorite subject for painters and photographers because of its nine ponds and the picturesque native brick buildings reflected in the water of Nubaunsit Pond.

The village of Chesham, part of Harrisville, took its name, not from the English town of that name, but from Cheshire County in which it is located. Cheshire County was named in 1769 for the county in England, which was the site of one of the Wentworth estates.

HINSDALE

HINSDALE, in the farthest southwest corner of the state, was incorporated in 1753 and takes its name from Colonel Ebenezer Hinsdale, one of the state's most illustrious pioneers.

He was descended from a prominent family in Deerfield, where his mother had once been captured by the Indians and taken to Canada. He attended Harvard and after his graduation was ordained in the Old South Church in Boston in order to be a missionary to the Indians and chaplain of Fort Dummer, then an important trading post on the Connecticut River near the Massachusetts border.

The entire area in which Fort Dummer was located, part of which is now Vermont, at one time contained four other forts — Fort Howe, Fort Shattuck, Fort Bridgman and Fort Hinsdale. Colonel Hinsdale's career as a missionary, however, was cut short by his enlistment as an officer and later by his establishing himself as a trader. He gained considerable prosperity and is said to have built the trading post at Fort Hinsdale at his own expense.

Fort Shattuck was named for Captain Daniel Shattuck, Fort Bridgman for Captain Orlando Bridgman, and Fort Howe for Lord Howe, all Hinsdale's military associates. Fort Dummer took its name from William Dummer, colonial governor of Massachusetts in the 1700's.

Captain Orlando Bridgman was the town's first moderator and among his fellow settlers, largely from Massachusetts border towns, were ten members of the Fields family, seven Wrights, six Strattons, and four each of the Stebbins and Holbrook families.

The Hinsdales in America were descended from an ancient Walloon family bearing the name de Hinnesdel. Hinsdale was the birthplace of Charles A. Dana (1819-1897), famous editor of the *New York Sun,* and today is noted for a paper mill and the Hinsdale Raceway.

JAFFREY

Rowley Canada was the name of the area, now comprising Jaffrey and parts of Rindge and Sharon, first granted in 1736 to Massachusetts soldiers (or their relatives) who had served in an ill-fated expedition to Canada. Most of them came from Rowley, Massachusetts—thus the name. The town was re-chartered, however, in 1749 as Monadnock No. 2, sometimes known as Middle Monadnock or Middletown. It was one of the first towns to be established following the New Hampshire proprietors' purchase of the undivided lands under the Masonian claim. By the terms of their grant, the settlers were required to set aside ten acres of land "for public use" and to build a "good convenient meeting house near the center of the town."

A re-grant of the town was made in 1767 by John Wentworth, and six years later it was incorporated as Jaffrey in honor of George Jaffrey, a member of one of the prominent families of Portsmouth. His father, graduating from Harvard College in 1702, had been treasurer when the province was under the jurisdiction of Massachusetts, its Chief Justice, and a son-in-law of Lieutenant Governor John Wentworth.

Jaffrey's son, known as George Jaffrey III, graduated from Harvard where he is said to have been fined for "playing at cards and dice," Nevertheless he became valedictorian of his class of 1736, served as proprietors' clerk in the new province and had charge of its surveying and clerical work. He was treasurer of the famous Louisbourg Expedition and in 1769 was made a life trustee of Dartmouth, giving it the official college seal which it still uses. He was also clerk of the Supreme Court, a member of the Governor's Council, and treasurer of the province.

George Jaffrey had grants in Londonderry, Gilmanton, Piermont, Tamworth and in the unincorporated settlement of Hadley, part of what is now Jaffrey. He died in 1802 and left property to his nephew provided he would become a permanent resident of Portsmouth and "never follow any profession except that of being a gentleman."

Jaffrey's fine old meeting house was erected in 1775, at the time of the Battle of Bunker Hill. One of the town's early settlers was Amos Fortune, a black slave who purchased his freedom and came to Jaffrey to establish a thriving tannery in 1769. Named for him is the Amos Fortune Forum which presents programs of cultural interest, as does the more recently established Jaffrey-Gilmore Foundation. Near Amos Fortune's grave in the old cemetery is that of Willa Cather, the famous novelist, who spent several summers here.

Standing in the western part of the town is the Grand Monadnock, the mountain which has given its name to this region of New Hampshire and has been celebrated by many poets and writers.

KEENE

THIS TOWN, now a city, was originally named Upper Ashuelot after the home of one of the friendly tribes of Pequot Indians who inhabited western Connecticut. First spelled Ashuelock, said to have meant "place of the ash," it gave the name Ashuelot to a river, valley and railroad in western New Hampshire.

Upper Ashuelot was granted by the Massachusetts government in 1735 to soldiers in the wars against Canada and was intended to be one of a line of "fort towns," of which Fort

Dummer was the center. The establishment of a new boundary line ultimately placed it in New Hampshire and the early grants were confirmed by that province in 1753. It then contained 25,248 acres and was one of the largest in New England.

Some of the first settlers, coming from the Massachusetts towns of Lancaster, Deerfield and Northampton, bore the family names of Adams, Colony, Nims, Darling, Holbrook, Nourse and Godfrey, and the first "clerk" or moderator was Colonel Benjamin Bellows of Walpole, who did the surveying.

Under the new grant, the town was given the name Keene, in honor of Sir Benjamin Keene of England, who was associated with Governor Wentworth in the Spanish West Indies trade and as agent for the South Sea Company was appointed consul at Madrid. Sir Benjamin was instrumental in bringing the war between England and Spain to an end and was described by Horace Walpole as being "one of the best kind of agreeable men, quite fat and easy with universal knowledge" and by Prime Minister Pelham as acting "ably, honestly and bravely." He died in 1757.

Keene was incorporated as a city in 1873. The county seat of Cheshire County, it is today becoming one of the foremost manufacturing cities of New Hampshire. It also has a branch of the University of New Hampshire, Keene State College.

LYNDEBOROUGH

LYNDEBOROUGH was first settled in 1735 by the sons and grandsons of soldiers who had fought in 1690 under Sir William Phipps in New England's first war with Canada. Five towns were granted by Massachusetts at the time, all named "Canada," and Salem-Canada, now Lyndeborough, was one of them, some of the settlers coming from Salem.

Among these was Benjamin Lynde, and he was accompanied by such Massachusetts families as Putnam, Cram, Epes and Blaney, whose names still persist in the area. Another early settler was Benjamin Pratt, who later became Chief Justice of New

York. They called a part of the settlement "Purgatory," perhaps because of its rugged nature, and that name also still persists.

Benjamin Lynde went to Harvard in the class of 1718, a member of which was Theodore Atkinson, afterward president of the Governor's Council in New Hampshire. In Harvard at that time were Governor Benning Wentworth of the class of 1715, John Hancock, first signer of the Declaration of Independence, and Archelaeus Putnam, cousin of General Israel Putnam and also a settler of Lyndeborough. After his graduation, Benjamin Lynde studied law in Boston, was made naval officer at Salem, and a member of the Massachusetts-New Hampshire Boundary Commission in 1737.

In 1763, under the new provincial government in New Hampshire, Mr. Lynde was regranted parts of Salem-Canada to be known as Lyndeborough. He also had grants in Weare, Chesterfield, Nelson, Winchester, and in Brattleboro, Vermont, then a part of New Hampshire. This land is said to have totaled 28,000 acres.

Benjamin Lynde had a distinguished career, succeeding his father as chief justice of Massachusetts, and presiding at the trial which involved the famous "Boston Massacre" in which John Adams and Josiah Quincy acted as defendants for the accused British soldiers. At the age of seventy-two Justice Lynde retired to his estates in Salem, Massachusetts, and Lyndeborough, dying at the age of eighty-one.

Lyndeborough was noted as a glass-making center in the latter part of the last century, and its hand-blown bottles are much sought after today.

MARLBOROUGH

First granted in 1752 as Monadnock No. 5, Marlborough was one of several towns in the Monadnock region, all known only by number.

Six members of the Morrison family of Marlborough, Massachusetts, together with five Willsons, four Cochrans, three

Moores, two Gilmans, and a number of others from that section of Massachusetts, were among the grantees. The terms of their grant required "the mowing or tillage" on at least thirty of their shares. Each of the grantees was called on to have built on his lot "a house of a room sixteen feet square besides the chimney-way, fit for a comfortable dwelling." The grant also called for a "convenient meeting house to be built within ten years" and ten acres "reserved for public use, such terms being subject to the improbability of there being an Indian war during the term allowed."

The town was at one time known as Oxford, but never so incorporated. In 1768 it appears to have been called New Marlborough, after the former home of some of the settlers, and in 1776 it was officially given its incorporated name of Marlborough.

Marlborough, Massachusetts, from which the New Hampshire town appears to have derived its name, dates back to the late 1600's when it was named for John Churchill, the great Duke of Marlborough, whose victory at the Battle of Blenheim in 1704 brought an end to England's war with France.

MARLOW

ADDISON was the original name of this town, a name known to every school student as that of Joseph Addison, editor of the English *Spectator* in the early 1700s. As Secretary of State for England he signed the papers appointing John Wentworth as Lieutenant Governor of New Hampshire under the jurisdiction of Massachusetts in 1717.

The name Addison, given in his honor in 1753, was intended to be that of a town six miles square under a grant to sixty families. It was made almost entirely to prospective settlers from a single New England town, Lyme, on the Connecticut River, and included such well-known names as Parsons, Beckwith, Peck, Sill, Ely, Selden and Brockway.

Not all of these families took up their grants because of the uncertainties of the French War which did not end until 1763. The underdeveloped land was regranted in 1761, and the town renamed as Marlow after Christopher Marlowe, another English scholar who achieved fame as an author and playwright.

The town became prominent in the 1870s as the birthplace of Calista M. Huntley, who taught herself to play the piano at the age of twelve, studied music in Boston and in Italy, and became one of America's well-known concert pianists. Also born in Marlow was "Rosina Delight" (Richardson) who weighed only five pounds at birth, and 515 pounds at the age of nineteen. She joined Barnum's Circus and toured the country as "Fat Rosie," along with the famous General Tom Thumb and Commodore Nutt, who was born in Manchester, this state.

MASON

MASON was first known as "Number 1" in a line of "border towns" which included the area allotted to this state by Massachusetts at the time the boundary lines were resurveyed by order of the English crown, and New Hampshire became a separate province, in 1741.

The town's charter, however, was not granted until 1749, and it continued to be known as Number 1 until Benning Wentworth was succeeded as governor by his nephew, John Wentworth, one of whose first acts was to rename it in 1768 in honor of New Hampshire's founder, Captain John Mason.

To Captain Mason New Hampshire owes not only its state name and that of the town of Mason, but also that of Portsmouth, New Hampshire, the city of that name in Hampshire, England, having been his home, and of which he was "governor." John Mason probably never came to New Hampshire, but under the patent giving him title to land here he sent over in 1631 a considerable colony of "traders, stewards, agents and workmen," together with building materials and a herd of Danish cattle. He later became Governor of Newfoundland.

Mason's New Hampshire title was finally purchased, in 1746,

after long litigation, from one of his descendants, Colonel John Tufton Mason, and came into the private ownership of a group of "proprietors". Ignoring profit to themselves, the proprietors instituted a unique plan of "self-colonization" among the many "grantees" who helped to establish most of the New Hampshire towns as they exist today. In 1874, to commemorate the two hundred and fiftieth anniversary of John Mason's New Hampshire settlement, the state, under the direction of Governor James A. Weston, arranged the erection of a bronze tablet in his honor in the Garrison Church at Portsmouth, England, his home.

Mason is the birthplace of "Uncle Sam", the nation's symbolic relative. Samuel Wilson lived here until he was thirty-four, when he moved to Troy, New York, to become a contractor supplying meat to the army during the War of 1812. The letters "U. S." were marked on his barrels. His house in Mason has been preserved.

MILFORD

MILFORD appears to have taken its name from its location near a shallow water-crossing on the Souhegan River below an early mill site which was long known as "Mill Ford." It was incorporated in 1794, prior to which date it was known as "The Falls" and "Mile Slip."

First granted in 1746, following the establishment of new boundary lines between Massachusetts and the border towns, Milford had been one of several settlements separated from the town of Monson, so named by Governor Benning Wentworth in honor of Sir John Monson (d. 1748), first Baron Monson, and Lord of Trade and Plantations. Monson as a town ultimately lost its identity, being absorbed by its neighboring towns; but the name still remains as that of the Massachusetts Monson.

A section of Milford was known in 1733 as Duxbury School Farm. It consisted of a thousand acres, and was intended to yield a revenue to support the schools of Duxbury, Massachusetts. This land was finally sold for 750 English pounds. Another section was known as Charlestown School Farm with a similar grant to Charlestown, Massachusetts.

Among Milford's original settlers were the Massachusetts families of Burns, Fiske, Livermore, Bruce, Putnam, Ward, Mansfield, Bradford, Wallis and Hutchinson. There were eleven Hutchinsons, who formed a group of choral singers, and the famous "Hutchinson Quartet" won fame for the town by touring the country in pre-Civil War days. Milford's rocky terrain led to the operation of extensive quarries of granite of exceptionally high quality and gave it the name "The Granite Town."

Milford has given the state two governors, George A. Ramsdell who was born here in 1834 and served from 1897-1899, and John McLane, born in Scotland and elected governor from Milford in 1905.

NELSON

NELSON, like others in the transition that took place in New Hampshire history, has had three names. It was first Monadnock No. 6; second Packersfield; and third its permanent name, Nelson. Monadnock No. 6 was the name given it by the New Hampshire proprietors in 1752 when, with other towns, it was laid out for settlement by a group of surveyors, one of whom was Ensign Breed Batcheller, who had served in the French war and in return for his services as surveyor had been given a large grant of land.

Ensign Batcheller was the leader of a group of settlers of the new town, said to have been the best planned of any at that date. This planning so attracted the admiration of the proprietors that in 1767 they renamed it Packersfield after Thomas Packer, one of their number, who was high sheriff of Portsmouth. In return for the honor Packer gave the son of Ensign Batcheller two lots, one for the name and the other for his having been the first child born in the new town, and bearing the name Thomas Packer Batcheller. Another of its early settlers was Ebenezer Tolman, who came here after serving in the Quebec expedition of 1776 and whose farmhouse still stands at Tolman Pond.

The town, which includes Munsonville, continued under the name Packersfield until 1814, when it was renamed Nelson after the naval hero, Lord Horatio Nelson, who died on board the British ship *Victory* in the English war against Napoleon.

The unincorporated village of Munsonville took its name from Alvin Munson who established a cotton factory near Granite Lake in 1843. Munson sold the factory to the Colony family in 1860, and many years later it burned.

Nelson was the site of one of the first ski-tows to operate in New England, begun at Tolman Pond in the early 1930's. In recent years the town has attracted many writers and artists and has been a center for the revival of early square dance music.

NEW IPSWICH

THIS TOWN, first granted in 1735, was named by early settlers from Ipswich, Massachusetts, which in turn took its name from Ipswich, England, so-called after the Saxon queen Ebba and the Saxon name "wich," meaning village, or "Ebba's village."

The New Ipswich settlers bore the New England family names of Foster, Kidder, Woolson, Farrar, Hoar and Preston, the grant having been first made to Colonel John Wainwright and John Choate. Later the town was incorporated under the New Hampshire provincial government in 1762, first being called Ipswich and later, in 1766, New Ipswich.

The famous academy at New Ipswich was one of the first in New England, and in 1789 was the recipient of a pair of geographic globes, then a new teaching device; a library of a hundred books; and $5,000, given by Samuel Appleton, who was born in New Ipswich. The academy was renamed for him and continues as a private school today.

New Ipswich had what was probably the first cotton mill in New Hampshire, built in 1804, the forerunner of the cotton-producing centers of Waltham and Lawrence in Massachusetts, and Manchester in New Hampshire. Samuel Appleton's brother Jesse, also born in New Ipswich, was a president of Bowdoin College and father-in-law of President Franklin Pierce.

The town has many fine examples of Georgian and Colonial architecture, outstanding among them the Barrett Mansion, built in 1799, the 1808 House, formerly an inn, and Appleton Academy.

PETERBOROUGH

PETERBOROUGH, first so called in 1738, probably bears the name of Charles Mordaunt, famous English admiral, third Earl of Peterborough, whose death occurred three years earlier. It was among the several "soldier's" towns named during the term of Governor Jonathan Belcher of Massachusetts, of which this state was then a province.

The Earl of Peterborough played an important part in the English wars with France and Spain, in which the surrender of Barcelona to his fleet was later followed by the Treaty of Utrecht, under the terms of which Gibraltar and a considerable portion of Canada became English territory, thus ending eleven long years of conflict. Under King William III, the Earl was made First Lord of the Treasury, and valued among his friends the writers of the times, Swift, Pope and Locke, who visited him at his manor Reigate. One of his titles was Baron Reigate; Reigate, Vermont, originally in New Hampshire, took its name from this barony.

Another theory as to the naming of Peterborough holds that it was originally "Peter's Borough," for Peter Prescott, of Concord, Massachusetts, the clerk of the Proprietors, who drew two lots in the town. The idea has also been advanced that it was named for St. Petersburg in Russia.

Most of the early settlers of Peterborough were from the Massachusetts towns of Concord, Roxbury, and Lunenburg, but they were soon joined by colonists from Londonderry, among whom were the Scotch families of Morison, Gregg, Scott, Wilson, Cunningham, Wallace and Ferguson. One of the early names in the town was Monadnock Hill, now known as "Little" or Pack Monadnock Mountain, a part of which is in the adjoining town of Temple. The mountain is the site of Miller State Park, named for General James Miller of Temple, a soldier in the War of 1812.

Peterborough had the first free public library supported by taxation, founded in 1833, and the first mill in the state (the Phoenix Mills) for weaving cloth mechanically. The town has given New Hampshire at least four of its governors; Jonathan Smith, 1809; John H. Steele, elected in 1844; Robert P. Bass, 1911-1913; and Walter R. Peterson, elected in 1968.

The MacDowell Colony in Peterborough, started as a memorial to the composer Edward MacDowell by his widow, offers quiet working conditions in beautiful surroundings to writers, artists, and composers. Among them have been such renowned figures as Edward Arlington Robinson, Leonard Bernstein and Aaron Copland. Here Thornton Wilder wrote his well-known play, *Our Town,* said to have been inspired by Peterborough.

The settlement of Noone, or South Peterborough, was named for Joseph Noone, whose family owned the Noone Mills there for over a century.

RICHMOND

RICHMOND was originally called Sylvester Canada. It was named by Governor Jonathan Belcher of Massachusetts (of which New Hampshire was then a part) in 1735. He selected four sites in New Hampshire for settlement by New England soldiers who had fought under Sir William Phipps against Canada in 1690 for the capture of Quebec, and thus established the so-called "Canada" towns of which Sylvester Canada was one, named for Captain Joseph Sylvester.

Captain Sylvester was one of seven children of Richard Sylvester of Scituate, Massachusetts, a member of the English Sylvester family which owned extensive sugar interests in Barbadoes, with the profits from which they purchased a large section of Long Island, New York. Another member of this family, Anthony Sylvester, married a daughter of James Lloyd, after whom Lloyd's Hills, now Bethlehem, this state, was named. Captain Joseph Sylvester served in Canada under Colonel Benjamin Church, and lost his life in that expedition. Sylvester Canada was granted in his memory to the sixteen surviving members of his company.

Soon after New Hampshire became a separate province, Governor Benning Wentworth reincorporated the "Canada" towns in 1752, and Sylvester Canada took its present name of Richmond in honor of the governor's English friend, Charles Lennox, Duke of Richmond. The Duke was a brigadier general in the English forces, and a Secretary of State.

As a member of Parliament he was a staunch advocate of colonial independence. In one of his speeches he proposed the withdrawal of English troops from America, insisting that resistance by the Colonies "was neither treason nor rebellion but perfectly justifiable in every political and moral sense." He was supported in this view by Lord Rockingham, an English relative of Governor Wentworth.

Richmond is the site of Camp Takodah, a summer camp for the schoolchildren of the region, and is the location of one of the state's fish hatcheries.

RINDGE

RINDGE was first granted by Governor Belcher of Massachusetts in 1736 as one of a chain of settlements in the western part of the state to descendants of soldiers who had fought in the war against Canada in 1690 under Sir William Phipps.

The area, which included most of present day towns of Rindge, Jaffrey and Sharon, was first named Rowley-Canada, in honor of a number of these soldiers who had come from Rowley, Massachusetts. Among them was Captain Daniel

Rindge, originally of Ipswich, and one of the thirteen children of John Rindge, an Ipswich chaise-maker. He later settled in Portsmouth and became a prosperous merchant there, representing the colony at one time in London. The Rindge family was related by marriage to Governor Benning Wentworth.

In 1749 the town was renamed with a group of other towns in the region of Mount Monadnock as Monadnock No. 1, or South Monadnock. It was finally incorporated as Rindge in 1768, and named for Daniel Rindge. In addition to his grant in Rindge, the proprietors gave Captain Rindge subsequent grants in Albany, Alexandria, Ellsworth, New London, Orange, Ossipee, Richmond, and Tamworth.

In the last decade Rindge has become a college town with the founding of Franklin Pierce College, a four-year liberal arts institution; the town also has two small private schools. The Cathedral of the Pines, which attracts thousands of visitors every year, is also located in Rindge. Here too are the headwaters of the Contoocook River, which flows north to join the Merrimack above Concord.

ROXBURY

ROXBURY was originally a "parish" in what was known as Monadnock No. 5, one of a series of early settlements in the western part of the state intended to contain grants to soldiers in the French wars. Monadnock No. 5 afterward became Marlborough, a number of its grantees having come from Marlborough, Massachusetts.

What is now Roxbury remained as a part of Marlborough until after the Revolution, but in 1812 a group of its citizens, largely from Massachusetts, applied for incorporation as a separate town, which they proposed calling Roxbury after their old village which is now a section of Boston, and their petition was granted.

Roxbury, Massachusetts was settled in 1630. It may have been named for the county of Roxburghe in the Scottish lowlands,

or the name may commemorate Robert Ker, first Earl of Roxburghe (1570-1650), privy councillor to James I and Charles I.
The name as used in America has been spelled in various ways:
Roxburgh, Rocksborough, Roxberry, and Rocksberry. It has
been for many years one of Boston's best known historical areas.

Roxbury, New Hampshire, was once suggested for annexa-
tion as a part of Keene, but the motion failed for lack of support by the voters of both towns, as required. One of Roxbury's
many respected natives was Cyrus Wakefield, founder of the
famous Wakefield Rattan Furniture Company, now known as
the Heywood-Wakefield Company of Boston.

SHARON

ORIGINALLY a part of Peterborough, Sharon began its existence
in 1738 under the name Peterborough Slip or Sliptown, and
became Sharon in 1791 following the readjustment of a number
of town lines after the war of the Revolution. Part of the town,
like Jaffrey and Rindge, was in the early Rowley Canada grant
of 1736. The name Sharon, that of the Connecticut town from
which some of its settlers had come, had been suggested in 1768
for the town of Mason, but was never adopted.

In proposing the separation of Peterborough Slip from Peterborough, the inhabitants made the modest proposal that their
territory might include one square mile from each of their
neighboring towns, a plan which those towns accepted.

Sharon's charter differed from previous New Hampshire
town charters in that it included the right "to levy taxes of one
cent per acre to repair its roads and bridges" and the right to
tax non-resident property owners for the purpose of "mending
and repairing our highways."

The tiny village of Sharon includes the small brick schoolhouse, built about 1833 and used for town meetings, and the
Sharon Arts Center, founded in 1947 to offer courses in arts and
crafts and to provide a gallery for exhibitions by artists of the
region.

STODDARD

MONADNOCK No. 7 was the name of this town when it was first granted in 1752. It was also known for a time as Limerick and was incorporated as Stoddard in 1774 by Governor John Wentworth. It was named in honor of Colonel Sampson Stoddard, who, like George Washington, began his career in life as a surveyor. Colonel Stoddard's New England ancestor was Solomon Stoddard, who married a niece of Governor Winthrop, and was the grandfather of Reverend Jonathan Edwards of Northampton, Massachusetts, a member of the class of 1662 at Harvard and its first librarian. Colonel Stoddard's father was Reverend Sampson Stoddard, Harvard 1701, Congregational minister at Chelmsford, Massachusetts, and Colonel Stoddard himself was Harvard, class of 1730.

Upon graduation, Colonel Stoddard fought in the Indian wars, and established a store and tavern in Chelmsford. He was later to be appointed by the colonial government to survey southwestern New Hampshire, including what is now Cheshire County. One of his assistants was Benjamin Pierce, father of President Franklin Pierce.

In partial return for his services Colonel Stoddard received large grants of land in the section which would later be called Fitzwilliam, and which was first named Stoddardstown in his honor. Other grants were made to him in the new towns of Goffstown, Dublin, Jaffrey, Acworth and Randolph. Colonel Stoddard died in 1777.

Stoddard is the site of Pitcher Mountain, but it is best known today for its glass manufacturing. Between 1840 and 1873 there were four glass factories operating in the town, and the dark-hued bottles and other glassware made there are much sought after by collectors. The glass factories were located at Mill Village, South Stoddard and "Stoddard Box" — the latter so named for the old tavern there — and employed several hundred glassblowers and other workers in their heyday. The plants finally closed in the depression after the Civil War.

SULLIVAN

THIS Cheshire County town, incorporated in 1787, bears the honored name of General John Sullivan of Revolutionary fame. Sullivan County to the north, which also honors General Sullivan, was not created until 1827.

Sullivan, which was chartered in the same year as the adoption of the United States Constitution, was carved out of the older neighboring towns of Gilsum, Stoddard, Nelson, and Keene. Like Roxbury, also formed after the Revolution, it is one of Cheshire County's "newer towns."

Some of General Sullivan's ancestors, prominent in Limerick, Ireland, first came to America in 1723. While Stoddard was once called Limerick and included land taken for the town of Sullivan, the connection is probably only a coincidence, as the town was first called by that name in 1752, when John Sullivan was only twelve.

General Sullivan deserves a place as one of the great soldiers in the Revolution. Commissioned as a major in 1772 while a young lawyer in Portsmouth, he was a member of the Continental Congress in Philadelphia, and was made one of the eight brigadier generals in the American forces. Two years later he was appointed Adjutant General to Washington, and a Major General of the Northern Army, under which title he completed a long and distinguished military career culminating in his election as President (governor) of New Hampshire in 1786. The town of Sullivan, named at that time in his honor, was created by combining parcels of land taken from Stoddard, Keene, Gilsum, and Nelson.

While General Sullivan never owned land in the town which bears his name, he had been previously given grants in Chatham, Sunapee and Dorchester. An imposing monument in his memory has been erected at Durham, where he died, and another commemorating the Mason claims, the only one of its kind, stands in the town of Sullivan. General Sullivan's brother James, also a Revolutionary soldier, served as Governor of Massachusetts.

SURRY

THE TOWN of Surry was chartered in 1769 by Governor John Wentworth, having originally been a part of Westmoreland. The town appears to have been named for the then Earl of Surrey, Charles Howard (1720-1786), who later became the tenth Duke of Norfolk and hereditary Earl Marshal of England. The Surrey title has been traditionally held by the eldest male heirs of the Dukes of Norfolk. The most celebrated Earl of Surrey in history was Henry Howard, handsome poet, soldier and scholar of Tudor times, who was beheaded in 1547 by Henry VIII. The young Earl, who was a victim of the aging king's vindictiveness and jealousy, was a first cousin of Catherine Howard, Henry's fifth queen, and of Anne Boleyn, both of whom had been executed several years earlier.

The county of Surrey in England, sometimes spelled "Surry" in old documents, is noted for its manufacture of "pleasure carts" or carriages called surreys which were introduced into America in 1872.

Surry, New Hampshire is one of the state's best known geological areas, containing large quantities of quartz, bearing veins of gold, silver, copper and lead. Surry Mountain was once the scene of extensive mining activities, and in 1879 a company known as the Granite Gold and Silver Refining Company was organized and put into operation at Surry. Although considerable metal was mined, its processing proved to be unprofitable, and the project was abandoned. Surry Mountain remains, however, as one of New Hampshire's most admired scenic attractions. The town is also the location of Surry Mountain Dam, built in recent years as a flood control project on the Ashuelot River.

SWANZEY

THIS TOWN, with a slight change in spelling, takes its name from Swansea, Massachusetts, which in turn was named for Swansea in Wales. The Welsh town is located on a coastal inlet which the natives called an "ey" and later called by them "Sweyn's Ey," probably after the Viking King, Sweyn Forkbeard; over the years it became Swansea. The first minister in Swansea, Massachusetts, the Reverend Ezra Carpenter, came from Swansea, Wales, and is said to have suggested the name. Spelling was more or less phonetic in the eighteenth century — there were no authoritative dictionaries then — and thus Swansea easily became "Swanzey."

Swanzey, New Hampshire secured its charter from Governor Benning Wentworth in 1753 who appears to have named it at the suggestion of Governor Brenton of Rhode Island, the owner of "Brenton's Farm" in Litchfield, New Hampshire, and a large landowner in Swansea, Massachusetts. Prior to that Swanzey had been one of the several defense or "fort" towns established by Governor Belcher and was granted by him in 1733 as "Lower Ashuelot" after the Ashuelot River. It was the scene of numerous Indian encounters and few settlements were made until its incorporation as Swanzey.

The earliest families included the Hammonds, Cressons, Gunns, Beldings and Whitcombs. One of the Whitcombs, Irvine, was the originator in the 1890's of the first vacation excursions to the White Mountains, a project which he expanded into the firm of Raymond Whitcomb and Company of Boston. Swanzey was the home of Denman Thompson, author of one of America's most successful and popular plays, *The Old Homestead,* which is still annually presented in Swanzey's "Potash Bowl."

TEMPLE

TEMPLE is named for provincial New Hampshire's last lieutenant governor, John Temple. Born in Boston in 1732, he was related to the Grenville-Temple family who were prominent politically in eighteenth century England. John Temple occupied the post of Surveyor General of the customs at Boston, and at his 500-acre estate at Ten Hills in Charlestown, Massachusetts, entertained many of those prominent in Boston society in the late 1700's, including the Apthorps, Sewalls, Lloyds, Nelsons, and Governor John Wentworth, then a student at Harvard.

Upon succeeding to the governorship of New Hampshire in 1767, John Wentworth named John Temple as lieutenant governor, which post he held until 1774, when he went to England. He later returned as British Consul General at New York. In 1786 he was knighted by King George III and became Sir John Temple. He married Elizabeth Bowdoin, daughter of James Bowdoin, governor of Massachusetts, for whom Bowdoin College is named. His brother, Robert Temple, married the daughter of Governor Shirley of Massachusetts.

The town of Temple, like Sharon, was originally called Peterborough Slip. It was first granted by Governor Benning Wentworth in 1750, and incorporated under its present name in 1768. In 1780 the Temple Glass Works was founded by Robert Hewes of Boston, employing Hessian glassblowers who were former soldiers in the British army. The operation did not last long, however, and Temple glass is rare and much sought after today.

Temple was the birthplace of General James Miller (1776-1851), hero of the Battle of Lundy's Lane in the War of 1812. Miller State Park is named for him. Another native son was Charles W. Tobey, former governor of the state, and United States Senator from 1939 to 1953.

TROY

TROY was originally a part of Marlborough from which it was legally separated in 1815, during the term of Governor John Taylor Gilman. Territory was also taken from the towns of Fitzwilliam, Swanzey and Richmond. Names from Greek and Roman antiquity were popular at this time, but the town actually appears to have taken its name from Troy, New York at the suggestion of Captain Benjamin Mann of Mason, a close friend of Governor Gilman, and whose company, enlisted from Marlborough and its surrounding towns, had fought in the Revolution at Bunker Hill.

Captain Mann's daughter Betsy was then living in the New York Troy as the wife of one of its most prominent citizens, Samuel Wilson, who achieved everlasting fame as "Uncle Sam." Among the original grantees of Marlborough were no fewer than seven Wilsons of the same family, all of whom appear to have approved the selection of the name Troy for the new town, after Troy, New York, which also was incorporated the next year, 1816. The house of Samuel Wilson (Uncle Sam), which he occupied in Mason, New Hampshire before moving to Troy, New York, is preserved as a landmark.

Troy was a granite quarrying center in its early days, and today is the home of the Troy Blanket Mills, its principal industry.

WALPOLE

WALPOLE on the Connecticut River bears the name of Sir Robert Walpole, first prime minister of England and later Earl of Orford. The first settlements were made as early as 1736 by Massachusetts when it was known as Great Falls or Lunenburg. A New Hampshire grant was not made until 1752, when it was called Bellowstown. The grant was renewed in 1761 as Walpole.

Robert Walpole came into prominence in England because of his efforts to establish sound finance and to end foreign wars and diplomatic intrigues. During England's war with Spain in 1740 he served as chancellor of the exchequer and treasurer of the navy, which brought him into direct contact with Governor Wentworth's shipping interests in the West Indies.

The town of Walpole, which now includes the village of Drewsville, comprised 23,000 acres and was settled largely by land speculators from Lunenburg, Massachusetts. Most of them were related by birth or marriage to Colonel Benjamin Bellows who, besides taking part in the French and Indian War, had done most of the surveying under which the Connecticut River towns were laid out.

Colonel Bellows, after whom the Vermont town of Bellows Falls is named, constructed at Walpole one of the several north country "forts" or palisades which served as defenses against Indian attacks, said to have been among the largest, being one hundred feet in length. He received grants, in addition to a ferry privilege, either by gift or purchase, in the New Hampshire communities of Keene, Dublin, Fitzwilliam, Marlow, Rindge, Temple and Jaffrey. There is an imposing monument in his memory at Walpole.

Walpole has one of the handsomest main streets in northern New England. Its many fine houses, Unitarian Church and the old Academy building are witness to the town's prosperity in the years before and after 1800. Walpole had a vigorous intellectual life at the time and was the home of *The Farmer's Museum*, a weekly newspaper edited by Royall Tyler and Joseph Dennie, both graduates of Harvard College. This lively journal had the largest circulation of any country paper in America at the time, and numbered among its subscribers President George Washington. Its editors, Tyler and Dennie, were the center of a circle known as "the Walpole wits." Royall Tyler later became Chief Justice of the Vermont Supreme Court.

Walpole was also the site of one of the longest covered bridges in New England, built across the Connecticut River in 1785.

WESTMORELAND

ORIGINALLY called "Great Meadows," Westmoreland was established in 1735 by Massachusetts Governor Jonathan Belcher, and listed by him as Number 2 in a line of Connecticut River "fort towns" first intended to be trading posts. However, disagreements with the Indians in bartering operations, as occurred also in other river towns, led to the construction at Number 2 of a square blockhouse or "stockade" made of horizontally placed logs. But like Fort Dummer to the south, it proved subject to Indian attacks, and few settlements occurred.

By 1752, however, following the separation of New Hampshire into an independent province, the founding of new towns became possible and one of these was granted as Westmoreland by Governor Benning Wentworth. It was named for his English relative John Fane, seventh Earl of Westmoreland, who was also honored in the same year by the naming of New Fane (Newfane) in Vermont, then a part of this province.

The Earl of Westmoreland, who died in 1762, had a distinguished military career, becoming lieutenant general of the English forces, keeper of the Wentworth estates at Rockingham, and later chancellor of the University of Oxford.

Westmoreland in New Hampshire drew its settlers from prominent Massachusetts families, among them the Howes, of whom there were seven; the Chamberlains with six; and the Wheelers with three. Other grantees included Joseph Bellows, Samuel Livermore, Josiah Willard, Ebenezer Hinsdale and Reverend Samuel Hunt, all pioneers in Connecticut River towns. One of the grantees in Newfane, Vermont, was John Adams, later to become second President of the United States.

Westmoreland has an unusually fine old meeting house, built in 1762, its belfry containing a Paul Revere bell.

WILTON

WILTON and part of the adjoining town of Lyndeborough, were originally called Number 2 in a group of towns at the state's border laid out in the 1730's. Intended to provide protection against Indian raids, these towns were first granted to Massachusetts soldiers who had fought in the "Canada Expedition" against the French in Canada. These were the so-called "Canada" towns of which there were ten, one of them being called "Salem-Canada," afterward Lyndeborough, grants there being given to soldiers from Salem, Massachusetts.

Wilton's first settlers were among these soldiers, and included the families of Putnam, Lovewell, Badger, Dale, Harriman, Powers, Blodgett and Cummings, who got their first grant in 1749 and a regrant as Wilton in 1762.

Evidence seems to indicate that the name did not come from the town of Wilton, England, as sometimes assumed, but from Sir Joseph Wilton (1722-1803), a famous English sculptor. He appears to have been a friend of Governor Benning Wentworth who made the grant and who lived in London prior to being made the first governor of the province of New Hampshire. Sir Joseph, who was one of a group of London artists (Sir Joshua Reynolds was among its leaders) is credited with having worked in gold, silver and marble as the creator of statues of Sir Isaac Newton, Francis Bacon, Swift, Chesterfield, Cromwell, General Wolfe and William Pitt, Earl of Chatham. In 1761 he was appointed by King George III to design the stage coach to be used in his coronation, and many years later this coach is said to have served as a model for New Hampshire's "Concord Coach." Sir Joseph was one of the charter members of the Royal Academy and held the office of sculptor to the King.

It has also been suggested that Wilton was named in honor of Wilton House near Salisbury, England, the famous estate of the Herbert family. Henry Herbert (1689-1750) succeeded as the ninth Earl of Pembroke in 1733, and it is for him that Benning Wentworth named Pembroke, New Hampshire three years before the naming of Wilton.

WINCHESTER

WINCHESTER, which came into existence in 1733 as one of those towns intended to protect the Massachusetts border at the Connecticut River boundary, was originally named Arlington. The name appears to have been given by Governor Jonathan Belcher in honor of Charles Fitzroy, Earl of Arlington and second Duke of Grafton. Fitzroy, who died in 1757, was a grandson of King Charles II.

The Arlington settlement, which in 1741 became a part of

the province of New Hampshire, was first granted to Colonel Josiah Willard of Lunenburg, Massachusetts, who had been in command of the famous Fort Dummer on the Connecticut River and who brought with him several members of his family and a group of other Lunenburg citizens at the time of the Indian wars. Colonel Josiah Willard was of the same family as Simon Willard, early New England clockmaker, who is credited with having designed the famous "banjo" clock.

Following the wars, the town was incorporated in 1753 by Governor Benning Wentworth as Winchester, bearing the name of Charles Paulet, Marquess of Winchester, and third Duke of Bolton. He was a lord justice and for many years governor of the Isle of Wight and constable of the Tower of London. Paulet, who derived his title from the ancient city of Winchester, capitol of England in Saxon times, died the year after the naming of the New Hampshire town. Two Vermont towns, then a part of New Hampshire, were also named in his honor, Pawlet and Bolton.

Winchester is the birthplace of Francis Parnell Murphy, elected governor of New Hampshire in 1937. A Republican, he was the state's first Catholic chief executive.

V

Seacoast Region

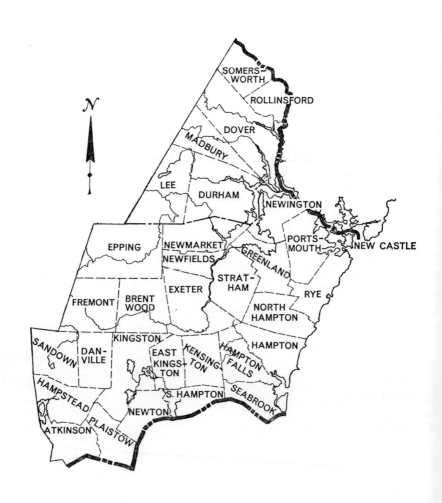

N

SOMERS-
WORTH

ROLLINSFORD

DOVER

MADBURY

LEE

DURHAM

NEWINGTON

EPPING

NEWMARKET

NEWFIELDS

PORTS-
MOUTH

NEW CASTLE

GREENLAND

STRAT-
HAM

RYE

EXETER

FREMONT

BRENT
WOOD

NORTH
HAMPTON

KINGSTON

HAMPTON

SANDOWN

DAN-
VILLE

EAST
KINGS-
TON

KENSING-
TON

HAMPTON
FALLS

HAMPSTEAD

S. HAMPTON

SEABROOK

NEWTON

PLAISTOW

ATKINSON

ATKINSON

THE TOWN of Atkinson, so-named in 1767, when it was set aside from Plaistow, does honor to Colonel Theodore Atkinson whose farm had once covered several hundred acres or practically its entire area.

Colonel Atkinson helped to raise and commanded a regiment in one of the French wars. He later served as collector of customs at Portsmouth and in 1748 was appointed by his brother-in-law, Governor Benning Wentworth, to be secretary of the colony, in which office he served until the Revolution.

When New Hampshire's more than two million acres of "undivided lands" were purchased from the Mason heirs, he became one of the group of proprietors who parcelled them out to the more than 30,000 colonizers who were selected to settle northern New England.

Colonel Atkinson is credited with having superintended the assembly of the lists of these colonizers, whose names are noted in the *New Hampshire State Papers*. He had graduated from Harvard in 1718, three years after Governor Wentworth, and his early records of prospective owners of "free lands" were compiled largely from the catalog of the then Harvard alumni.

Colonel Atkinson died in 1779 and beside bequests of money and silver to what is now St. John's Church in Portsmouth, he helped to establish Atkinson Academy at Atkinson with a fund afterwards augmented by means of a lottery of $2,000 authorized by the legislature. In 1809 the state also granted the academy approximately 13,000 acres in Coos County, now known as the Atkinson-Gilman Grant.

New Hampshire has a mountain named in honor of Colonel Atkinson, as are one of Portsmouth's principal streets, and Atkinson Hill in Dover. His son, Theodore Atkinson Jr., married Frances Deering, his cousin. After young Atkinson's death, his widow became the wife of Governor John Wentworth. Among the prominent citizens of Atkinson were William Cogswell, first professor of education and history at Dartmouth, and William C. Todd who was instrumental in securing the funds subscribed by Edward Tuck for the present building of the New Hampshire Historical Society.

BRENTWOOD

ORIGINALLY known as Brentwood Parish, this town was one of several which were a part of Exeter. It appears to have taken its name from Brentwood, England, a suburb of London, once a part of the king's forest, the burning of which caused it to be called "Burnt Wood."

Exeter's Brentwood Parish became a separate town in 1741 during the first year of the governorship of Benning Wentworth, who at that time authorized the division of a number of the older and overgrown New Hampshire towns into separate units. It was at one time unofficially known as Keeneborough, a name afterward given to the town of Keene, so called for the governor's friend, Sir Benjamin Keene.

Among the early Brentwood families appeared the names of Gilman, Roberts, Dudley, Edgerly, Kimball, Sanborn, and Leavitt, most of whom had first settled in Exeter. The name Brentwood has since become a popular name for American towns, among them those located in Maryland, Missouri, New York, Pennsylvania, and California.

DANVILLE

DANVILLE was originally one of the several parishes of the ancient New Hampshire town of Kingston, or Kingstown, as it was first called, the settlement of which dates back to 1694.

Among the earliest land-owners of Danville parish, then called Hawke, were Daniel Brown, Daniel Sanborn, and Daniel Gilman, and it was probably from them that the town got its present name.

The separation of the town from its parent occurred in 1760, and when the proprietors gave it its charter name of Hawke, it was in honor of a great English admiral, then very much in the public eye.

Admiral Sir Edward Hawke went to sea at the age of fourteen, and at the age of twenty he was made captain of the ship *Portland*, assigned to the Mediterranean fleet. In 1739 at the outbreak of England's war with Spain, he was transferred to the West Indian fleet with orders to guard American shipping, of which Governor Benning Wentworth's Portsmouth vessels were an important factor. During the Seven Years' War which followed, Admiral Hawke was associated with several prominent admirals — Warren, Boscawen, and Vernon, all of whose names were given to New Hampshire towns. His fleet defeated the French in 1759, capturing five ships.

The town name Hawke, while that of a famous naval officer, was never popular. It had associations with the bird of prey. In 1836 the town was renamed and incorporated as Danville by general consent of the inhabitants, in honor of the early settlers.

DOVER

Settled in 1623, Dover on the Piscataqua River ranks with Portsmouth as one of the state's "oldest plantations with an unbroken history." Together with Exeter and Hampton, established in the 1630's, these towns remained the only communities in the New Hampshire wilderness for over half a century — until the founding of Kingston in 1694. Dover was first called Hilton's Point after William and Edward Hilton who began the original settlement at Dover Point in 1623. It was also called by the Indian names, Newichwannock, meaning "place of wigwams," and Cocheco. For a time it became Bristol, after Bristol, England, and Northam, after its minister Thomas Larkham's home in Northam, England.

Finally the town was incorporated as Dover in 1641. The name appears to have been taken from Robert Dover (1575-1641), English soldier and lawyer and founder of the "Cotswold Games", originated in protest against the growing severity of Puritanism at the time. It has also been suggested that the town is named for Dover, England, the famous seaport on the English Channel.

Dover, like other New England coast towns, was never laid out topographically but consisted largely of a group of small settlements (listed in the early records as more than one hundred), among them such colorful names as Pudding Hill, Bloody Point, Poor Town and Plum Swamp. In 1689, Dover suffered from a severe Indian attack in which its leading citizen, Major Richard Waldron, then spelled Walderne, was killed and a considerable number of its citizens captured and taken to Canada.

At one time plans were drawn up in Dover for what was intended to be called Franklin City, after Benjamin Franklin, but the War of 1812 prevented their being carried out. The town's location on the Piscataqua and other rivers helped to make it a thriving trading and manufacturing town in the early years, and it was incorporated as a city in 1855. Parts of the original town have been annexed from time to time by the surrounding neighborhoods of Newington, Madbury, Somersworth, Rollinsford, Durham and Lee. Dover continues as the county seat of Strafford County.

One of Dover's notable citizens was the Reverend Jeremy Belknap (1744-1798) minister of the Congregational Church there in the years before and after the Revolution. Belknap wrote the first history of New Hampshire, published in 1784. No other history of the state written since has equalled it for interest or style. Belknap County was named for him in 1840.

DURHAM

DURHAM was named and incorporated in 1732 after having existed as a Dover "parish" since 1669, when it was known as Oyster River Plantation. It was the home of many early Dover settlers who had come from England to establish that colony.

The name Durham appears to have been suggested as a town name by the plantation's first minister, the Reverend Hugh Adams, Harvard graduate in 1697, after Richard Barnes, Bishop of Durham, England. Barnes was famous as the first "Puritan bishop" in the seventeenth century. In his application for a town charter for his congregation, once numbering more than one hundred, Mr. Adams is said to have desired its government to be modeled after that defined by the English bishop of Durham in administering the affairs of his diocese, which plan was also referred to in the grant of King Charles I to Captain John Mason of New Hampshire. Hugh Adams was minister at Durham for twenty-one years.

In its early days Durham, like its neighboring towns, was often the center of Indian troubles, and maintained a total of fourteen garrisons for defense. One of the first settlers was Ebenezer Thompson, whose descendant, Benjamin Thompson, bequeathed the family estate known as the "Warner Farm" to be used for the establishment of an agricultural college. The state agricultural school, which had been set up at Hanover in 1866, was moved here in 1890 after the Thompson grant. In 1923 it became the University of New Hampshire, and since then has greatly expanded its curriculum in the liberal arts and sciences. In his will Benjamin Thompson expressed the hope that "all nations shall beat their swords into ploughshares and their spears into pruning hooks, so that nation shall not lift up its sword against nation, neither shall they learn war any more."

Durham was the birthplace of General John Sullivan of Revolutionary fame, who was chosen "president" of this state in 1786 and again in 1789. His homestead is still standing.

EAST KINGSTON

EAST KINGSTON originally bore the name "Kingston East Parish" when it was a part of Kingston. It secured its independence in 1738 when it was granted a separate charter by Governor Jonathan Belcher of Massachusetts, after some of its inhabitants had petitioned to the effect that its location was "too distant from the Kingston school and place of worship," and that they "desired to establish their own."

Among East Parish families named in the grant were four Bachelders, three Cloughs and those with the names Webster, Sweatt, Gale, Call, Merrill, Greeley, Stevens, Fifield, Eastman, French, Judkins and Sanborn. It is believed that the first settlers were William and Abraham Smith. Among its most prominent citizens was Major Ebenezer Stevens who later received a grant of north country land to be named Stevens-town, which is now Salisbury. This land was regranted in 1749, and among the grantees was Ebenezer Webster of East Kingston, adopted son of Major Stevens, and father of Daniel Webster.

Major Stevens had a distinguished career in the French war, and was one of the five commissioners delegated by Governor Benning Wentworth to survey and plot the long series of new towns to be established in northern and western New Hampshire.

East Kingston shares with Sandown and Danville the distinction of having had Kingston, or "King's Town" (its early name) as its parent community. It endured a long period of litigation concerned with the establishment of its boundaries, one of them involving its parsonage land, and the other what was then known as the "Exeter Road," both problems having been ultimately settled to the satisfaction of both towns.

EPPING

GRANTED in 1741, Epping was the last of several towns chartered during the term of Massachusetts Governor Jonathan Belcher, who was succeeded in that year by Benning Wentworth, governor of the newly-established independent province of New Hampshire. It was one of several towns created out of the parent town of Exeter, and appears to have been named for Epping Forest, a parklike suburb of London, with which Governor Belcher must have been familiar and admired during his visits to England.

The land which became Epping in New Hampshire was carefully parcelled out to fifty-six Exeter residents, and bordered on the Lamprey River, over which they erected a bridge paid for and maintained by means of a lottery.

Epping gave the state three governors. William Plumer was first elected in 1812, and again in 1816. Governor Plumer also served as United States Senator from 1802 to 1807, and was the author of more than nineteen hundred biographical sketches of persons living in his lifetime. He was first president of the New Hampshire Historical Society. David Morrill served as governor from 1824 to 1827, and Benjamin Franklin Prescott was elected for two years in 1877.

EXETER

EXETER is one of the four original towns established in New Hampshire, the others being Portsmouth, Dover and Hampton. First settled in 1638, and known as Squamscott, it was managed by the "Exeter Combination," a group of English colonizers headed by the Reverend John Wheelwright who gave it its permanent name. Exeter takes its name from the English town, the county borough of Devonshire, famed for its beautiful cathedral. The town derives its name from the River Exe.

Exeter, New Hampshire, at first contained what are now the towns of Epping, Newmarket and Brentwood, all of which were allowed to become separate towns. Its river location enabled it to become an early New England shipbuilding and West Indies trading port. Exeter is the second largest town and county seat of Rockingham County, which was named in 1769 for Charles

Watson-Wentworth, Marquess of Rockingham. The Marquess was a staunch friend of the colonies and a cousin of the New Hampshire Wentworths. Exeter is one of the few New Hampshire towns never officially incorporated. Prior to and during the Revolution, Exeter was New Hampshire's capital, the home of its legislature. Its "Provincial Congress" in 1776 adopted a state constitution, the first to be adopted in America by direct action of the people.

Phillips Exeter Academy, endowed in 1781 by Colonel John Phillips, a wealthy merchant, is the oldest in the state. The academy's fine old buildings dominate the town and many of its alumni have distinguished themselves in all phases of American life. Among the town of Exeter's native sons was John Taylor Gilman (1753-1828), member of Congress and governor of the state for fourteen years. Exeter was also the birthplace of Daniel Chester French, sculptor of *The Minuteman* at Concord, Massachusetts and of the imposing figure of Lincoln at the Lincoln Memorial in Washington, D.C. Another of its citizens was Judge Henry A. Shute, author of *The Real Diary of a Real Boy,* who has been called "second only to Mark Twain as a chronicler of American boyhood."

FREMONT

THE FIRST presidential candidate of the Republican Party, John C. Fremont, has his name perpetuated in New Hampshire. Our town of Fremont in Rockingham County was originally Poplin, so called by Governor Benning Wentworth in 1764 after the thriving English mill town. Fremont was part of Exeter until its incorporation. It got its present name at the height of General John C. Fremont's popularity in 1854. A decade earlier, another of our towns, Coventry, in Grafton County, was renamed Benton, after Senator Thomas Hart Benton, Fremont's father-in-law, whose famous daughter Jessie he married in 1841.

While Fremont as a youth took Horace Greeley's advice, "Go west, young man," he was not in reality the explorer the name

"Pathfinder" suggests. It is true the name Fremont's Peak is in his memory, but most of his journey into the West was over the old trails set by Lewis and Clark. He did, however, seek gold in California in 1849, and came away a comparatively rich man, only to lose his fortune by 1870, and have to depend on the writings of his wife, Jessie, to save him from poverty.

Fremont's political prominence was recognized by President Abraham Lincoln, who made him a major general at the beginning of the Civil War in 1861. Impulsively, he predated Mr. Lincoln by a slavery emancipation proclamation, for which he was dismissed from office for disobeying orders. Arizona honors Fremont as its first territorial governor, 1878-1883. Governor William Haile, who campaigned for Fremont in New Hampshire, carried the state for him in the presidential election of 1856, the first Republican campaign in America.

GREENLAND

GREENLAND was among the earliest towns to be settled in this state, originating in 1638 as one of several Portsmouth "parishes." It appears to have been named in honor of Henry Greenland, one of its leading town officers, not, as sometimes supposed, from Denmark's Greenland, although that country was named as early as the year 984, nor from the fact that its fertility has made it a "green land."

The residents of our Greenland parish, who had purchased their estates from Captain Champernowne of Devonshire, England, and who had soon prospered to the extent of desiring a church and a school of their own, were granted a separate town in 1704. In the same period Leonard Weeks erected a substantial house which is thought to be the oldest brick house in New Hampshire still standing.

The Greenland, Weeks, Haines, Brackett, Wingate, Wiggin and McClintock families have contributed a long list of illustrious names to the history of this state. One of them was Senator John W. Weeks of Massachusetts who was responsible for "the passage of legislation that saved the White Mountains from the lumberman's axe," through the establishment of the White Mountain National Forest.

HAMPSTEAD

HAMPSTEAD, one of the earliest to be established as a result of the change, in 1739, of boundary lines between Massachusetts and the new province of New Hampshire, was originally known as Timberlane Parish because of its heavy growth of native trees. In 1749 it became Hampstead, so-named by Governor Benning Wentworth after the English residence of William Pitt, Earl of Chatham, advocate of colonial independence and a close friend of the governor. It had originally been part of Haverhill and Amesbury in Massachusetts.

Hampstead, New Hampshire, contained plots of land granted to Daniel Little, its first moderator, and Reverend Henry True, Harvard class of 1750, its first minister. The early settlers included no fewer than nine members of the Little family, and other families represented were those of Cleveland, Bond, Stevens, Gile, Huse, Colby and Shaw, all from neighboring Massachusetts towns.

The old Congregational Church at Hampstead is one of the few in the state to possess a Paul Revere bell in its belfry.

HAMPTON

THE TOWN of Hampton takes its name from Hampton, England, where its founder, the Reverend Stephen Bachiler, had preached before coming to America in the 1630's. First called Winnecunnet, the Indian name for "Pleasant Pines," our Hampton was one of the first "self-colonizing" projects established in New Hampshire by the Massachusetts government. It was one of the four original towns in the province. Its charter, granted under the direction of Governor Thomas Dudley by the Massachusetts legislature in 1635, was intended to "induce men to build houses," the cost of supervising them to be borne by the state.

The Hampton project, covering approximately 45,000 acres, and actually begun in 1638, included land which now comprises the areas of Seabrook, Kensington, Danville, Kingston, East Kingston, Sandown, North Hampton, South Hampton, Hampton Falls and Great Boar's Head.

Stephen Bachiler, having come from England in his late seventies, had been a preacher at Ipswich and Lynn, Massachusetts. Under authority of Massachusetts he "gathered" a group of his parishioners who were to settle on approximately sixty lots in the then Winnecunnet, and establish a town into which they voted that "no person can come without our consent." The new colonists obtained incorporation rights in 1639, renaming the town Hampton. Reverend Bachiler received 300 acres, and his son-in-law, Christopher Hussey, a "farm" of 250 acres. The project appears to have been successful from the start, and is recorded as having at one time had 400 cattle.

Mr. Bachiler is credited with having served as minister without recompense in one of the earliest New Hampshire "meeting houses" built under his direction. He retired in his eighties, much revered by his congregation, and returned to England to live to the age of one hundred. One of his direct descendants was the American poet, John Greenleaf Whittier.

Hampton Beach, a coastal section of the town, began to develop as a resort in the 1850's with the construction of the railroad. It is today one of the most popular seaside vacation areas on the eastern seaboard.

HAMPTON FALLS

HAMPTON FALLS was originally a part of Hampton, which was one of the four towns listed as the earliest New Hampshire settlements in existence under the Massachusetts government, the others being Portsmouth, Dover and Exeter. It was first known as Hampton's "Third Parish", and received its grant as an independent town in 1726, from Lieutenant-Governor John Wentworth. It then contained what are now the towns of Kensington and part of Kingston.

Located on the Taylor River, Hampton Falls provided water power for Weare's mills, operated by the ancestors of Meshech Weare, who in 1776 became New Hampshire's first "president", afterward called "governor", and from whom the town of Weare is named. Meshech Weare was born and lived in Hampton Falls and was host here to President George Washington when he visited New Hampshire in 1789.

Other New Hampshire families who were early settlers at "The Falls" bore the names of Dearborn, Sanborn, Cotton, Tilton, Moulton and Cram. A descendant of the last named family was Ralph Adams Cram (1863-1942) who was born in Hampton Falls and became a famous architect. Among his many buildings are the Cathedral of St. John the Divine in New York and the chapels at West Point and Exeter Academy. Another native son is Wesley Powell who served as governor from 1959 to 1963.

KENSINGTON

THIS TOWN was one of twenty-seven granted in what is now New Hampshire by Governor Jonathan Belcher of Massachusetts, in the 1730's, when it was part of that province.

All but three of these towns were named by him with numbers only, or were the "Canada" towns granted to soldiers in the French wars as a reward for their military service. These three bore the names of prominent Englishmen of the period: Arlington, Peterborough and Kensington, the last being that of Edward Rich, Earl of Holland and Baron Kensington, who once owned the famous Kensington Palace in London. He derived his title from an ancestor who owned land in the borough of Kensington, now a part of London.

Governor Belcher's grant of Kensington originally comprised

one of the several parishes of Hampton, another of which became Hampton Falls; and the selection of its grantees in 1737 was largely entrusted to the Reverend Jeremiah Fogg of Hampton and Portsmouth, who was a college classmate of the governor at Harvard and who served as the town's beloved and respected minister for many years.

The English borough of Kensington, as laid out and developed by Heneage Finch, Earl of Nottingham, became one of London's most beautiful sections, and was the birthplace of Queen Victoria. Its palace and public gardens were designed by Sir Christopher Wren, and are now the site of a royal residence and museum. To William Forsythe, keeper of Kensington Gardens, the world is indebted for the name of the flower, forsythia.

KINGSTON

THIS was the fifth town to be established in New Hampshire, an act made possible in 1694 by peace treaties with the Indians following what was known as King William's War, in the reign of William and Mary.

The settlement, sometimes called King's Town, appears to have been named Kingston by a group of its colonizers from Kingston, Massachusetts, then a part of Plymouth, which had been given its name by Lieutenant-Governor William Dummer in honor of Evelyn Pierrepont (1655-1726), a member of Parliament and Privy Councillor who became fifth Earl of Kingston-on-Hull in 1690. He was later created first Duke of Kingston. It has also been suggested that "King's Town" was named for William of Orange who came to the throne in 1689 as King William III. The ancient town of Kingston-on-Thames in England is so named for the early Saxon Kings who were crowned there.

Kingston, New Hampshire, carried on a prosperous trade in fish and lumber with Spain, Portugal, and the West Indies. It was noted for having once been the home of Dr. Josiah Bartlett, "president" of the state from 1790 to 1794, delegate to the Continental Congress, first signer of the Declaration of Independence, and founder of the New Hampshire Medical Society.

It is also noted for having contributed from its population fifty-four out of the group of fifty-seven grantees of the town of Salisbury, New Hampshire, then called Stevenstown after Major Ebenezer Stevens, a large grant-holder. Among the families so transplanted were those with the well-known New Hampshire names of Sanborn, Calef, Bailey, Scribner, Bohanon, Call, Fifield, Bartlett, Webster, Cram, Eastman, Colcord, Elkins, and Fellows.

A section of Kingston known as Kingston Parish was legally separated from its parent town in 1739 and named East Kingston.

LEE

ESTABLISHED in 1766, Lee was one of the last towns to obtain a charter among the total of one hundred twenty-nine granted in this state during the governorship of Benning Wentworth.

Governor Wentworth named the town for his friend and relative, General Charles Lee, an officer in the English army during the French and Indian War. General Lee, then a colonel, had come to America with the forces under command of General Braddock, and had fought with Washington at Fort Duquesne, with General Johnson at Ticonderoga, and with General Amherst at Montreal.

At the close of the war in 1763 he returned to England, but later came back to America and took sides with the Colonies in the Revolution. He was in the battle for the defense of Boston, and throughout the war is said to have been "second in command" to General Washington. His loyalty, however, came into question, and, after being court-martialed for "disobedience to orders and disrespect to his commander-in-chief," he retired to his estate in Virginia.

At the time of the granting of Lee in 1766, General Lee was

referred to by Governor Wentworth as his "kinsman." In England he had married Isabella Bunbury whose brother, Charles Bunbury, had come to Portsmouth in the 1750's to engage in the West Indies trade, and had married Hannah Wentworth, the governor's niece.

A portion of the Bunbury estate, among England's wealthiest, became the property of General Lee upon the death of Lee's father-in-law, Sir Henry Bunbury, but was confiscated when he joined the American army, a loss compensated for by a congressional grant. General Lee died in 1782 and is buried in a church cemetery in Washington.

Lee in New Hampshire contains Wheelwright Pond, one of the state's most attractive scenic spots. It was once part of the large tract in the claim of the Reverend John Wheelwright, the founder of Exeter.

MADBURY

MADBURY was formerly a part of Durham and of a section of Dover called Barbados, so named because of the West Indies trade carried on between that island and the New Hampshire coast settlements. It appears to have at one time been the farm of Sir Francis Champernowne of Greenland. Sir Francis was a nephew of Ferdinando Gorges, and came to America in the early 1640's to take up what was then understood to be his grant in the vicinity of Dover. Sir Francis's English home was called Modbury, and he is thought to have named his farm Modbury, or Madbury, in its honor.

The name Madbury Parish appeared for the first time in a grant made in 1755 by Governor Benning Wentworth, and town privileges were granted by Governor John Wentworth in 1768.

Many of the names contained in the early Madbury records were those of Barbados traders, six of whom, Clark, Daniel, Demerit, Gerrish, Tasker, and Twombly, built "garrison houses" for protection against the Indians, probably the largest number in any New Hampshire coast town. The name Barbados remains in the present names of Barbados Pond, Barbados Springs, and Barbados Woods.

NEW CASTLE

THIS ancient island town appears to have taken its name not from the English town of Newcastle-on-Tyne, as is sometimes assumed, or from the Dukes of Newcastle, but from the famous Fort William and Mary, which was built during the reign of William and Mary, and, because of its structure, was known as "The Castle."

Once a part of Portsmouth, New Castle was originally called "Great Island," being the largest of several islands at the mouth of the Piscataqua River. It was first chartered as a "parish" in 1679, and in 1693 a grant of incorporation was made by Lieutenant-Governor John Usher of Massachusetts when New Hampshire was under the dominion of that state. It is thought to have been one of the few "William and Mary" charters in existence in New England.

Fort William and Mary came to be of special historical significance in pre-revolutionary days, when its supply of ammunition was removed by the Portsmouth colonists in order to prevent its remaining in the hands of the English whose fleet had been sent there to protect it in 1774. Following the Revolution, having fallen into disrepair, it was rebuilt during tthe War of 1812, and its tower strengthened. It is now known as Fort Constitution and is a historic landmark. New Castle itself was one of the "coast towns" in New Hampshire to suffer severely from the Indian depredations which followed its incorporation, culminating in "King William's War" in the late 1690's.

New Castle is connected to the mainland by bridges, and is unique in the state as the only town made up entirely of islands. The Old Fort Point Lighthouse was first built in 1784 and rebuilt in 1877. Located in New Castle is the historic Wentworth-By-The-Sea hotel, site of the Russo-Japanese Peace Treaty of 1905, which was mediated by Theodore Roosevelt.

NEWFIELDS

THIS TOWN, on the west bank of the Squamscott River, was first part of Exeter until 1727 and then a part of Newmarket. It was called "Newfield Village," as early as 1681, and then known as South Newmarket. It was one of the then several parishes or "divisions" of Newmarket itself, the others having been called Piscasset, Lamprey River and The Plains. It was not officially incorporated as Newfields until 1895.

The name Newfields, as restored in 1895, after having been called South Newmarket, came about through the recommendation of Dr. John M. Brodhead, a Newfields native and descendant of its first minister, Elder John Brodhead, who was appointed to "do the town's preaching until the worth of which he expended." The elder John Brodhead, after being state representative for several terms, was elected to the United States Senate where he served from 1817 to 1827. An imposing full-length portrait of him hangs in the New Hampshire Capitol.

Dr. John M. Brodhead in 1880 presented his own library and $10,000 to the town on the condition that it be renamed Newfields, which was done fifteen years later. It was so named because of the beautiful meadow lands bordering the Squamscott River. Newfields was at one time a thriving shipbuilding center. Early families bore the names of Hilton, Kittredge, Wiggin, Bryant, Hersey, Norris, Varney and Tarlton. It was also the home of Samuel Smith, the builder of what is said to have been the first railroad in New Hampshire, the Bangor and Piscataqua Canal R.R. Co.

NEWINGTON

NEWINGTON originally bore the graphic name of "Bloody Point," in memory of the defeat by the early colonists of a roving band of Indians who had made a night attack on Dover, of which it was then a part, in the late 1600's.

The entire territory was once known as the Squamscott Patent, but some time before 1714 the "Bloody Point" section was renamed Newington Parish, and so designated by Governor Joseph Dudley of Massachusetts, the parish residents considering themselves as having officially separated from Dover with full township status. Newington appears to have taken its name from a village of the same name in England.

Soon after this date Newington erected its imposing, sturdily built colonial-style church, with its "Paul Revere bell" cast in 1755. According to all available records it appears to be among the oldest of New England churches; and its minister, Reverend Joseph Adams, Harvard 1710 and uncle of President John Adams, began his ministerial career there as a schoolmaster, serving the parish for the probably unequalled period of sixty-eight years.

The Reverend Adams declined to accept the full salary offered him, amounting to approximately $400 a year, and frequently distributed portions of it to his needy parishioners. He was active in the first years of his term in helping to secure the charter for Dartmouth College.

Another of Newington's prominent early citizens was John Pickering, at one time chief justice of the New Hampshire Supreme Court.

Newington is surrounded on three sides by the Piscataqua River and the Great Bay. Nearly three-fifths of the town's area is now taken up by Pease Air Force Base.

NEWMARKET

THIS TOWN is one of six granted by the Massachusetts government of which the province was then a part, by Lieutenant Governor John Wentworth in 1727, the last year of the reign of King George I. Four of these towns, Canterbury, Chichester, Epsom and Newmarket, bore English town names, among the first to find a place in the long list of such names in New Hampshire history.

Newmarket was originally one of several parishes in Exeter, and long after its separation it gave up a piece of its territory to form Newfields. It was granted full town privileges by the legislature in 1737.

The Lamprey (Oyster) River, which runs through the town, has long been subject to discussion. Its name appears not to have been taken from the lamprey eel, as sometimes assumed, but from an early settler, John Lamprey, whose name was derived, as was Lamphier, from the Saxon word "land frith" meaning "a woodland enclosure where peace is to be found." Newmarket was once called Lampreyville.

Newmarket's water power made possible the erection of prosperous lumber mills, and it became a center for New England shipping trade with the West Indies, rivaling Portsmouth and Kittery. Its famous Chapman Spring has long been reputed to have supplied the purest water found in New Hampshire, not varying in quantity in wet, dry, or cold weather.

Newmarket in County Suffolk, England, from which the town name appears to have come, is the site of the Newmarket Heath racetrack, on which horse races have been run annually since the reign of King James I.

NEWTON

NEWTON, on the Massachusetts border, was the tenth town to be established under the administration of Benning Wentworth, first governor of the province. It was the sixth to be granted in the great Masonian land purchase of 1746, and was one of a group of new towns in the Rockingham district set up at that time, most of them having been originally parts of other long-settled towns in the area.

First incorporated as "Newtown" in 1749, it had been for some time a part of South Hampton, a number of whose residents considered themselves too far away from its church for their convenience. Among these were the families of Bartlett, Peaslee, Currier, Hoyt, Chase and Rowell. The residents appear to have adopted the name to describe their "new town" and did not take it from an older community of the same name.

While it was still a part of South Hampton, a section of Newtown was known as "Loggin Plain," a tract devoted to tree cutting. In the early 1700's it had been subject to Indian attacks, one of the settlers, Joseph Bartlett, having been captured and sold to the French in Canada and released by them after a period of four years.

Newtown bore that name for nearly one hundred years. In 1846 the New Hampshire legislature voted to contract it to Newton. The United States has no fewer than ten other Newtowns or Newtons in as many states and Great Britain has nearly an equal number.

NORTH HAMPTON

NORTH HAMPTON was one of several towns carved out of the old settlement of Hampton. Settled in 1639 by Massachusetts colonists under the leadership of Reverend Stephen Bachilor, it was first known as "North Hill" and later "North Parish."

Residents of this section first began petitioning to be made a separate town as early as 1719 but were not successful until 1742, following the separation of the province of New Hampshire from Massachusetts. The new governor, Benning Wentworth, with his group of "Proprietors," then began granting new towns of which this was the third, the first two being Epping and Windham.

One of the arguments used by the North Hampton settlers was that they desired to have a "church of their own" and that they might be exempted from Hampton's "minister's tax." The separation resulted in the appointment of the Reverend Nathaniel Gookin as their own minister. The first settlers, who also built their own "garrison" house, one of the first in New Hampshire, included the families of Dearborn, Batchelder, Haynes, Page, Lamprey, Marston, and Brown.

Prominent among these families were the Dearborns, who were the ancestors of General Henry Dearborn, who was born here in 1751. He fought at Bunker Hill and later was commander-in-chief of the American forces in the War of 1812. In this war he led the forces which captured York, in Canada, now Toronto, and established Fort Dearborn, now Chicago. General Dearborn served as Secretary of War under President Thomas Jefferson, and was elected a member of Congress. He died in 1829. Dearborn, Michigan is also named for him.

PLAISTOW

PLAISTOW, once a part of Haverhill, Massachusetts, came by its picturesque name in 1749 when it was set aside as an English "plaistowe," meaning an "open space or greenwood, near the center of a village where the maypole stood and where sports at holiday times were carried on." Other names in this locality, since long forgotten, were Timburlain, Policy Pond, Spicket Meadow, and Amesbury Peak.

John White, descended from William White who came from England in 1650, was said to have been the "richest man in town" and his son, Deacon Nicholas White, was appointed to administer the affairs of Plaistow. Some of the residents had previously joined with Ebenezer Eastman in 1725 to settle the town of Penacook, afterward Concord, and others were among the group which included the Hazens, Peasleys, Whittiers and Cogswells, who went north to take up new grants in Haverhill, New Hampshire.

Nathaniel White of Hillsborough, a direct descendant of Deacon Nicholas, became one of New Hampshire's "stage coach pioneers" in the 1830s and was associated with Benjamin P. Cheney who founded Boston's Canada Express Company which afterward became the American Express Company and is now the Railway Express Agency.

PORTSMOUTH

THE CAPITAL of colonial New Hampshire and one of the most thriving seaports on the eastern seaboard in the eighteenth century, Portsmouth's history goes back some 350 years. It is a town so rich in historical lore that it is impossible in this brief space to touch on more than a few of its events and personalities. Portsmouth was one of New Hampshire's original settlements. What is now Portsmouth was first colonized in 1630, two earlier fishing villages having been established in 1623 at Rye (then part of Portsmouth) and Dover. It was first called Piscataqua, the name of the river on its eastern boundary, and very soon thereafter "Strawbery Banke," after a field filled with wild strawberries, a name it retained until 1653.

In that year the settlement became Portsmouth, after Portsmouth, England, where the founder of the New Hampshire colony, Captain John Mason, had been captain of the port. Among the early settlers of the town were the families of Hilton, Neal, Colcord, Larkham, Vaughan, Pickering, Seavey, Sherburne, Wiggin, Champernowne, Martyn, and Hunking. The last named were ancestors of Benning Wentworth, governor of the province from 1741 to 1766, who was responsible for the naming of so many of its towns.

Portsmouth became the capital of New Hampshire in 1679, when New Hampshire legally became a separate province. Even at that date, though trade in lumber and fish were beginning to flourish, there were still only four towns in the colony — the fifth, Kingston, was not granted until the 1690's, and others soon followed. The Provincial Assembly, sitting in Portsmouth, passed laws during this period forbidding men from wearing long hair and banning the sale of "strong drink" and firearms ("except for hunting purposes") to the Indians. The executive authority of the province was often administered by the Governor of Massachusetts, until 1741 when Benning Wentworth assumed the office.

It was after this that Portsmouth came into its "golden age." The colony expanded rapidly, commerce thrived, the town grew and many fine Georgian mansions were built. Portsmouth was not only the home of Governor Benning Wentworth, whose house is still preserved, but of his nephew and successor John Wentworth, governor from 1766 to 1774. Among its citizens were the Revolutionary War patriots William Whipple, signer of the Declaration of Independence; Governor John Langdon, first president of the United States Senate; and Captain John Paul Jones, who built the famous ship *Ranger* at what later became the Portsmouth Navy Yard. A notable literary figure was Thomas Bailey Aldrich, whose delightful *Story of a Bad Boy*, written in 1870, was based on his boyhood in Portsmouth.

Portsmouth, which was incorporated as a city in 1849, is noted for its many fine examples of colonial architecture, among them the homes of two governors, Levi Woodbury and Ichabod Goodwin. The latter is in the old section called Strawbery Banke. This historic area was retrieved from decay in 1957 and is being preserved, like Williamsburg, Virginia, as a recreation of a colonial American town. Over thirty houses, inns and shops have been saved in the Strawbery Banke project and are being restored to recapture their original historical and architectural features. The restoration will eventually include the Old State House and "Puddle Dock," the old harbor inlet, named for the famous Puddle Dock in the Blackfriars district of London.

ROLLINSFORD

A CAREFUL SEARCH will probably reveal few American marriages, if any, where the bride and groom received a wedding gift of having a town named for them. Yet that is what happened when, in 1849, Edward H. Rollins and his new wife, Ellen West, returned to Rollinsford, New Hampshire, from their honeymoon and found the town had just been officially named in their honor. Rollins was twenty-five years old at the time.

It is true that there had been Rollins at the "ford" and at nearby Salmon Falls in Somersworth for several generations, since the original James Rawlings came up from Ipswich, Massachusetts, to settle. Edward, his great-great-grandson, had hoped to enter Dartmouth, but had to go to work instead, finding employment in a drug store in Concord. Later he got into the wholesale drug business in Boston, and returned with enough savings to buy out the store where he had once begun his business career. Two years later Rollinsford was set apart from Somersworth and became a separate town, the same year of his marriage.

From then on Rollins rapidly rose to fame. He went to the legislature, became Speaker of the House (in 1856), was chairman of the State Republican Committee, and became a Congressman from New Hampshire from 1861 to 1867. Later he served as assistant treasurer of the newly formed Union Pacific Railroad, and from 1877 to 1883 was United States Senator from this state. He then founded the banking firm of E. H. Rollins & Sons in Boston, in which he was succeeded by his son, Frank W. Rollins, who was New Hampshire's governor in 1900 and the originator of "Old Home Week."

Rollinsford, when still a part of Somersworth, was the site of the landing place of James Stackpole in 1680 on the Salmon Falls River. The town includes Salmon Falls, named for the Salmon River.

RYE

THE COASTAL TOWN of Rye was the site of the first settlement in New Hampshire, made by David Thompson in 1623 at Odiorne's Point. This primitive fishing village was first called Pannaway. In the same year another small pioneer settlement was made at Dover by the Hilton brothers.

Rye was originally part of Portsmouth and was incorporated as a parish of New Castle in 1726 by Lieutenant Governor John Wentworth. It bears the name of the twelfth century English borough of Rye, once a flourishing England Channel town. Rye and its neighbor, Dover, are two of the historical "Cinque Ports" of England.

Rye, New Hampshire, with an eight-mile stretch of seacoast is dotted with such sectional place-names as Wallis and Jenness Sands, Locke's Neck, Ragged Neck, Biddy Beach, Pig Beach, and Foss Beach, Cone and Odiorne Points, and Rye Beach.

Long famous as a summer resort, Rye lists among its first land owners the families of Seavey, Locke, Jenness, Rand, Marden, Wallis, and Odiorne. Its early colony of inhabitants was frequently the scene of Indian attacks, one of which, in 1696, is said to have resulted in the capture of a group of Indian fishermen who were encamped for an early morning feast, on what became known as Breakfast Hill.

Rye has the distinction of being the only New Hampshire town to contain Atlantic islands, four of the ISLES OF SHOALS, which were annexed to the town in 1876. The remaining five islands in the group belong to Maine. Three centuries ago the word "Shoals" meant fishing grounds, and thus the islands got their name. Gosport, the once busy and properous New Hampshire fishing town, on Star Island, is said to have been originally named "God's Town." During the days of the early European wars it was frequently the first port in America for the landing of foreign ships bringing news from abroad, and it is said the name became recast as if taken from "Gossip's Town." In fact it was probably named by the earliest emigrants for Gosport, in the county of Hampshire, England, which lies directly across the bay from the English town of Portsmouth.

Star Island is the largest of the New Hampshire islands, the others being Lunging, White and Seavey. Gosport was at one time inhabited by several hundred families. It had its own church, stores and hotels in the center of extensive fishing grounds, having grown to that size since its discovery in the early 1600's. It abounds in legends, one of them being the tale of a minister who urged his parishioners not to fish on Sunday, promising that those who did not do so, but remained in church, would be rewarded on the following Monday. The tale records that thirty stayed and five went out, the latter getting only four fish, while the faithful who went next day caught five hundred.

Gosport's first church was said to have been built from the

timbers of wrecked Spanish vessels, but was reconstructed in 1790 from stone. It was at one time supported by Church of England missionary funds. Together with several modern buildings, it is now owned and occupied during the summer months by national religious organizations. The three remaining larger islands of the Isles of Shoals, Appledore (Hog Island), Cedar and Smuttynose, are part of Maine. It was on Appledore that Celia Thaxter, the poet, lived and is buried.

SANDOWN

SANDOWN, once a part of Kingston, became an incorporated town in 1756. Like Epsom, Chiswick, Kensington, and Plaistow, which took their names from picturesque and fashionable English parks and resorts, Sandown on the Isle of Wight was so recognized by Governor Benning Wentworth in the naming of this town. The governor had been a frequent London visitor during his long career as a shipping merchant in Portsmouth.

Most of the grantees of our Sandown came from Hampton, Salisbury and Kingston, and as usual they included whole families, of which four were Shaws, three were Tuckers and two were Huses and Pressys. The first minister was the Reverend Joseph Cotton, a son of Seaborn Cotton, who began his services with the building, in 1773, of the famous Sandown Church with its eleven foot high pulpit, its "sounding board," its "deacons' pews," and its marble columns supporting the gallery. According to the records, the builders were supplied with a barrel of New England rum to aid them in their work, and are said to have refused to work when it ran out, until more could be secured from Newburyport. The building itself, in a fine state of preservation, is one of the outstanding examples of early New England church architecture still remaining.

SEABROOK

THE SOUTHERN border of Seabrook was first settled in 1638 when it was a part of Hampton. It was incorporated in 1768 by Governor John Wentworth, and named Seabrook after the Seabrook River into which flow several brooks before it empties into the Atlantic Ocean.

Its first moderator was Nathaniel Weare, agent for New Hampshire in England, one of whose descendants was Meshech Weare, the state's first "president." Other early settlers included the families of Gove, Robie, Brown, Leavitt, Dow, Hussey, Philbrick and Dearborn, the last named being the ancestors of General Henry Dearborn who fought at Bunker Hill. Seabrook's Dearborn Academy had as its donor Dr. Edward Dearborn, a member of that family.

Another famous Seabrook personage was Edward Gove who organized what was called Gove's Rebellion, in revolt against the English Governor Edmund Andros, and was imprisoned in the Tower of London, afterward to be released and returned to his native town.

The town of Seabrook contains several small industries inland from its marshlands, harbor and coastal waters. A boundary dispute with Hampton, which began two centuries ago and has cropped up periodically since then, was finally settled by a court decision in 1953.

SOMERSWORTH

SOMERSWORTH, bordering Maine on the Salmon River, was originally a "parish" in Dover, where it was first called Sligo after the Irish county, which was the home of one of the early colonial governors. Later it became Summersworth, the name being finally contracted into Somersworth when it was incorporated as a town in 1754 by Governor Benning Wentworth. It became a city in 1893. Somersworth is the only town in the

United States or England so named, and the origins of its name
are obscure.

Somersworth owes much of its early existence to the fact that
it is located on what was then one of New Hampshire's busiest
manufacturing streams, the Salmon River. Here, as in most
river towns, grew up the usual sawmills and grist mills, several of which were consolidated, or torn down, to provide a
site for what turned out to be one of the largest and earliest
cotton and woolen making establishments in New Hampshire.

First incorporated as the "Mill and Works on the Salmon
Falls River in Somersworth," the undertaking was renamed as
the Great Falls Manufacturing Company. It was owned and
built by Isaac and Jacob Wendell of Boston in 1823, who produced their own bricks from nearby kilns and their own iron
from native mines. In their first year the mills operated more
than three thousand spindles under the direction of an experi-
enced weaver from Manchester, England.

Somersworth gave New Hampshire one of its governors, Fred
H. Brown, who also served as United States Senator from New
Hampshire from 1933 to 1939.

SOUTH HAMPTON

ONCE A PART of Amesbury and Salisbury in Massachusetts,
South Hampton is one of the first towns granted in this state by
Governor Benning Wentworth, who became governor of the
province in 1741. Chartered in 1742, it was one of the Hampton
"border towns" which resulted from the establishment of a new
and permanent boundary line between the two governments.

South Hampton combined several groups of settlers located
in what were known as Loggin (Logging) Plain and Rocky and
Pow-wow-Hills, the latter so named because it had been the
scene of an Indian peace-talk or "pow-wow."

Soon after its incorporation, South Hampton lost part of its
territory to form the town of Hampton Falls, and later lost
more to the new towns of Seabrook to the east and Newton to

the west. It gained, however, in 1824, additional land from East
Kingston.

South Hampton was said at one time to have more religious
sects within its borders than any other New Hampshire town.
In 1834 some of its church property was sold for $2585.47, the
income from which was voted to be divided among the follow-
ing denominations: Baptists, Quakers, Congregationalists,
Deists, Naturalists, Episcopalians, Methodists, Free Baptists,
Universalists, Second Universalists, Philanthropists, and Free-
Thinkers.

STRATHAM

THE TOWN of Stratham was incorporated in 1716 by Governor
Samuel Shute of Massachusetts, of which this state was then a
part. It was the sixth town to be incorporated in New Hampshire. Bordering the Great Bay and the Squamscott River, it
was originally called by the Indians Winnicutt and was part of
a large coastal area known as the "Squamscott Patent" or "Point
of Rocks." The area was first settled in 1631 under the leadership of Governor Thomas Wiggin of Massachusetts.

The name Stratham comes from the English town of Streatham, now a residential district of south London. In old English
it means a place on a street or paved road. The towns of Strafford, Stratford and Stratton have a similar derivation.

Stratham, New Hampshire appears to have been named for
a nobleman who took his title from the English town. Wriothes-
ley Russell (1680-1771), who was a friend of Governor Shute's,
was summoned to Parliament in 1695 as Baron Howland of
Streatham. His mother, Elizabeth Howland, was the heiress to
the Streatham title and estate. Russell later became the second
Duke of Bedford.

While not a large town, Stratham bears the distinction of
having subscribed more than ten thousand pounds toward the
expenses of the colonies during the Revolutionary War. In
addition, the town raised and enrolled 170 soldiers, among

them one colonel, two majors, four captains, eight lieutenants, two ensigns, and 153 privates — a record perhaps unequalled by any town of its size in New England.

VI

White Mountain Region

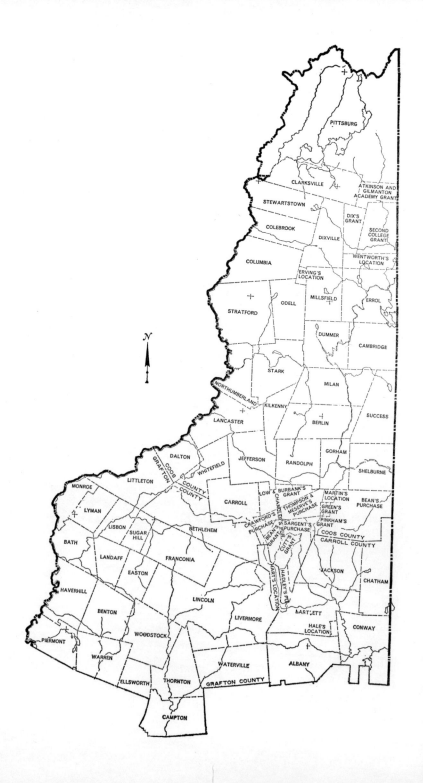

ALBANY

THE TOWN of Albany, which is famous for having New Hampshire's much-loved Mount Chocorua in residence, was originally chartered in 1766 as Burton and probably named for General Jonathan Burton of Wilton. The town was one of the last granted in the term of Governor Benning Wentworth, and the origin of its name has also been attributed to Henry Paget of England, who became second Baron Burton and Earl of Uxbridge in 1743. Paget died in 1769.

It was one of several "soldiers' grants" made at that time, most of the land being allotted to men who fought the French at Louisbourg in America's first "world war" for Canada in 1745. Among those to whom land in Burton was given were Colonel Jonathan Moulton, Captain Israel Gilman, Captain Jeremiah Folsom, Lieutenant Joseph Senter and members of their families, there being in the list eight Gilmans, seven Senters, and four Folsoms.

The area included in this grant, while it proved to be suitable for raising considerable flax from which linen was made, an art which the Senters brought with them from their native Londonderry, is generally mountainous. Among its peaks are — in addition to Chocorua — Paugus, Three Sisters, Pequawket and South Moat mountains.

The town continued under the name of Burton until 1833, which was the year the railroad from New York to Albany, later the New York Central, was chartered, when, perhaps for that reason, it was incorporated and renamed Albany. The town has rich deposits of what was known in the 1870's as "Albany Granite", although no quarries seem to have ever been put into operation in that section. Much of Albany is now part of the White Mountain National Forest.

ATKINSON AND GILMANTON GRANT

LOCATED in the far reaches of the north country along the Maine boundary, this uninhabited tract of land was granted by the legislature in 1809 during the administration of Governor Jeremiah Smith. The grantees were Gilmanton Academy and Atkinson Academy, which were to hold the land in equal shares and derive the income from it. The academies, named for two prominent New Hampshire families of the Colonial and early Federal period, were then important educational institutions in the state. The grant followed by two years that of an adjoining tract, six miles square, to Dartmouth College. These unincorporated areas remain on the state's official list of towns and places. The Atkinson and Gilmanton Grant consists of about 13,000 acres, mostly timberland.

BARTLETT

THIS TOWN was named in 1790 in honor of Dr. Josiah Bartlett of Kingston, who in that year became New Hampshire's first chief executive to have the name "governor," both of his predecessors under the new government having been called "president."

A part of the area now included in the town of Bartlett was originally granted in the 1760's to four officers in the French War. One of these was Captain William Stark, brother of General John Stark. Another was Major James Gray, who fought with Amherst in Canada, while another was Lieutenant Andrew McMillan of Bow, and the fourth was Colonel Vere Royse who came from England and fought with Washington at the time of Braddock's defeat in Pennsylvania, and who surveyed the territory.

None of these officers appears to have taken up his grant prior to the Revolution, so that the land was available for new assignment under the colonial government. Dr. Bartlett, to whom the title descended, was a practicing physician at Portsmouth. He was elected to represent New Hampshire at the Continental Congress, and there he was one of New Hampshire's three signers of the Declaration of Independence, being the first to place his name under that of John Hancock at the head of the list. He was the founder, in 1791, of the New Hampshire Medical Society.

In 1823 the town of Bartlett annexed a part of Jackson including the villages of Glen, Lower Bartlett, and Intervale, which are today popular winter and summer resort areas.

BATH

THE CHARTER of the town of Bath was granted in 1761, and set aside land in equal shares for sixty-two families, with a church and a school.

The name Bath was that of one of England's prominent statesmen of the times, William Pulteney (1684-1764), first Earl of Bath, who served as Secretary of War and a member of the Privy Council. He was a graduate of Oxford, noted as a brilliant scholar and one of the best orators in the English Parliament. The town of Poultney, Vermont, once a part of New Hampshire, also is named for him.

Among the early grantees and settlers of Bath was the Reverend Andrew Gardner, who deserves to be remembered as its "patron saint." Graduating from Harvard in 1712, he became minister of the church at Brookline, Massachusetts, later at the church at Lunenburg, Massachusetts, and served as chaplain at the famous Fort Dummer on the Connecticut River. Another fort was erected under his supervision at Bath, where he was moderator of the first town meeting. Mr. Gardner was a cousin of President John Adams, and Gardner Mountain, which divides the towns of Monroe and Lyman, is named for him.

Bath is famous for having had as its first settler Jaaziel (biblical for "God's Created") Harriman, and one of its ministers, the Reverend David Sutherland, born in Scotland and a noted evangelist, preached to the entire countryside and was known as "Father" Sutherland. Among the grantees and early settlers were the Bedels, who fought, father, son, and grandson, in the Revolution, the War of 1812, and the Civil War. The town is said to have once been "the most important" north country town, having had at one time a population of nearly two thousand people.

This Connecticut River town has several fine colonial houses and the old Woods-Goodale law offices, a two-story brick building, erected in 1816 for State Chief Justice Andrew S. Woods and Ira Goodale.

BEAN'S GRANT

THIS unincorporated mountainous area, located above Crawford Notch, was granted by the state in 1835 to Charles Bean of Maine and contained about 3,300 acres. This grant and several others in the vicinity of the Presidential Range were made possible by an act of the legislature in 1831 authorizing the governor to sell and apportion unassigned public lands. Governor Samuel Dinsmoor appointed James Willey of Concord as land commissioner. Commissioner Willey was responsible for apportioning about a dozen such unincorporated townships in the 1830's. Bean's Grant includes Mount Jackson, 4,052 feet, named for President Andrew Jackson, and Mount Eisenhower, 4,775 feet, formerly Mount Pleasant, recently renamed for the late President Dwight D. Eisenhower.

BEAN'S PURCHASE

A LARGE unpopulated wilderness area stretching east from Pinkham Notch to the Maine border, Bean's Purchase was one of the largest grants made by James Willey, state land commissioner, in the 1830's. The mountainous tract, comprising about 33,000 acres, was made to Alpheus Bean of Bartlett in

1832 for one thousand dollars. The unincorporated township, which includes the headwaters of the Wild River and the site of the Wild River Camping Ground, is now entirely within the White Mountain National Forest. Within the area is Mount Moriah, a biblical name meaning "provided by Jehovah" and so-named for a mountain in Jerusalem. The Carter range, which includes Carter Dome, Carter Mountain, Carter Ledge and Carter Boulders, was named for Dr. Ezra Carter, a physician in Concord in the early 1800's who made frequent explorations in this section in search of medicinal herbs, roots, and plants. The Bean's Purchase Grant also includes Wildcat Mountain, now popular as a ski area.

BENTON

THIS TOWN, the site of Mount Moosilauke, was originally granted in 1764 as Coventry, taking the name from an old Connecticut town, which, in turn was given its name in 1711 by an early New England pioneer, the Reverend James Davenport who was born in Coventry, England. It was also the surname of George William Coventry, who became sixth Earl of Coventry in 1751 and died in 1809.

The list of grantees of Coventry, New Hampshire included a considerable number of Connecticut families. Among these were the Weeds, of whom there were no fewer than eleven recorded in the charter, the Crisseys, Fanchers, Seeleys, Lounsburys and Fitches, one of the last of whom, Theophilus Fitch, had come from Coventry, Connecticut. As first moderator of the new town, he suggested the name to Governor Wentworth, a close friend of one of his relatives, the Reverend Jabez Fitch, who taught at Harvard while the Governor was there, and whose son, the Reverend James Fitch of Lebanon, Connecticut, was probably the first in America to preach to the Indians in their own language.

The town retained the name of Coventry for more than seventy-five years. In 1839 Governor Isaac Hill proposed re-

naming it Benton, after his friend Thomas Hart Benton, senator from Missouri, and it was so incorporated in 1840. Senator
Benton had then served in Congress for more than twenty
years and achieved fame for his championship of the cause of
Western expansion through the establishment of the express,
railroad, navigation and telegraph interests. He was the father-
in-law of the Western explorer, General John C. Fremont,
after whom the New Hampshire town of Fremont was named
in 1854.

BERLIN

THE CITY of Berlin provides an example of the odd turns in
place naming which occur so often in this state.

The name Berlin does not, as first might seem, come from
the capital of Germany, but instead from a small but ancient
town called Berlin in Worcester County, Massachusetts, which
probably did get its name from that source. Thus the people
of our own Berlin have no need to insist, as they sometimes do,
that their name should be accented on its first, instead of second, syllable to distinguish it from the European city.

New Hampshire's Berlin began its identity in 1771 as Maynesborough, a name suggested by Governor John Wentworth in
honor of his friend Sir William Mayne of London, who was
associated with him in his extensive West Indies trade with
Barbados, the colony which got its unique name because the
long strands of moss which hung from its trees looked to the
early colonists like beards.

Governor Wentworth not only named the New Hampshire
town to honor a fellow Barbados trader, but secured grants
there for a dozen others, including Sir Robert Needham, for
whom Needham, Massachusetts, and Needham Point in Barbados are named. Our own Portsmouth still has its "Barbados"
section.

None of the Barbados grantees of Maynesborough, however,
seem to have ever settled or visited here, and their grants ex-

pired with the American Revolution, the land remaining being gradually occupied by colonists from the Worcester County towns of Lancaster, Bolton and Berlin in Massachusetts. Prominent among these were the families of Bean, Cates, Greene, Ordway and Wheeler, the last being from Berlin, from which Maynesborough was renamed in 1829. The Wheelers built the first mill in their new settlement, and it thus became the commercial ancestor of the thriving enterprises in the present city.

Berlin includes the town of Cascade, located on the Ammonoosuc River.

BETHLEHEM

AMONG the several Granite State town names which are derived from places in far-away lands, that of Bethlehem indicates an especially pleasing choice. The name was first selected on the last Christmas Day in the century which gave America its freedom, and the incorporation papers were signed on December 27, 1799 by Governor John Taylor Gilman.

Prior to this event, Bethlehem had existed since 1774 under the obscurely inscribed and almost forgotten name of Lloyd's Hills and most records treated the identity of the name as a matter of uncertainty. Recent researches, however, have established certain facts relating to the origin of the name Lloyd in connection with Lloyd's Hills.

It appears that there were Lloyds who were among the leading Boston families in pre-Revolutionary days, and that James Lloyd was a prosperous Boston merchant whose father, Charles Lloyd, had been secretary to George Grenville, English Prime Minister in 1764, and noted for his alliance with the Rockingham or Wentworth administration against war with America.

James Lloyd of Boston had ten children, one of whom was Dr. James Lloyd who became a well-known Boston physician, and another who became the wife of Commodore Joshua Loring, Boston shipping merchant, later high sheriff of Massachusetts. The records indicate that in 1773 James Lloyd of Boston either purchased or was granted land by the proprietors in the new town of Dummer, and that another grant was made to him the following year in what was to be called Lloyd's Hills. This tract comprised some twenty-three thousand acres, and James Lloyd was the sole proprietor.

Upon the death of James Lloyd, the New Hampshire Lloyd's Hills grant was transferred to Commodore Loring who, through his friendship for Governor Wentworth named his son John Wentworth Loring. He afterwards became Sir John Wentworth Loring of England.

Dr. James Lloyd built one of the imposing "mansions" with their extensive gardens which surrounded the King's Chapel section of Boston at the foot of Beacon Hill, and his son, James Lloyd 3d, became United States Senator from Massachusetts from 1808 to 1813, succeeding John Quincy Adams. He was a staunch Federalist and sided in Congress with Daniel Webster during his first New Hampshire term in opposition to the War of 1812.

Bethlehem has the distinction of being the last of the provincial land grants.

One of its hills is Mount Agassiz, named for Jean Louis Rudolph Agassiz, the great explorer and naturalist who visited the area in the 1840's.

CAMBRIDGE

CAMBRIDGE took its name from Cambridge, Massachusetts, where Governor John Wentworth graduated from Harvard College in 1755. Its charter was prepared in 1773, during the last years of his administration, but does not appear to have been ever issued.

The Cambridge land grants under this charter included land to be awarded to a number of distinguished individuals, including Nathaniel Rogers and the Reverend Samuel Locke, who became president of Harvard in 1770. Another was John Adams, later to be President of the United States, who was a classmate of Governor Wentworth at Harvard, while another classmate was the Reverend Jacob Bailey, who afterward became minister of a church in Nova Scotia which Governor Wentworth attended during his residence there.

Cambridge is located in the line of towns along the Maine border at the northern peak of New Hampshire, through which the Governor proposed to establish a direct North-and-South highway to Canada, from Portsmouth to Montreal, a project to be completed many years later.

The original grantees of Cambridge were required under the charter "to build and maintain a church with a settled minister of the Church of England, forever," and a school for which the land was provided.

Cambridge contains over 23,000 acres, but today is virtually uninhabited. The township was never incorporated.

CAMPTON

IT HAS BEEN suggested that Campton, granted in 1761 by Governor Benning Wentworth, took its name from an early surveyor's camp-site in the vicinity. It is much more likely, however, that the name commemorates one of the governor's influential English friends, Spencer Compton, Earl of Wilmington (1673-1743). Wentworth named the great majority of his New Hampshire grants for business and political friends, and it was due in part to Compton's influence that Wentworth became governor in 1741.

The Earl was paymaster of the land forces, and afterwards became speaker of the House of Lords, a Lord Justice, and for a brief time Prime Minister. Governor Wentworth also named one of his Vermont towns Wilmington in 1752, and the cities of Wilmington in Delaware and North Carolina were named for him. Spelling in the eighteenth century was more phonetic and not so formalized as at present, and pronunciation of the letter "a" was broader, as one might hear it spoken by a Scotsman or Irishman today. Thus "Compton" easily became "Campton."

Most of the settlers of Campton came from one of the river towns in Connecticut, East Haddam. One of them was Deacon Daniel Brainerd, whose grandson, David, associated with the Reverend Jonathan Edwards, was an Indian preacher and Bible translator. At Stockbridge, Massachusetts, David Brainerd established an Indian mission which served as a model for Eleazar Wheelock, the founder of Dartmouth College. Among the other early grantees were several members of the Spencer family, from whom Sir Winston Churchill was descended.

Another of the Campton grantees was John Marsh, also from East Haddam, whose grandson, Sylvester Marsh, after a successful career in Chicago, revisited his boyhood home and built the famous cog-railroad to Mount Washington. It was chartered by the legislature in 1858 whose members had misgivings as to its possibilities, naming the inventor "Crazy" Marsh and calling their act a "charter to the moon." The railroad's original cost was $139,000 and appears to have well justified the expense.

CARROLL

IN THE SELECTION of names for New Hampshire places the name Carroll has been chosen twice, once as the name of a county and again as the name of a town. For an adopted name, Carroll has taken to itself a considerable portion of New Hampshire history.

The town of Carroll is named for Charles Carroll of Carrollton, Maryland, who signed the Declaration of Independence. Through his large land holdings in his native and neighboring states he is said to have been among the richest men in America in Revolutionary days. His connection with New Hampshire is derived indirectly from his visit here in 1776.

At that time, just prior to our alliance with France, it was proposed by Benjamin Franklin that the possibility of a union with Canada be explored, and a committee consisting of Franklin, Charles Carroll, his cousin, Father John Carroll, and Samuel Chase, congressman from Maryland, was appointed by Congress for this purpose. The two Carrolls were to confer with the French-Canadian clergy, and Franklin and Chase with the laity. Their route to Canada lay through what is now Carroll County. The committee visited Montreal, but was not successful.

Charles Carroll was a congressman and senator in the first and subsequent Congresses, but was opposed to the War of 1812 with England. He was a member of the first board of directors of the Baltimore & Ohio Railroad. His cousin John, affectionately known as "Jackie", taught school as a Jesuit in France, and returned to become a founder and first president of Georgetown College. He had the honor of being the first Roman Catholic bishop in America.

The town of Carroll was originally granted as Bretton Woods, after the distinguished English jurist, Henry de Brachton who, in 1268, built the famous Bretton Hall which later became the estate of the ancestors of New Hampshire's provincial governor, John Wentworth. Its owner in 1772, the year the Bretton Woods charter was granted, was Sir Thomas Wentworth, who was named one of the grantees. BRETTON WOODS, which continues today as part of the town of Carroll, gives its name to the historic conference held here in July 1944, resulting in the creation of the International Monetary Fund.

The town of Carroll, which is in Coos County, took its present name in 1832, the year of the death of Charles Carroll, and Carroll County was so designated in 1840, eight years later.

The town includes the original settlements at Crawford Notch (Crawford House), Fabyan's (Fabyan House), Twin Mountain, and the Zealand Notch Camping Area. FABYAN'S, though never incorporated, has appeared on all our maps since the 1870's. It takes its name from Horace Fabyan, a provision dealer from Maine who built an inn there in 1837 which became one of the most popular in the White Mountains.

Calling it the Mount Washington House, Horace Fabyan

is said to have listed as one of its features his famous six-foot tin horn which he blew at sundown each evening so that his patrons might hear the reverberating echoes from the surrounding mountains.

The Fabyan family was one of the oldest in New England, spelling their name Fabens, Fabins and Fabians, and engaged in a prosperous fishing and boat-building enterprise in Marblehead, Massachusetts. Samuel Fabyan, who moved to Newington, New Hampshire in the 1700's, is recorded as having had twelve children who attained an average age of seventy-three, their added ages, including those of their parents, totaling more than one thousand. Samuel Fabyan's daughter Lydia is also said to have had twelve children, with sixty grandchildren and ninety-three great grandchildren. One of the Fabyans, an extensive traveler, was once the promoter of a project to import camels into the American southwest.

The New Hampshire Fabyans built a seven-mile long bridle path along the Ammonoosuc River to the foot of Mount Washington, which became known as the Fabyan Turnpike, now Fabyan's Path. Their Mount Washington House burned in 1858 and was rebuilt in 1874 as the Fabyan House. It burned again in 1951.

NASH AND SAWYER'S LOCATION, now part of Carroll, comprised the strip of territory extending north from Crawford's Notch to a point beyond the present Fabyan's House. It took its name from two pioneer surveyors, Captain Timothy Nash and Benjamin Sawyer, who in return for clearing the first trail through the Notch were granted the tract by Governor John Wentworth in 1773. Two years previously Nash, while hunting a moose, had climbed a tree and discovered the pass which was to become an important gateway through the mountains to the upper Connecticut River Valley. Eleazer Rosebrook, father-in-law of Abel Crawford, settled in the area in 1792, and in 1803 the Tenth New Hampshire Turnpike was built through the Notch. Nash and Sawyer also received grants in several other towns: Conway, Lancaster, Bath and Northumberland. Parts of Nash and Sawyer's Location were annexed to Carroll in 1848 and 1878, and the whole grant was absorbed in 1887.

CHANDLER'S PURCHASE

CHANDLER'S PURCHASE, a narrow strip of land covering part of the western approaches to Mount Washington, was granted in 1835 to Jeremiah Chandler of Conway for three hundred dollars. The grant was one of those made by James Willey, the state land commissioner, of hitherto unassigned public lands, mostly in the vicinity of the Presidential Range. The Chandler's Purchase tract is now entirely within the White Mountain National Park, and the Mount Washington Cog Railway has its starting point there.

CHATHAM

THIS SCENIC but sparsely populated town on the Maine border bears the name of William Pitt, the Earl of Chatham, one of the greatest names in English history. But for Pitt, New England and perhaps a good part of North America, as well as Canada, might have come under the dominion of France, and there could never have been a United States of America as we know it today.

Pitt, himself beginning as a member of the House of Commons from old Sarum, an English "small town," rose to be the Secretary of State of England at a time when everything seemed to be going against her. His nation was about to lose its war with Spain and with France. But Pitt looked to America with his famous words, "I am sure I can save this country as no one else can." Pitt was almost alone in joining the Rockingham, or Wentworth, government in proposing that England "adopt a more gentle mode of governing America," saying that "this country has no right to tax the colonists." As supreme director of the war and of foreign affairs, he sent Generals Amherst and Wolfe to conquer Quebec, British troops to win victories abroad, and laid the foundations for American independence.

Chatham was originally granted by the New Hampshire proprietors in 1767 to a group of seventy-three grantees, none of whom, because of its being a "wilderness" inhabited by the Pequawket Indians, dared to settle there. It contained the famous "Baldface" mountain, and Mount Pigwacket, recently renamed without especial reason "Kearsarge North," due perhaps to an error in map-making in the early days.

Chatham was later regranted in 1770 to another group which included Abiel Chandler, founder of the Chandler Scientific School at Dartmouth and Samuel Langdon of Boston, president of Harvard College while Governor John Wentworth was a student there. Langdon was chaplain of the New England troops at Louisbourg and made the famous "Blanchard Map" of the North Country, assisted by Colonel Joseph Blanchard, the surveyor.

Also among the new grantees was the son of Reverend Timothy Walker of Concord, Timothy Walker Jr., who kept a store on South Main Street in Concord, and had charge of supplying the troops who took part in the French War, and who had attended Harvard at the same time as Governor Wentworth.

CLARKSVILLE

CLARKSVILLE was originally a part of a large tract of more than 40,000 acres of north country land which, as proposed by New Hampshire President (afterward governor) John Sullivan, was deeded by the legislature to Dartmouth College in 1789.

The college was then twenty years old and in the process of expansion following the Revolution. But the trustees considered their need for cash greater at that time than a need for new land, and accordingly voted to offer it for sale, which was done three years later. The purchasers were two Dartmouth graduates Joseph Murdock, of Norwich, Vermont, brother-in-law of Dartmouth treasurer, Mills Alcott, and Benjamin Clark of Boston, friend of former Governor John Wentworth and a member of the Society for the Encouragement of Trade and Commerce. The price paid for the section of the eight mile square portion they acquired was said to have been a shilling an acre, a total of approximately $10,000.

Settlements and sales by the new owners were slow in coming but by the late 1820's Mr. Clark and members of his family had cleared enough of the rich intervale Connecticut River land to attract a group of settlers, who called it Clarksville in his honor, a name appearing on the early maps. It was so incorporated in 1853, although the name "Dartmouth College Grant" also continued until 1872 when the last indebtedness to the college was cleared up. Other "college land," long subject to litigation, was located in the present "Second College Grant," and also in the Vermont town of Wheelock, some of which still yields the institution an income.

Only one New Hampshire town, Pittsburg, is farther north toward the Canadian border than Clarksville.

COLEBROOK

COLEBROOK, granted in 1762, was originally named Dryden, after the English poet and playwright, John Dryden, then very popular in college courses of the time. Dryden was in those years much in the public eye, and his death in 1700 had preceded Governor Wentworth's courses in Harvard by but a few years.

Added to this was the fact that Dryden was a cousin of Anne Marbury Hutchinson, a religious "liberal" of her time who was banished from Massachusetts in 1637 for her unorthodox beliefs.

One of the incidents relating to the choice of the early grantees of Colebrook was the selection of some twenty Dutch landholders from New York State, apparently in an effort by the New Hampshire government to colonize the territory west of the Connecticut River with Dutch settlers not in sympathy with the New York government. The actual result was the final formation of the separate state of Vermont.

Because of the failure of the early grantees to settle Dryden,

it was regranted in 1770 by Governor John Wentworth to a
new group of colonizers, and renamed Colebrook after Sir
George Colebrooke of England, chairman of the board of the
East India Company.

Colebrook attracted national attention when in the 1830's a
large group of its citizens subscribed to a purchase agreement
and "went west" under the leadership of Dr. Horace White,
buying up a large area which is now Beloit, Wisconsin at a
considerable profit. Colebrook, incorporated in 1896, encompasses the unincorporated town of Kidderville, named for Reuben Kidder, an early settler from New Ipswich, New Hampshire.

COLUMBIA

COLUMBIA on the Connecticut River was originally chartered
as Preston in 1762, taking the name from Richard Graham,
Viscount Preston of Scotland. The grantees, mainly from Long
Island, consisted of a group of members of the Society of
Friends, led by Captain John Seaman, the prosperous owner of
a large estate in Queens County, New York, which they called
Jerusalem because they considered it similar in topography and
fertility to the Holy City of biblical times.

Captain Seaman had sixteen children and his eight sons
were all given grants, along with their relatives, the Motts,
Pearsalls, Jacksons, Dotys, Willetses, Coleses and Hegemans.

Failure of a number of these grantees, due to the uncertainties of the times, to satisfy the terms of their titles, however,
caused Governor John Wentworth to regrant the land in 1770
as a new town which he called Cockburntown after his friend
Sir James Cockburn. Cockburn came from a notable Scottish
family that included the admirals George and Alexander Cockburn, and the eighteenth century poet, Alicia Cockburn, author
of *The Flowers of the Forest.*

The town continued under that name until 1811, when it
was renamed Columbia by Governor John Langdon, reflecting
the period of national patriotism which preceded the War of

1812. Only six other United States places seem to bear the honored name of Columbia.

CONWAY

THE MAN for whom Governor Benning Wentworth named Conway in 1765 was Henry Seymour Conway (1721-1793), the dashing and ambitious younger son of a prominent English family who rose rapidly in politics and the army. Elected to the House of Commons at the age of twenty, Conway soon joined the army, distinguishing himself in Europe and at the Battle of Culloden. He rose to the rank of Major General before he was thirty-five. In the years before the Revolution, General Conway joined vigorously with Pitt, Rockingham, Burke, and Fox in espousing the cause of the Colonies against the policies of the king and Lord North. For this and his opposition to the Stamp Act he incurred the disfavor of George III. In 1765, the year our Conway was named, he was made Secretary of State in the Rockingham ministry.

The early settlers of Conway, New Hampshire, had arrived prior to its incorporation and first called their settlement Pequawket, known colloquially as "Pigwacket", after the nearby mountain. Among them were Hugh Stirling of Londonderry and Archibald Stark of Dunbarton who had secured grants of 2,000 acres.

Among Conway's landmarks are Cathedral Ledge, Echo Lake State Park and the Mount Cranmore Ski Area. The town has three covered bridges within its borders. A scenic resort center, Conway includes the villages of North and South Conway, Conway Center, part of Intervale, and Redstone, a granite quarrying center. It also contains the unincorporated town of Kearsarge, which takes its name from Cowissewaschook, an Indian name which the white settlers variously interpreted as Keewiss-aga, Caresarga, and Kyarsarga. The name Kearsarge was given at one time to Mount Pequawket rising to the north of the town in Chatham. This caused considerable confusion, however, as there was already an earlier named Mount Kearsarge in Merrimack County. After numerous discussions and appeals to Concord and Washington, it was decided in 1958 that Mount Pequawket might be called Kearsarge North, but the original name was to remain with the Merrimack County Mountain.

Conway was the center for a group of well-known American artists who came to the region in the period following the Civil War. Among these painters were Benjamin Champney, Thomas and Edward Hill, Thomas Cole, and Chester Harding.

CRAWFORD'S PURCHASE and CRAWFORD NOTCH

OF ALL the names associated with the White Mountains, none is more renowned than that of the Crawfords: Abel, the pioneer and his son, Ethan Allen Crawford, the guide and explorer. Crawford Notch, one of the most famous of nature's prehistoric indentations dividing New Hampshire's majestic White Mountains, was named for its early explorer, Abel Crawford. Working from his rude cabin built in the early 1800's near what is now known as "The Giants' Grave", and once the home of his father-in-law, Captain Eleazer Rosebrook, Abel Crawford moved the huge rocks and cut down the great trees to make the first path through the notch, thus providing for man's ascent to Mount Washington in the days to come. He is said to have been the first, at the age of seventy-five, to make the climb on horseback.

The building of the road, or turnpike, followed under the leadership of his son, Ethan Allen Crawford, and was financed in part by a state-authorized lottery from which the $32,000 worth of chances sold netted the project in its final accounting a total of only $1,500. Ethan Allen Crawford, who served for many years as a guide to the region, where he used to fire off his cannon so that his guests could hear the reverberating echoes, lived to see the establishment of the great resort hotels, the Glen House, Fabyan's and the Profile House, in what is now the White Mountain National Forest.

Many a legend has grown up, including that of Daniel Webster's visit, when, in company with Crawford, Mr. Webster is said to have climbed the mountain and delivered a solitary oration on its grandeur, paying his guide a twenty-dollar bill for the privilege. Crawford's records are preserved in a book on the White Mountains, written by his wife, Lucy, in 1845, the first edition of which is in the New Hampshire State Library and is a great American rarity. The book has recently been re-issued in a new edition.

CRAWFORD'S PURCHASE, lesser known than its neighbor "The Notch", comprises an unincorporated tract of land to the east of Fabyan's and Bretton Woods and includes the approach roads to the Mount Washington Cog Railway. One of the grants of public lands made by Commissioner James Willey, it was granted in 1834 to Ethan Allen Crawford and Thomas and Nathaniel Abbott. The area includes 15,712 acres and was bought by the grantees for $8,000. The state also named one of its mountains Mount Crawford in honor of the father and son explorers.

CUTT'S GRANT

CUTT'S GRANT, an unincorporated territory of mountainous terrain adjacent to Mount Washington and above Crawford Notch, was granted in 1818 to Thomas Cutts of Maine during the administration of Governor John Langdon. The area's most prominent landmark is Mount Webster, named in the middle of the last century for New Hampshire's celebrated native son, Daniel Webster, who died in 1852. Cutt's Grant is now part of the White Mountain National Forest.

DALTON

DALTON was once a part of what is now Littleton, the entire area being known in 1764 as Chiswick after the Duke of Devonshire's castle, then in 1770 as Apthorp for the Apthorp family, relatives of the Wentworths. It took its present name in 1784, honoring the memory of one of New England's foremost colonial merchants, Tristram Dalton.

That was the year in which New Hampshire became a state, and much of the Connecticut River land which is now Dalton had been purchased by Colonel Moses Little, whose son, Tristram Little, had a daughter Mary, who became the wife of Colonel Michael Dalton, prominent Boston merchant and father of Tristram Dalton. Tristram Dalton attended Harvard in the same class as Governor John Wentworth, and had become associated with him in the West Indies shipping business, at the same time inheriting his great-grandfather's north country lands.

Tristram Dalton represented Massachusetts in the first American Congress, and built a handsome residence at Newburyport, where he is said to have entertained General Washington and John Adams, his Harvard classmate, and many other dignitaries including King Louis Philippe of France and Talleyrand.

Among the early grantees of Dalton were fourteen related members of the Avery, Gallup and Fancher families of Stonington, Connecticut, some of whose prosperous farms were in the section long known as Dalton Hills.

DIXVILLE

THIS New Hampshire name is one of wide significance in the state's history, having been derived from Colonel Timothy Dix, whose land holdings in Coos County once included the present day scenic attractions of Dixville Notch, Dixville Peak and the other Dixville Mountains, Mount Gloriette, Mount Sanguinari, Mount Abenaki, Cave Mountain, Table Rock, and the "Old Man" profile of Dixville, all for the most part in the town of Dixville itself.

The ancestor of the Dix family was Jonathan Dix of Ipswich,

Massachusetts, who settled first in New Ipswich, New Hampshire, then in Pembroke, where he received a land grant and ferry rights, and finally in Boscawen, where he became a prosperous merchant.

Colonel Timothy Dix, his grandson, and Colonel Timothy Dix, Jr., received by purchase in 1805 a total of nearly 30,000 acres in the Dixville area and were authorized by the legislature in 1811 to raise money by lottery to construct a roadway through the notch to the Maine boundary. The project was completed under the supervision of Daniel Webster and his brother Ezekiel, then lawyers for Colonel Dix in Boscawen, and the work was done by John Whittemore of Salisbury, son of Reverend Aaron Whittemore of Pembroke.

One of Colonel Dix's descendants was General John A. Dix who brought fame to the family through having been Secretary of the Treasury under President Buchanan, and whose orders during the Civil War to the pro-Southern captain of a United States revenue cutter at New Orleans having been disobeyed, caused him to issue his famous command, "If any one attempt to haul down the American flag, shoot him on the spot." General Dix afterward became Governor of New York.

Dixville remains an unincorporated township, as does the adjoining territory to the east, known as Dix's Grant, which was granted to Timothy Dix, Jr. in 1809.

DUMMER

THIS TOWN on the Androscoggin River was granted in 1773. It was named for Governor William Dummer of Massachusetts, in honor of whom Fort Dummer, one of New England's earliest and most famous "Indian" forts, is also named, as well as the equally famous Governor Dummer Academy in Massachusetts, said to have been the first of New England's private academies. Governor Dummer, one of the three sons of Jeremy Dummer, a leading Boston silversmith, served as chief magistrate of Massachusetts in the early 1720's. One of his many achievements was the arrangement of a peace treaty with the Indians which lasted almost without interruption for more than twenty years. His wife was Kate Dudley, daughter of Governor Joseph Dudley, one of his predecessors.

When granted by Governor John Wentworth, the town of Dummer contained approximately 23,000 acres and its long list of grantees included the names of a number of prominent Massachusettes and New Hampshire citizens, among them John Winthrop, Governor Wentworth's professor of mathematics and natural philosophy at Harvard, who achieved fame for his astronomical observations in Newfoundland of the planet Mercury, the earliest purely scientific expedition in America, and for his researches into the cause of earthquakes, one of which occurred in 1755.

Among the other grantees was Jeremiah Powell of Boston, who was related to Governor Dummer by marriage, served as his secretary, and was a member of the Council. The list also includes the name of the Reverend Samuel Langdon, under whom Governor Wentworth studied at Harvard, and who became its president in 1774.

Dummer was not incorporated until 1848. Dummerston, Vermont, once a New Hampshire town, shares with New Hampshire's Dummer the origin of its name.

EASTON

AMONG the earliest settlers of the small town of Easton, before it split off from Landaff nearly one hundred years ago, was the famous Kinsman family after whom Mount Kinsman, Kinsman Notch, and the Kinsman range were named.

The name Easton appears to be a corruption of the word "eastern," the town having been known as "Eastern Landaff" until 1867 when it was incorporated as Easton, during the administration of Governor Person Cheney.

Asa Kinsman, for whom Mount Kinsman is named, was a pioneer settler of the town. He came north to take up his grant, "with his wife and household goods piled on a two-wheeled cart pulled by a yoke of oxen," and literally had to hew his way through the forest to reach the new settlement.

The Kinsmans came originally from Ipswich, Massachusetts. One of them, Colonel Nathan, afterward moved to Concord, New Hampshire, where he engaged in the hat business after having fought with General Stark in the Revolution. His brother Aaron Kinsman moved to Hanover, where his daughter Abigail married a grandson of President Eleazar Wheelock of Dartmouth. He is credited with having built the first Dartmouth Commons, largely at his own expense.

Either through their own industry or by the sale of land in New Hampshire, the Kinsmans became prosperous enough to purchase in 1804 a large tract in the grants offered New England colonizers in Ohio, which they named for themselves, Kinsman, Ohio. There for many years they operated a large farm.

ELLSWORTH

ELLSWORTH, described in the gazeteers as "a romantic hamlet, a great basin among the hills, isolated from the rest of the world and full of tarns, brooks, and mountains," was first called Trecothick, unique among American town names.

Barlow Trecothick, from whom the name came, was Lord Mayor of London and head of the East India Company. He was associated with John Thomlinson of London, and together they played an important part in English politics, inducing the crown authorities to set up New Hampshire as a separate province having its own governor, and free from Massachusetts under whose jurisdiction it had been for many years.

Among the grantees in 1769 were Tobias Lear, William Whipple, John Langdon, James Bowdoin, and John Winthrop, all of whose names became famous in American history. The town originally contained approximately 25,000 acres.

Few settlements were made in Trecothick until after the

Revolution. In 1802, the name was changed and the town incorporated as Ellsworth, after Chief Justice Oliver Ellsworth of Connecticut, who had negotiated the peace treaty with France in that year, a treaty which resulted in the Louisiana Purchase under which the lands west of the Mississippi were ceded to the United States. Ellsworth is one of the smallest towns in the White Mountain region.

ERROL

CHARTERED by Governor John Wentworth in 1774, Errol was named in honor of James Hay of Scotland, fifteenth Earl of Erroll, a member of one of the most ancient Scotch families, and owner of the famous Linlithgow Castle, birthplace of Mary, Queen of Scots and King James V. Errol is among the last of the many New Hampshire towns chartered by the Wentworth governors.

Although few settlements were made until after the Revolution, the roll of grantees included many names of prominent Massachusetts people, including that of Brigadier General Timothy Ruggles of Hardwick, who became the largest landholder in Errol, due in part to his friendship with Governor John Wentworth with whom he was a fellow graduate of Harvard College.

Known throughout New England as "the Brigadier," General Ruggles served at Ticonderoga under Sir William Johnson in the war with France which ended in 1763, and was a commanding officer in Amherst's expedition which resulted in the conquest of Canada. Timothy Ruggles became speaker of the Massachusetts House of Representatives and a chief justice, receiving in return for services a grant of land in Princeton, Massachusetts.

Another grantee of Errol was the Reverend Benjamin Stevens, Harvard 1740, who afterwards became minister of the church at Kittery, Maine.

Errol, which borders on Maine and Umbagog Lake, was not

incorporated until 1836 during the administration of Governor Isaac Hill.

ERVING'S GRANT

A SMALL wilderness tract of land southwest of Dixville Notch in the north country, Erving's Grant is one of the state's official "unincorporated places." The grant was made in 1775 to Captain William Erving of Boston, who had served as a soldier in the French and Indian Wars. Erving's Grant contains about thirty-five hundred acres and is site of the headwaters of Phillips Brook which flows into the Upper Ammonoosuc River. It is surrounded by three mountains, Dixville Peak, Mount Kelsey and Whitcomb Mountain.

FRANCONIA

THE NAME Franconia applies not only to the town and to Franconia Notch, but to the region which ranks foremost among the many New England scenic areas. It is thought to have derived the name from the Franconian Alps in Germany which it resembles if not surpasses in natural beauty.

First called Indian Head, and originally granted by the New Hampshire Proprietors in 1764, its charter required the building of at least thirty houses in five years, a restriction which the grantees, although listing a number of wealthy and influential Boston and Portsmouth merchants, either could not or did not comply with, possibly due to the mountainous and rocky nature of the terrain.

In 1772, during the governorship of John Wentworth, it was therefore regranted under the new name of Morristown, after Corbyn Morris of Boston, one of the original grantees. Several others in the early lists also were given new leases, among them governors Bernard of New Jersey and Hutchinson of Massachusetts, John Temple, John Nelson, and John and Oliver

Wendell of Portsmouth, the last named being an ancestor of Oliver Wendell Holmes. Allowances were made in the new deeds for "unimprovable land, mountains and waters."

Franconia remained Morristown until 1782 when the town became Franconia. Within its boundaries are the Profile (Old Man of the Mountain); Profile, Echo and Lonesome Lakes; and Mounts Lafayette, Lincoln, Haystack, Garfield and Twin Mountains. The Cannon Mountain Aerial Tramway is the first such passenger tramway ever to be built in North America.

Considerable copper and iron were once mined in the western section of the town, an activity which gave the name FRANCONIA IRON MINES to a small village near the geological site. The discovery of iron in the years immediately following the Revolutionary War resulted in the establishment in 1805 of the Franconia Iron Factory Company. Its mines were actually located on Concord Mountain in the neighboring town of Lisbon, once called Concord. The mountain was then known as Ore Hill.

Charles H. Hitchcock, New Hampshire's first state geologist, has described the mines in considerable detail in his three-volume geological history. A surface vein of magnetic iron, he says, approximately four feet wide and several hundred feet deep, at least six miles long, was pronounced, when discovered, "the richest iron deposit in the United States," yielding from fifty-six per cent to sixty-three per cent pure iron from its ore.

The "factory" to which the ore had to be transported over a three-mile roadway consisted of a blast furnace, reservoir of water to be used in case of fire, an air furnace, steel furnace, pounding machine, trip-hammer shop, and a forge with four fires. Here a prosperous business was in operation for more than fifty years, a period which ended only because the cutting down of much of the timber in the neighborhood deprived the owners of the necessary charcoal then used for smelting.

Franconia iron, widely known and marketed by the name throughout the country in the pre-railroad era, was largely employed in the making of stoves, horseshoes, anchors, hinges, chains, and iron kettles. In 1855 the company is said to have produced more than 300 tons of the finest "granular magnetic" iron yearly.

GORHAM

THE TOWN of Gorham, the eastern gateway to the White Mountains, was originally a part of Shelburne which was first chartered in 1770 by Governor John Wentworth. It was renamed Gorham and incorporated by Governor Isaac Hill's administration in 1836. The name Gorham was proposed by a resident, Sylvester Davis, formerly of Gorham, Maine, and a relative of the Gorham family who had founded that town in 1764.

The Gorhams played an important part in New England history. Captain John Gorham, whose ancestor Hugh de Gorran came to England with William the Conqueror, settled in Barnstable, Massachusetts, in 1643, and one of the early Gorhams led a company of rangers in the famous "Canada Expedition" against the French, his band being known as "Gorham's men." Another Gorham, Captain Nathaniel, fought in the Revolution, signed the commission making John Stark a major general, and served as president of the Continental Congress in 1786.

Gorham, New Hampshire has one of the state's outstanding scenic attractions, the "Alpine Cascades" on the Androscoggin River, bearing the same name as the famous Alpine Hotel or "Station House," operated in the 1890's by the Grand Trunk Railroad. It was managed by the popular Mrs. Sarah Frost Hayes, after whom Mount Hayes is named. Among Gorham's early settlers were the Ordway, Goodnow, Messer, Burbank, Lary, and Willey families.

GREEN'S GRANT

GREEN'S GRANT, one of the unincorporated places adjacent to Mount Washington, is now part of the White Mountain National Forest. It lies in the Mount Washington Valley along the main highway between Pinkham Notch and Gorham, immediately to the north of Glen House. The grant was one of the last made by New Hampshire's provincial governor, John Wentworth, before the Revolutionary War. The area takes its name from the grantee, Lieutenant Francis Green of Boston, who had been a soldier in the French and Indian War. Green's tract comprised about two thousand acres.

HADLEY'S PURCHASE

ANOTHER of the unincorporated grants in the heart of the White Mountains, Hadley's Purchase was granted by the state in 1834 to Henry G. Hadley of Eugene City, Oregon for $500. It was one of the pieces of hitherto unassigned public lands sold by Commissioner James Willey during that period. The area, now entirely within the White Mountain National Forest, contains a little over eight thousand acres in a long narrow strip of mountainous land above Crawford's Notch and east of the village of Hart's Location.

HALE'S LOCATION

HALE'S LOCATION is a small uninhabited square of land, surrounded by the towns of Bartlett, Conway and Albany, and is now a part of the White Mountain National Forest. The area takes its name from Samuel Hale of Portsmouth, to whom the original grant was made in 1771 by Governor John Wentworth, New Hampshire's last provincial chief executive. Hale received a 1,215 acre tract a few miles to the west of the present town of North Conway, but no settlement was ever made. The northeast corner of Hale's Location borders on Echo Lake and Echo Lake State Park.

HART'S LOCATION

HART'S LOCATION encompasses the dramatic grandeur of Crawford's Notch and the valley to the south surrounded by sheer rock walls nearly a thousand feet high. The town was originally one of several plots of undivided land remaining for disposal by the proprietors at the time Governor John Wentworth took office in 1766. It was given the name of Colonel John Hart of Portsmouth but has never been officially incorporated.

Colonel Hart's people had owned Portsmouth land as early as 1702, and were related to the Stoodley, Cutts, Willey and other prominent families. His son, Captain Samuel Hart, held an important position as manager for Colonel Joseph Whipple's estates at Jackson and Conway. Colonel Hart fought in the French War and the Louisbourg Expedition, and appears to have received what is now called Hart's Location as a reward for his services.

In 1772 a re-grant of this land was made to Thomas Chadbourne of Portsmouth, a descendant of Humphrey and William Chadbourne who arrived from England in 1632, and are said to have built the famous "Great House" or Manor in the Strawbery Banke colony. Thomas Chadbourne appears to have been associated with Captain Hart in another grant at Conway.

Hart's Location was the scene, in 1826, of the famous "Willey's Slide," a White Mountain avalanche which swept to their death Samuel Willey and his entire family. Mount Willey is named in their memory. Hart's Location has a village named Avalanche, as well as one called Bemis. The latter commemorates an early settler known as "The Lord of the Valley," Dr. Samuel Bemis, who named many of the mountains nearby. Here also is the site of the grave of Abel Crawford, the famous pioneer.

HAVERHILL

HAVERHILL, which includes the towns of Woodsville and Pike, was one of several to be settled by groups of citizens coming almost entirely from a single New England neighborhood. Those of Haverhill, New Hampshire, came from Haverhill in Massachusetts and its surrounding countryside near the mouth of the Merrimack River. The earliest colonists supposed that the Merrimack ran west, not north, and much of New Hampshire's history was influenced by this error, so that the inhabitants of the early towns clung to the seashore as a result.

As populations increased, the explorations to the north led the surveyors into what was known as Lower Coos, the early name of New Hampshire's Haverhill. Coos was a St. Francis Indian tribal name, variously spelt Cowass, Kohass, Cohas and Cohos, all meaning "crooked river," later translated into "ox bow." Coos County takes its name from the same source.

The first settlers, under the leadership of Captain John Hazen and his brothers William and Moses, included the Youngs, related to the Wheelock presidents of Dartmouth, the Johnstons, Baileys, Petties and Pages, and approximately sixty other Haverhill, Massachusetts, families, many of whose names persist in today's records.

Haverhill, granted in 1763, was among the first in New Hampshire to call for a court test of the validity of its charter. This charter, like others in the new or "north" country, required the grantees to build a church, school and parsonage, implying that otherwise it might be cancelled. Land was provided for that purpose.

Through the influence of the English Society for the Propagation of the Gospel, several young men in New England were sent abroad and were ordained ministers by the Bishop of London, among them Samuel Peters and Rene Cossitt, or Cossette, and a church was planned by them at Haverhill to serve the entire "north country" section. The society claimed that, having helped finance the establishment of Dartmouth College, it might also promote new churches here under town charters on the land designated. This opinion was opposed by some of the grantees, but supported by Colonel Asa Porter and Chief Justice of New Hampshire John Hurd, one-time secretary to Governor Wentworth, both large Haverhill land owners, in whose favor the courts decided. Their ruling, however, was set aside by the legislature in 1777.

Reverend Samuel Peters afterward established a church at Hebron, Connecticut, and Reverend Rene Cossitt, who married Ruth Porter of Connecticut, a relative of the Haverhill Porters, became the Episcopal minister at Claremont.

Haverhill was the terminus of the Old Province Road, built before the Revolution to connect the northern and western settlements with the seacoast at Dover. In 1773 Haverhill became the county seat (or "shire town" as they called it then) of Grafton County. The present court house is at Woodsville.

WOODSVILLE, one of the several named sections of the town of Haverhill, ranked at one time as second only in importance to Concord as a railroad center. Woodsville was not, as might be supposed, named for the dense woodlands which surrounded it, but instead from John L. Woods who came to this state in 1830 from the neighboring town of Wells River, Vermont. Woods first operated a sawmill on the Ammonoosuc River and, with the coming of the Boston, Concord and Montreal Railroad, expanded his business to include a prosperous enterprise dealing in railroad supplies.

Woodsville and its vicinity was once known as the "Governor's Farm" or "Governor's Reservation." It is believed to have been the land awarded in the original Haverhill grant of 1763 to Governor Benning Wentworth himself. It was customary for the Wentworth governors to retain 500-acre tracts in many of the towns they granted to assure them of a voting voice in future town affairs. Such appears to have been the case in the Woodsville section. There seems to be no record of these "Governor's Lands" in any of these towns ever having passed into the hands of speculators, most of them having been ultimately returned to the towns in which they were located.

The minature village of PIKE located in the southern section of Haverhill dates back to 1860 when it was first settled by future employees of the Pike Manufacturing Company, which afterward became the world's leading makers of whetstones. The first of the Pikes to appear in this state was Isaac, descended from the Reverend John Pike who came from England in 1635. Alonzo Pike, Isaac's grandson, guided by the state geologist, Charles H. Hitchcock, first located here what was then designated an immense rock bed of "Bethlehem gneiss" near Little

Black Mountain. From these quarries he mined the materials used in making the famous Pike tool grinders and sharpeners, known throughout the world as "Pikestones." Beginning in 1860 and organized as the Alonzo Pike Company, in 1883, the company later became the Pike Manufacturing Company, headed by Colonel E. Bertram Pike.

At one time Pike Village, consisting mainly of houses built by the company, was inhabited by no fewer than sixteen members of the Pike family, most of whom were Pike employees. The corporation closed its doors in recent years, due in part to a declining market and in part to the exhaustion of the Haverhill quarries.

Other sections of Haverhill had such colorful names as Horse Meadow, Slab City, Bangstown, and Cobleigh's Landing. The town has many fine Colonial houses and is believed to have been the point of return of Rogers' Rangers from their Canadian expedition.

JACKSON

THE GREAT SCENIC area, of which this town is now a part, originally consisted of several large land grants by Governor John Wentworth.

The first of these grants, made in 1771, consisted of some 8,000 acres to Governor Wentworth's friends, Daniel and Charles Rogers, and Jacob Treadwell of Portsmouth, who later sold their rights for 50,000 pounds to John Brown of Providence, ancestor of the founder of Brown University. Other portions were granted to the Pinkhams, after whom Pinkham Notch was named, to Daniel Gilman of Pembroke and to Richard Gridley of Boston, in 1773, in return for service in the French Wars.

Gridley, who later became a Major General of Engineers in the Revolution, deserves to be among Jackson's "patron saints." He studied engineering as a boy in Boston, and designed the forts at Boston Harbor. Enlisting in 1745 as a lieutenant colonel for the invasion of Louisbourg, the maps for which he had made, for Governor Shirley, without ever having seen Louisbourg, he returned to make designs for forts on the Kennebec River and Fort William Henry on Lake Champlain.

Gridley served as a commander of artillery at Crown Point under General Amherst, and later under General Wolfe at Quebec. Previous to the Revolution he designed the fortifications on Breed's Hill which played so important a part in the Battle of Bunker Hill, where he was made a general officer.

In addition to his land grant of 3,000 acres at what is now Jackson, General Gridley was given a grant of the famous Magdalen Islands of Quebec in the St. Lawrence River.

Jackson was first called New Madbury, after the New Hampshire seacoast town, and was later named for two presidents. The town became Adams in 1800 in honor of President John Adams who was then in office. It remained so until 1829, when it became Jackson in response to the election of the hero of the Battle of New Orleans. 1829 was the year of General Andrew Jackson's first inauguration as president. The town appears to have changed its name largely through the influence of Governor Benjamin Pierce, a Democrat and staunch backer of Andrew Jackson.

JEFFERSON

THE TOWN now bearing the name of President Thomas Jefferson, was originally called Dartmouth, after William Legge, second Earl of Dartmouth, the English patron of Dartmouth College, and friend of the colonies.

Granted in 1765, along with a group of other new towns following the close of the Seven Years War, its location was at the mountainous center of a wild and unexplored country, to which few of the grantees ever came to take up their titles.

One of these who did settle here, however, was the wealthy merchant and shipowner of Portsmouth, Colonel Joseph Whipple. To him goes the credit of having cut a path through the forests to build his famous "manor" where he entertained Reverend Jeremy Belknap and his associates, who were the first to climb Mount Washington and give it its name.

Colonel Whipple not only was the true founder of the town of Dartmouth, but through wise investment purchased for the modest sum of a few hundred dollars the entire area of seventy rights, amounting to nearly 25,000 acres, a part of the proceeds of which he willed at his death in 1816 to found an academy to "encourage manufacturing and to pursue such studies as tend to a love of peace and an aversion to war and the continuance of the republican form of government, wishing that experiment to be tried over the next century."

Colonel Whipple became an ardent Jeffersonian Democrat, and in the days following the Revolution, in 1796, was instrumental in having the town's original name changed to its present one of Jefferson. He was a brother and partner of William Whipple who was one of New Hampshire's three signers of the Declaration of Independence, of which Thomas Jefferson was the principal author. The town received its name four years before Jefferson's election to the presidency.

Riverton, a part of Jefferson, was the birthplace of Thaddeus Lowe (1832-1913), early student of the atmosphere and aeronautic scientist.

KILKENNY

THE OLD township of Kilkenny, which was never incorporated and is now a wilderness area in the White Mountain National Forest, was first granted in 1774 just prior to the Revolution by Governor John Wentworth. A grant of over twenty-six thousand acres was made to Jonathan Warner and several others. Kilkenny, adjoining Lancaster to the east, is one of the few towns this far north to appear on Samuel Holland's map of New Hampshire of 1784. The name Kilkenny is that of the county, town, and castle in southeastern Ireland, the county having been established during the English occupation in the reign of King John in the 1200's.

Kilkenny, New Hampshire, was intended by Governor Wentworth to be a town mainly for the merchants of Portsmouth. Besides Warner, the grantees included Henry Sherburne, blacksmith; John Dennet, blockmaker; William Welsh, chaisemaker; William Stanwood, perukemaker; Richard Truesdale, butcher; Joseph Walton, cooper; Isaac Smith, husbandman; Joseph Pierce, merchant; and John Briard, mariner.

Due, perhaps, to the approaching American Revolution, not many of these grantees apparently ever settled in Kilkenny, which was later described by John Farmer, the historian, in the 1820's, as containing "very few inhabitants and they are very poor and for aught that appears to the contrary they must remain so as they may be deemed actually trespassers on that part of God's heritage which he designed for the reservation of bears, wolves, moose and other animals of the forest."

During the last century Kilkenny, New Hampshire, was the "solitary retreat in the forest" of the recluse Jonathan Willard, who came here from Francestown. Willard was a cousin of Henry Hubbard, governor of the state from 1842 to 1844, and it is for him that Mount Willard and Willard Basin are named. Kilkenny also includes Mount Waumbec and Mount Cabot.

LANCASTER

LANCASTER, granted in 1763, constitutes one of the early settlements along the northern section of the Connecticut River, to which few came because of Indian troubles, but for those who did come and stay, the land brought almost unlimited prosperity.

The early settlers, David Page, known as "Governor Page" although he was never governor, together with Edwards Bucknam and Emmons Stockwell, found a country they first named "Upper Coos" which at that time seemed almost worthless because of the overflowing Connecticut River, but later ranked as among the most fertile lands in New England.

The section was permanently named Lancaster at the suggestion of Joseph Wilder of Lancaster, Massachusetts, one of the early settlers. Another of the grantees was Reverend Joshua Wingate Weeks, who, with Adino Brackett, Richard Eastman, Charles Stuart and Ethan Allen Crawford, formed the first White Mountain naming expedition. They designated what became known as the "Presidential Range," which included Mounts Washington, Jefferson, Madison, and Monroe, and later, Mount Franklin and Mount Pleasant. The exploring party "drank a health" to the mountains and the presidents whose names they bore, while atop Mount Washington. Almost a century later a descendant of Joshua Wingate Weeks, Senator John W. Weeks of Massachusetts, led the movement in Congress which resulted in the establishment of the White Mountain Forest Reservation. His son Sinclair Weeks, a resident of Lancaster, was also a United States Senator and Secretary of Commerce in the Eisenhower administration.

In the original grant of Lancaster were inscribed the names of Nash and Sawyer, the two surveyors who discovered "White Mountain Notch" making possible a short route to Portland, and who were thus rewarded. Captain Joseph Wilder, who named the town, also was a surveyor and received as his remuneration some ten grants in other New Hampshire towns. Among them was one in Wilder, Vermont, then a part of New Hampshire. His name is also commemorated by the Wilder Dam on the Connecticut River.

As early as 1791, Lancaster and other north country towns petitioned to be set off from Grafton County. In 1803 the legislature heeded their request and established Coos County with Lancaster as the county seat.

A section of Lancaster called EGYPT is one of the many "villages" which were parts of New Hampshire towns in early days, and while never becoming large enough to be towns by themselves, still retained their early names. The land which Egypt comprised was that of Colonel Sylvanus Chessman who was an officer in the War of 1812 and a prosperous tavern keeper. This land was in what was known as "Brook Meadows," and was said to have been the only land in the north country where corn would ripen despite early frosts.

Colonel Chessman's secret, which enabled him to have corn to sell when his neighbors had none, was his plan of surrounding his cornfields with a circle of hay and dried leaves which he would set afire on cold nights, thus keeping his corn warm and protected against frost. So his estate became known as Egypt, a name arising from the remarks of his biblical-minded fellow-citizens who needed corn, that they were "goin' to Egypt" to get it. Colonel Chessman also set up a "factory" on his estate, where he made "plaster of paris" from gypsum, and part of the area was known as Paris.

LANDAFF

THIS REMOTE TOWN got its Welsh name, spelled Llandaff in the charter, from the Bishop of Llandaff, chaplain in England to King George III.

Bishop Llandaff's surname was Shute-Barrington, and he was one of six sons of John Shute-Barrington, Viscount Barrington of Dublin, Ireland. Another son was Admiral Samuel Barrington of the British Navy. The elder Shute-Barrington was the brother of Samuel Shute, governor of Massachusetts from 1716 to 1723, who deserves fame as having welcomed the Scotch-Irish settlers from Ulster to New England in 1718. Barrington in Strafford County is also named for the family.

The bishopric of Llandaff in Cardiff, Wales, dating back to the sixth century, is one of the oldest in the British Isles and much prized in the English church. Llandaff was the home of Sir Thomas Mathews, who commanded the famous warship Kent in the Mediterranean under Admiral Byng in the war between England and Spain.

Landaff in New Hampshire, first known as Whitcherville, was originally granted by the proprietors in 1764 to some sixty prospective settlers; but by 1770 it was found by Governor John Wentworth that a considerable number of the grantees had not fulfilled the terms of their grants. The governor at that time was endeavoring to find a site for the proposed Dartmouth College, and suggested Landaff. It was found, however, that some of the land holders refused to relinquish their claims, causing the college to lose its proposed title, and Hanover was chosen instead. Landaff was reincorporated in 1774, and its original charter renewed that year.

LINCOLN

Our town of Lincoln is not, as is sometimes supposed, named for President Abraham Lincoln, although nearby Mount Lincoln was. This imposing summit, however, is not in the town of Lincoln but in Franconia to the north.

Lincoln, the New Hampshire town, was named in 1764, many years before Mr. Lincoln's birth, after Henry Clinton (1720-1794), ninth Earl of Lincoln, and a cousin of the Wentworth family. The Earl was a member of the Privy Council and Comptroller of Customs for the port of London under George II and George III. The latter position, as Governor Wentworth knew, was an important one in relation to trade between the colonies and the mother country. In 1768 the Earl of Lincoln inherited the title of Duke of Newcastle from his uncle, Thomas Pelham Holles. A cousin of the Earl's who bore the same name was Sir Henry Clinton, British general during the Revolutionary War.

The original charter of the town of Lincoln listed a total of sixty-two grantees, but apparently the number of actual settlements was insufficient to satisfy its terms and the town was re-granted in 1772 to a former governor of Massachusetts, Sir Francis Bernard, who had since returned to England and never took up the claim. By odd coincidence, Sir Francis was a native of the English city of Lincoln, and at one time he held an important office there.

Part of Lincoln was once known as PULLMAN, one of New Hampshire's earliest "lumber towns," located in the 1890's in the Zealand Valley section. It was probably so called because of its being in an important north country railroad center, to which large amounts of timber were hauled for cutting and processing. Other names used in the section were Henryville and Sawdust Boulevard, and at one time the whole section was known as the "Grand Duchy of Lincoln."

The lumbering enterprise here was established in 1892 by J. E. Henry. His company purchased more than 100,000 acres of forest which they expected to cut over a period of thirty years, at the end of which time a new growth would be available. At least three logging railroad lines were constructed across the adjacent mountains, rivers, swamps and valleys, the most important being that from Lincoln to North Woodstock, N. H., and the Henry Company operated what was said to have been the "longest sawmill in the world." The company is thought to have been the first to practice "forest conservation," holding to the rule that no tree less than twelve inches at the stump should be cut. The proprietors suffered from frequent fires, but prospered, and built a complete village of houses for their employees. At one time the Henry Company extended its operations into Mexico. The entire establishment, including its buildings, locomotives, and other railway and logging equipment, was taken over in 1917 by the Parker-Young Company.

LISBON

LISBON received its present name after having undergone several changes since it was first granted in 1763. It was named Concord, but in that year a settlement was reached after long boundary litigation between the towns of Bow and Rumford, and the latter town, now our state capital, was given the name Concord, from the Latin *concordia*, meaning harmony.

Lisbon was renamed Chiswick the following year after Chiswick Castle in England, which was owned by the Duke of Devonshire, a relative of Governor Benning Wentworth's. The town was re-granted in 1768 as Gunthwaite, after Sir William Bosville of Gunthwaite, England, who was a lieutenant in the French War and was related to Governor John Wentworth.

The name Lisbon, adopted for the town in 1824, apparently was suggested by Governor Levi Woodbury, whose friend, Colonel William Jarvis, had been consul at Lisbon, Portugal during the administration of President Jefferson. It was through Jarvis' efforts that a shipment of 3500 merino sheep was sent to America, many of which came to New Hampshire. Governor Woodbury's political platform in 1824, the year Lisbon was re-named, was headed "Young America Faction," in which he defined his objectives as being "soil surveys, diversified crops, scientifically selected; more production, exhibits of useful in-ventions and county lectures on agriculture and mechanics." Colonel Jarvis, who at one time owned considerable land in Claremont and had an extensive sheep farm in nearby Weathers-field, Vermont, once sent to President Jefferson from Lisbon a herd of merino sheep for his home in Monticello. Mr. Jefferson acknowledged the sheep with this comment: "I consider them as 'deposited' with me for the general good of the country and divesting myself of all views of gain, I propose to devote them to the diffusion of the race throughout our country."

Lisbon once comprised the town of Littleton, which separated in 1770, and Sugar Hill, New Hampshire's newest town, incorporated in 1962.

LITTLETON

LITTLETON was a part of Lisbon, then called Chiswick, until 1770 when it was granted by Governor John Wentworth as Apthorp. It did not receive its permanent name of Littleton until 1784 after the Revolution. The name Apthorp came from George Apthorp and his son Charles, heads of one of the wealth-iest mercantile establishments in Boston in the 1700's. In com-pany with Samuel Adams, Tristram Dalton and others, the

Apthorps formed a syndicate and either purchased, or were granted for the purpose of improvement, a total of 40,865 acres in the north country area of which Littleton is now a part.

George Apthorp's son, Charles, of Boston, succeeded his father in this grant. He is said to have had eighteen children, one of whom married Thomas Bulfinch, whose son Charles Bulfinch was the famous architect. His son, Henry Apthorp, was a grantee of Wolfeboro, and another son, East Apthorp, was the founder of Christ Church in Cambridge. Charles Apthorp gave the money to rebuild King's Chapel in Boston, and there is a monument in his memory in the church.

Just prior to the Revolution the Apthorp family's New Hampshire land came into possession of a group of their associates from Newburyport, Massachusetts, headed by Colonel Moses Little, who had occupied the highly remunerative post of "Surveyor of the King's Woods" under Governor Wentworth, and had fought the French at Louisbourg and in the Battle of Bunker Hill.

Colonel Little was an officer in the 17th Massachusetts Regiment, and later was made a brigadier general. At one time his holdings on the Connecticut River were said to have totaled fifteen miles. Littleton was named in his honor in the same year that New Hampshire became a state.

LIVERMORE

GHOST TOWN might aptly describe Livermore, a once thriving lumber town now deserted and nearly all traces of its village gone. Its name comes from an early grantee, the first Chief Justice of New Hampshire, Samuel Livermore.

Livermore graduated from Princeton in 1752 and carried on a successful law practice in Portsmouth, where he became "King's Attorney." He was later counsel for the New Hampshire "proprietors" who helped to make the colonial land grants in northern New Hampshire and Vermont in pre-Revolutionary days. He served as New Hampshire's Chief Justice in 1782-90 and represented the state in the Constitutional Convention in Philadelphia, which ratified the American Constitution. Justice Livermore, whose family name was derived from the "Leather-mores" of England, married the daughter of the Reverend Arthur Brown, rector of Queen's Chapel, now St. John's Church, of Portsmouth. He purchased considerable land in Holderness, his property including the "Governor's Farm" of 800 acres for which he paid fifty pounds. Mount Livermore in Holderness is named for him, and the state has its Livermore Falls, as has Maine. There are Livermores in Pennsylvania, Kentucky, Missouri, California and Colorado, all of which appear to have been named in his honor. His portrait by Trumbull hangs in the Supreme Court at Concord.

Livermore's friendship with Governor Benning Wentworth resulted in the naming of this north country grant in his honor. Later the governor awarded some of the land covered by this grant to Captain Stephen Holland of Londonderry, who had distinguished himself at Quebec as a member of the British and American forces in the war against France in 1759. Captain Holland never settled on his grant, having been ordered deported to England because of his sympathies with the English government in its pre-Revolutionary controversy with the American colonies. His land was sold in 1770 to a group of settlers bearing the names of Elkins, Bean, Sargent, Hatch, Cleaves, Raymond and Gilman.

The name Livermore was retained, however, and it was incorporated as a town in 1876. In the following year the Saunders Company built a railroad to the town as access to its lumber mills there from Bartlett six miles away. Livermore had a population of about 160 in 1890; it had dwindled to twenty-three by 1930 and zero by the 1950's. Livermore's incorporation was revoked in 1951, and today this remote town has reverted to wilderness — part of the White Mountain National Forest. Within the town boundaries are Mount Bemis and Mount Carrigain.

LOWE AND BURBANK GRANT

ONE OF the unincorporated sections of the White Mountain region, the Lowe and Burbank Grant lies to the north of Mount Washington and includes Mount Madison, Pine Peak, and Mount Sam Adams. The land was purchased from the state in 1832 by Clovis Lowe of Jefferson and Barker Burbank of Shelburne. Clovis Lowe was the father of Thaddeus Lowe, who was born in the same year as the Lowe and Burbank purchase and became a noted scientist, inventor, and one of the first American authorities on aeronautics. He was a man far ahead of his times and died in Pasadena, California in 1913. Mount Lowe, near that city, is named for him.

Mount Madison in New Hampshire's Lowe grant is of course named for James Madison, fourth President of the United States. Mount Sam Adams, to be distinguished from the other mountains named for his cousins, the presidents, John and John Quincy Adams, honors the man who probably had more to do with making the United States an independent republic than any other man of his time. He was a delegate to the Continental Congress, a signer of the Declaration of Independence, and a governor of Massachusetts. He is said to have been the "first voice to urge the Revolution" and the "first American who openly in any public assembly proposed absolute independence for the colonies." In his famous Faneuil Hall speech in 1769 he urged the country to "take up arms immediately and be free, and seize all the king's officers," adding, "We will not submit to any tax nor become slaves."

Samuel Adams' father, who hoped he would be a clergyman, left him a legacy of a thousand pounds, part of which he lost through an unsecured loan and part through speculation. Entering politics as a young man, he became a power in his town meeting, clerk in the legislature, and was instrumental in organizing a large group of Massachusetts towns for an exchange of ideas and civic improvement.

LYMAN

THIS TOWN, granted in 1761, came by its name through the honor paid to one of New England's ablest, but least known generals, Phineas Lyman. Graduating from Yale in 1738, and married to a daughter of one of its college presidents, Timothy Dwight, General Lyman commanded troops and fought in no less than eight campaigns in the Seven Years War with France and Spain which preceded our Revolution. To him goes the credit for having captured Crown Point; and Fort Lyman, afterward named Fort Edward on the Hudson River, was built by him. He was in command at Fort Ticonderoga and was with General Amherst at Montreal. In the war against Spain, General Lyman's two thousand three hundred Connecticut soldiers fought in Cuba when Havana was taken, only to have it ceded back to Spain at the Peace of Paris in 1763.

At the close of the Seven Years War General Lyman visited England to propose large land grants to the New England colonists who had fought in those wars, the grants to be located on the Mississippi and in Ohio, and called "Georgiana." The impending American Revolutionary War, however, prevented action on this project, but it was finally undertaken by the colonists themselves in 1803, led by General Rufus Putnam and Manasseh Cutler, in what was known as "The Western Reserve."

General Lyman was compensated for his services to the colonies not only by his grant in the town of Lyman, but by grants in Grantham, Lisbon and in eleven other towns originally a part of New Hampshire but now in Vermont. It is not likely, however, that he came here to settle, although members of his family did so. He died in 1774. The town of Lyman originally had a considerable acreage, but a part of the town was taken by the legislature in 1854 to form the new town of Monroe.

MARTIN'S LOCATION

MARTIN'S LOCATION, situated in the Pinkham Notch section, takes its name from Thomas Martin of Portsmouth, a conductor of artillery stores in the French and Indian War, who was among the grantees of about two thousand acres awarded here in 1773 by Governor John Wentworth. The area was never incorporated. Martin's Location is the site of the famous Dolly Copp Forest Camp, operated by the Appalachian Mountain Club. Its name comes from Dolly Emery who was the wife of Hayes Copp, one of the first settlers of that region. Dolly Emery was the daughter of Lieutenant Nathaniel Emery of Bartlett, and granddaughter of Enoch Emery who came there from Haverhill and Newbury, Massachusetts, in the early 1800's. Her husband's father was Lieutenant Samuel Copp of the family which once owned Copp's Hill in Boston. Hayes Copp, Dolly's husband, settled on land first granted to Daniel Pinkham, one of his relatives, at Martin's Location; the area is now a part of the White Mountain National Forest. Together the Copps built a log cabin which grew into a farmhouse and finally a prosperous inn presided over by Dolly, whose excellent and modestly priced fare and lodgings, combined with the surrounding scenery, attracted many an early New Hampshire tourist. The view of Mount Imp, one of the state's several face-formations which adorn its mountains, has long rivaled the "Old Man of The Mountain" for popularity.

MILAN

THIS TOWN north of Berlin was not named for Milan, Italy, as is sometimes supposed, but for Milan Harris of Harrisville, New Hampshire.

In its charter, first granted in 1771 by Governor John Wentworth, the town was called Paulsbourg after Paul Wentworth, the governor's English cousin. Although he apparently never came to America, Paul Wentworth represented the Wentworth shipping interests in the West Indies. At one time he was appointed to the Governor's Council, but declined to serve as he was not a resident.

While the first grants were made in Paulsbourg in 1771 to a number of prominent prospective settlers, only a few occupied their new land. Among those who did, however, were relatives and descendants of the Cheshire County Harrises and Twitchells who had established one of the first woolen mills in America at Harrisville, owned and operated by Milan Harris, whose mother was Deborah Twitchell, and for whom, as its leading citizen, the town of Harrisville was named.

By 1810 the town of Paulsbourg had only fourteen persons listed as inhabitants, but in the next decade the population increased by the addition of members of the Plumer, Livermore, Ellingwood and other families. In 1824 Governor Levi Woodbury, who was much interested in expanding wool culture and manufacturing in New Hampshire and a close friend of Milan Harris, authorized a change of name for the town to Milan, in his honor. In the same year Governor Woodbury renamed Lisbon.

Milan came into prominence in the middle 1800's by the establishment of one of the earliest starch mills in New England, and also by the discovery of what was thought to be an extensive vein of gold which was mined for several years. The mines were operated by nearly a hundred people. They were soon exhausted, however, and the town returned to its original occupations of lumbering and agriculture. Milan is the site of the Berlin ski jump and the Milan Hill State Park.

MILLSFIELD

MILLSFIELD's charter was granted in 1774 and the town took its name from Sir Thomas Mills of London, a prominent trader in lumber and other commodities which he imported from the American colonies and Russia. Sir Thomas was a member of Parliament from Canterbury, and had fought with Sir Roger Mostyn's famous dragoons in the Seven Years War. Sir Thomas Mills was an associate in Parliament with the Earl of Dart-

mouth and the Earl of Nottingham, both advocates of conciliation with the New England colonies as proposed by the Rockingham government in pre-Revolutionary times.

Many of the grantees of Millsfield were from Connecticut
towns, among them being Captain Israel Morey and his brothers, from Lebanon, Connecticut, where Eleazar Wheelock,
founder of Dartmouth College, was once minister. Captain
Morey's friendship with Governor John Wentworth, who made
the grant, grew out of his efforts to have the college located in
New Hampshire. Later he settled in Orford, where he obtained a patent for his "rotary steam engine" and developed
his model for a Connecticut River steamboat, which predated
that of Robert Fulton by several years.

Millsfield has never been incorporated and its population in
the 1960 census had dwindled to seven.

MONROE

MONROE, which at one time formed a part of Lyman, secured
its separation in 1854, taking the name of James Monroe, fifth
President of the United States. It was at that time known as
West Lyman, and previous to that as Hurd's Location.

The petitioners for the right to a new town, located on the
Connecticut River at the Vermont border, included a number
of old Connecticut families, with the names Emery, Heath,
Scarritt, Duncan, Blodget, Paddleford and Buffum. Also included were several members of the Hurd family, descended
from John Hurd, secretary to Governor John Wentworth, who
was active in North Country affairs and whose brother, Nathaniel Hurd, had designed the seal for Dartmouth College.
The Hurds, who received Wentworth grants in Lyman, Bath,
Haverhill, Lisbon and Whitefield, were associated with a group
which had once hoped to establish a Church of England colony
in this area, with Hanover as its center.

The choice of the name Hurd for the new town appears to
have been sponsored by a faction descended from the early
Hurds, and was led by Jacob Hurd of Bath and his son Timothy

of Lyman. They were defeated by an "opposition" group whose only reason for the substitution of the name Monroe appears to have been the fact that one of the mountains in the Presidential Range had recently been given the name in honor of the president, and that he had toured the section while in office.

Monroe is a part of what has been described as the "Ammonoosuc Gold Fields," whose supposed extensive mineral deposits have never been successfully mined. It is also the site of the Comerford Dam.

NORTHUMBERLAND

NORTHUMBERLAND, which includes the unincorporated but more populous town of Groveton, was first named Stonington in 1761, probably because of Governor Benning Wentworth's friendly relationship during the French and Indian War with the shipbuilding interests in Stonington, Connecticut. It was renamed Northumberland by Governor John Wentworth in 1771 in honor of Hugh Smithson, Earl Percy and first Duke of Northumberland. Percy was also the name of another town, later changed to Stark, and the Percy Peaks and Percy Lake in the White Mountains still remain in his memory.

The Duke, a close adherent of Rockingham and William Pitt, joined in the opposition to the king's American policy. A Knight of the Garter and Lord Lieutenant of Ireland, he expressed his attitude toward the colonies in a verse:

> Though to my sovereign's grace I owe
> My garter and commission,
> A sneaking kindness still, you know,
> I've shown for opposition.

The Duke of Northumberland did more than give his name to a New Hampshire town. To his son, James Smithson, America is indebted for a great gift, the Smithsonian Institution. A graduate of Oxford, James Smithson devoted his life to scientific research in chemistry and metallurgy. At his death in 1829 he expressed his well-known political sympathy with the American republic, which he had never visited, by a legacy ultimately amounting to more than half a million dollars to found the Smithsonian.

Northumberland is the site of old Fort Wentworth, a stockade built in the 1750's that was used by Rogers' Rangers in their expedition to Canada.

ODELL

AN UNINCORPORATED township of the White Mountain region, Odell's population had dwindled from eighty-two in the census of 1940 to zero in the 1960 census. This large wilderness tract of timberland east of Stratford was granted in 1834 to Richard Odell of Conway for $1,863. The grant, containing nearly twenty-four thousand acres, was one of those made by Land Commissioner James Willey, who had been authorized by the legislature to dispose of public lands still held by the state. Within Odell are Phillips Pond, Nash Bog Pond, and Little Bog Pond.

PIERMONT

THIS Connecticut River town was named in 1764, probably from Piedmont in the Italian Alps, a section which the Italians called Piemonte. The spelling was transcribed into Piermont when used here, and it was one of several New Hampshire towns whose names seemed to anticipate the later slogan "the Switzerland of America."

Piermont, Franconia, Heidelberg (the original name of New London), and Danzig (that of Newbury), were all famous European scenic areas which must have impressed the proprietors as similar in beauty and grandeur to New Hampshire.

Piermont, containing Tarleton Lake within its picturesque

surroundings, described in the early records as "a crystal scene in an emerald setting," well deserves the simile. The lake itself once bordered on, or was the property of Colonel William Tarleton who settled in Piermont in the 1700's and kept a tavern there in 1774. He fought in the Revolution, was a delegate to the famous Constitutional Convention of 1791, and was a presidential elector, in 1804 and member of the Governor's Council in 1808.

Colonel Tarleton expressed his patriotism by naming his sons George Washington, born 1800, Thomas Jefferson, born 1802, Benjamin Franklin, born 1806, and James Madison Tarleton, born 1809.

One of the original grantees of Piermont was Lieutenant Governor Sir John Temple, whose father, Robert Temple, married the daughter of Governor Wentworth's wealthy patron, John Nelson of London, one-time governor of Nova Scotia, who was given grants in no less than twenty-seven New Hampshire towns. Temple in Hillsborough County is named for Sir John Temple.

PINKHAM'S GRANT and PINKHAM NOTCH

THIS unincorporated section east of Mount Washington in Coos County takes its name from the Pinkham family of Dover who began their settlement there as early as 1789, when Joseph Pinkham built the road running through what afterwards became the famous Pinkham's Notch, a defile between mountains not more than a quarter of a mile wide.

The road was afterward improved in 1824 so that it ran from Jackson to Gorham. Daniel Pinkham, its builder, appears to have been reimbursed for his work by receiving, as a grant from the state in 1825 the land which now appears on the maps as Pinkham's Grant. The Pinkhams are said to have been the first in northern New Hampshire to display the United States flag at the top of Mount Washington.

The auto road to Mount Washington begins at the northern end of Pinkham's Grant, and the area includes the Crystal Cascades, Glen Ellis Falls and Emerald Pool, as well as the entrance to the Wildcat Mountain ski area.

PITTSBURG

THE TOWN of Pittsburg is the largest in area in the state, and the farthest north. It was originally known as Indian Stream Territory, through which flowed the river called Indian Stream. It contains Lake Francis and the three Connecticut Lakes and the famous international boundary post erected at its northern border on the 45th Parallel, halfway between the North Pole and the Equator, to designate the meeting-point of New Hampshire, Vermont and Canada.

While Pittsburg did not receive its present name until 1840, long after it was first settled, few New Hampshire places have so interesting a history. Following the Revolution, a dispute arose between Canada and the United States over the Indian Stream land (thought by Professor Agassiz, the explorer-geologist, to be the most ancient on the American continent). Here a colony led by David Gibbs of Concord, and Nathaniel Wales of Haverhill, had prospered as a result of a treaty with Philip, chief of the St. Francis tribe of the Abenaki Indians. Under this treaty the chief was guaranteed a perpetual supply of clothing and provisions, and was assured that the right of his people to fish and hunt in their former territory would not be interfered with. The treaty is still in existence, bearing the signatures of Philip and other Indians.

To protect this colony, Indian Stream settlers under the leadership of Luther Parker established, in 1832, an entirely separate government which they called the "Indian Stream Republic," electing their own officials under a private constitution. It remained in existence for more than four years, but finally, prior to the Treaty of Washington in 1842, it became a part of New Hampshire and was incorporated as Pittsburg in 1840.

Although there appears to be no connection between the

adoption of this name and the towns or cities of the same name in Pennsylvania, Kansas and California, it is probable that all four were named in honor of William Pitt, England's great eighteenth century statesman and defender of the Colonies, who is ranked with Churchill as one of Britain's greatest Prime Ministers.

RANDOLPH

RANDOLPH was originally named Durand in the charter of 1772, after John Durand, a member of the London Board of Trade. Durand was a direct descendant of Alexander Bryan, a large landholder in southern Connecticut, engaged in the West Indies trade and closely connected with his friend, Governor Benning Wentworth in the early 1700's. John Durand's father married Elizabeth Bryan, and inherited her father's estates. At the time when Randolph was chartered, the Durands were located in London and associated with Governor John Wentworth's shipping interests.

The name Durand continued as the name of the town until the year 1824 when, at the instigation of Governor Levi Woodbury, it was renamed Randolph. This was the same year in which Governor Woodbury was also responsible for renaming Milan and Lisbon. Randolph was named for the governor's close friend John Randolph of Virginia, long-time member of the House of Representatives, a follower of Jefferson and advocate of states' rights. Randolph was later a United States Senator. He was a descendant of Pocahontas and member of a prominent Virginia family.

One of the early settlers of the town of Randolph was Clovis Lowe, father of Thaddeus Lowe, the inventor and scientist. Randolph has three well-known mountains, Mount Randolph, Crescent Mountain, and Black Crescent Mountain. Its White Mountain names also include Randolph Hill and Randolph Path. The Durand name is commemorated by Durand Ridge.

SARGENT'S PURCHASE

This unincorporated mountainous section of New Hampshire is one of the group of communities in Coos County surrounding Mount Washington, and never formally granted by the Wentworth governors. The grant was finally made in 1831 — one of those awarded by Commissioner James Willey — and the grantees were Jacob Sargent of Thornton, Samuel Colby, William Dearborn and others. They paid three hundred dollars for the tract.

Jacob Sargent, after whom it is named, was the descendant and namesake of one of the leading settlers of Chester. The first Jacob Sargent had served as that town's surveyor when it was granted by Governor Shute as Cheshire, and was its moderator, town treasurer and member of the committees which built its church and school. Under the New Hampshire government Jacob Sargent, known as Ensign Sargent, and members of his family received grants in Whitefield, Warner, Manchester, Candia, and Hill (New Chester). He was with the Continental Army at the siege of Boston.

Sargent's Purchase contains some of the most magnificent scenery in New Hampshire. It includes the summit of Mount Washington, Lakes of the Clouds, Mount Monroe, and Tuckerman Ravine. The last takes its name from Dr. Edward Tuckerman, an eminent American botanist, who for almost twenty years explored the area for rare plant specimens. Dr. Tuckerman, born in Boston in 1817, graduated from Union College and Harvard Law School, after which he studied botany in Sweden, where he achieved a reputation as a leading authority on lichens. In his annual visits to the White Mountains it is said that "no portion of the region, however dark its glens or inaccessible its peaks, was untrodden by his footsteps." The ravine which bears his name is thought to have been directly in the path followed by the early Indian climbers of Mount Washington. Its rock cleavage ranks with the deepest to be found in the Alps, and is so great that a snowfall which remained through the summer once measured thirteen feet in depth and was packed so hard as to bear travellers.

Tuckerman Ravine, with its companion points of interest, Oake's Gulf and Bigelow's Lawn, all named for famous botanists, was first noted on Bond's White Mountain map published in 1858.

SECOND COLLEGE GRANT

THIS IS one of several unincorporated sections of northern New Hampshire which were directly related to the founding of Dartmouth College. The first of these, now the town of Landaff, was intended by Governor Benning Wentworth as a definite gift of the New Hampshire government to provide what he considered an ideal college site. Some time later there was proposed another site which had been granted by the new state of Vermont, appropriately named Wheelock, and land originally assumed to be a part of New Hampshire.

Landaff appears to have been the first choice of Governor Wentworth because of its proximity to a large tract still owned by the Indians, whom he hoped to see converted and educated by the college, or "Indian School" as it was first called. He also hoped to keep the school directly under the eye of the New Hampshire government and thus under English jurisdiction. When it was found that the choice of Landaff would involve litigation among previous incorporators, its selection as a site for the new college was abandoned and several other plots were proposed. The area finally selected, adjacent to the Maine border, continues to be called "Second College Grant." While the college was not finally built on this site, but at Hanover, this "Second Grant", along with Clarksville and Wheelock ultimately became the source of considerable income to Dartmouth both through sales of land and timber.

In 1807 the legislature made the official grant of this land (to be six miles square) to Dartmouth College. The decision to retain the "Second Grant" in New Hampshire's list of towns was permanently confirmed in 1919 by the legislature's passage of an act authorizing the college to use for its general purposes "so much of its avails and income granted to it by the state as may not reasonably be required for the purpose specifically declared in such grant, namely the education of indigent youths and the alleviation of the expenses of necessitous families in the state".

SHELBURNE

SHELBURNE, first chartered in 1769, bears the name of one of America's staunchest friends in the English Parliament during the pre-Revolutionary days when the rights of the colonies were debated, William Petty Fitzmaurice (1737-1805), Earl of Shelburne.

Made a colonel and aide-de-camp to the king for distinguished service in the French war in Europe, Lord Shelburne became President of the Board of Trade and Foreign Plantations, in which position he was brought directly into colonial affairs where he had an opportunity to show his desire to promote conciliation and justice toward America.

Lord Shelburne joined Rockingham and William Pitt in securing the repeal of the Stamp Act, and became a secretary of state under Pitt. He later urged the withdrawal of British troops from Boston, and condemned the "madness and injustice of coercing the Americans into a blind and servile submission." In one of his speeches he declared that "much as he valued America and fatal as her final separation from England might prove, he would be much better pleased to see America forever severed from Great Britain than restored to England's possession by force of arms and conquest." Shelburne became Prime Minister in 1782, and it was because of his insistence that the king recognized the independence of the United States. He later became first Marquess of Lansdowne.

No settlement appears to have been made in Shelburne, New Hampshire in the years immediately following its first granting, probably because of the coming Revolution. By the time of its incorporation in 1820, however, it had grown into a thriving village, the voters of which chose to retain the original name in honor of Lord Shelburne.

STARK

PERCY was the name given to Stark when it was first granted in 1774. Like its neighbor Northumberland, the name was given in honor of Hugh Smithson, Earl Percy and first Duke of Northumberland. It continued as Percy until 1832, when it was renamed Stark after the state's renowned General John Stark, the hero of Bunker Hill and Bennington. The small settlement of Percy retains the original name, as do the Percy Peaks nearby.

General Stark's memorable career is said to have been unequalled in American military history. His skillful war strategy at the Battle of Bunker Hill, where he successfully led two thousand untrained New England troops, mainly from New Hampshire, against a British force more than twice as large, brought him at once into prominence as a leader. As the War for Independence progressed and Fort Ticonderoga was forced to surrender, the danger to the north country in New Hampshire, and what is now Vermont, required immediate action. The colonists, unable to secure help from the American Congress, "drafted" General Stark as the head of its New England forces to halt Burgoyne and his advancing army of Hessians and "Brunswickers" in their mass march down the Hudson valley. Stark's well-planned victory at Bennington, a masterly undertaking, was hailed by the Congress which belatedly made him a brigadier general and expressed its gratitude and that of the new nation.

It is to General Stark that New Hampshire owes its official motto *Live Free or Die*. The words were written by the General in July 1809 in commemoration of the Battle of Bennington, which had taken place thirty-two years before. Replying to an invitation to be present at the anniversary celebration that year, General Stark wrote as a sentiment for the occasion: "Live free or die — Death is not the worst of evils." It is noteworthy that Stark was the first to carry the new thirteen-star American flag into battle — at Bennington on August 16, 1777 — and symbolically his motto contains thirteen letters.

New Hampshire has paid its respects to General John Stark in numerous other ways as well. It gave him, during his lifetime, grants of land in Dunbarton and his native Londonderry, and in Conway, Gilsum and Dublin, as well as in Pawlet, Vermont, once a part of New Hampshire. Starksborough, Vermont, is named for him, and so is Stark's Hill in Washington, New Hampshire.

At his death in 1822, John Stark was acclaimed as the "last surviving Revolutionary general," and in 1890 the state provided the funds for his imposing statue which graces its Capitol grounds in Concord. In 1894 it gave another to the National Statutary Hall in Washington.

STEWARTSTOWN

GOVERNOR John Wentworth made the first grant of this town in 1770. Situated on the Connecticut River, with Canada at the north and Vermont on the west, it became highly disputed territory, and Governor Wentworth's grant appears to have been intended to be passed on to a group of "developers" who would carry out its colonization.

These agents included John Nelson, associated with the Portsmouth Wentworths in the West Indies trade and the governor's relative by marriage, Sir George Colebrooke and Sir James Cockburn, both connected with the East India Company in England, and Sir John Stuart who, as Lord Bute, had considerable influence with the English crown under the new king, George III. This group paid their respects to Lord Bute by naming their six thousand acre grant Stuart, in his honor.

Among the first settlers to be attracted were Daniel Brainard, largest landholder in the Connecticut River town of Haddam, Connecticut, and Jeremiah Eames, Elisha Dyer and Clement

Miner, with whom he shared his grant. They cultivated a large area of farm land with flax and potatoes, and carried on a prosperous trade with the famous Penobscot Indian chief Metallak, whom they befriended in the blindness of his late years, and whose memory is preserved by a plot in the town cemetery.

Following the Revolution, the English grants in Stuart reverted to the colonies, and when the town was incorporated in 1799 the name Stewartstown was chosen. Thus the spelling reverted to the original Scottish form of the name Stuart. Stewartstown was the site of a fort during the War of 1812.

STRATFORD

THE TOWN of Stratford on the Connecticut River was originally called Woodbury, many of its early grantees having lived in Woodbury, Connecticut. The original grant was made in 1762 by Governor Benning Wentworth. The name Stratford was not given to the town until 1773, it being that of a Connecticut town adjacent to Woodbury, from which a number of the settlers also came. At least forty of the original sixty grantees, however, were from Woodbury, Connecticut.

As was often the case in the early grants, land was given on this occasion to entire families, and of these six were members of the family of Captain Joseph Tomlinson of Woodbury, six members of the family of Captain Stiles Judson, five Worcesters, four Averills, and four Hinmans. Other Connecticut names listed among the grantees were Bronson, Beardsley, Curtis, Wells, Strong, Baldwin, Munn, and the first minister, the Reverend Izrahiah Whittemore.

Because of the prevalence of Indian troubles in the north country section of New Hampshire at the time the Woodbury grants were made, few were taken up, and the regrant was made a decade later by Governor Wentworth as Stratford. The entire tract granted was one of the largest ever made in New Hampshire, amounting to 48,603 acres.

Stratford is the site of Sugar Loaf Mountain, and the Percy

Peaks are in the southeast corner of the township. At North Stratford are the Brunswick Mineral Springs, location at one time of a popular resort spa.

The name Stratford calls to mind William Shakespeare, and it is undoubtedly to the Bard's home, Stratford-on-Avon, that the American Stratfords ultimately owe their names. Besides the two New England towns, there are Stratfords in New Jersey, Oklahoma, Texas, Virginia, Wisconsin, and Ontario.

SUCCESS

SUCCESS was one of a group of ten towns granted in the years 1773 and 1774 which contained the last land grants made under the authority of Governor John Wentworth and the English crown. The grant was for over 30,000 acres.

The name "Success" was thought to have been chosen by Governor Wentworth in 1773 in recognition of the increasing evidence in the English Parliament of an attitude of concilia-tion toward the colonies prompted by its repeal of the Stamp Act. On this occasion bells were rung, cannons fired and ser-mons were preached with the title, "Good News From a Far Country." Governor Wentworth expressed his exuberance by naming an island on his Wolfeboro estate "Stamp Act Island." It was also in 1773 that the colonists refused to allow the impor-tation of British tea into Boston, an act which may have been also considered by the governors as a "success."

The town of Success, like its neighbors, Cambridge and Mar-tin's Location, both granted the same year, was never incorpo-rated. These three towns listed among their grantees many prominent Portsmouth names, including the MacKays, Harts, Langdons, Seaveys, Shillabers, Sherburnes, Waltons, Marches, Fernalds, Salters, Clapps and Havens. The Revolution appears to have prevented most of these grants from being taken advan-tage of, and the towns including them still remain "unincorpo-rated" on the New Hampshire map. Success, according to the census of 1960, also remains uninhabited.

SUGAR HILL

New Hampshire's youngest town was set off from Lisbon and incorporated in 1962 after considerable litigation. Sugar Hill is among forty-seven other New Hampshire towns which at one time or another have officially been carved out of parent New Hampshire towns to become independent voting units of their own. In addition to its large grove of sugar maples from which its name comes, a seldom-mentioned feature of the town is its many brooks, one of which, flowing into the Ammonoosuc River, contains the famous "Salmon Hole" where fishermen were once said "to have never exhausted the supply of fish."

A resort town, Sugar Hill also contains the iron ore deposits which were mined in the 1800's and processed at Franconia Iron Mines in neighboring Franconia.

THOMPSON AND MESERVE'S PURCHASE

The so-called Thompson and Meserve's Purchase comprises a grant of some twelve thousand acres and includes the northern slopes of Mount Washington. Within the area are the Cog Railway and the Mount Washington Summit Road. The grant was one of those made by James Willey, the state land commissioner, of as yet unassigned White Mountain lands, and was awarded in 1835 to Samuel W. Thompson of Conway and George P. Meserve of Jackson for five hundred dollars.

In addition to part of Mount Washington, Thompson and Meserve's Purchase is the site of two other peaks in the Presidential Range, Mounts Adams and Jefferson, as well as Mount Clay, named for Henry Clay, who never made it to the White House — but not for lack of trying; he ran for the presidency three times. Twelve New Hampshire mountains have presidential names, though not all of them are in the range of that name.

The plan of adopting such names dates back to 1820 when a group of enthusiastic Lancasterites, headed by John Weeks and Adino Brackett, explored the mountains near the summit already named for President Washington, and proposed to create a "Presidential Range," to be so called in honor of Washington and the three then-living ex-presidents, John Adams, Thomas Jefferson, and James Madison. In proposing the original Presidential Range the name of President Monroe, then in office, was also included in the first five, and later the names of John Quincy Adams and Andrew Jackson were placed on the roll. Four other presidents, Franklin Pierce, James A. Garfield, Grover Cleveland and Abraham Lincoln have been added to the list in more recent years, although not as part of the Presidential Range. The last to be added is Dwight D. Eisenhower.

THORNTON

CHARTERED in 1763 by Benning Wentworth, Thornton was named for one of the proposed settlers, Matthew Thornton. Dr. Thornton received land from the proprietors in return for having served as a surgeon in the famous Pepperell expedition of 1745 which resulted in the capture of Louisbourg, Nova Scotia, by New England troops, of which New Hampshire volunteers were a part.

Dr. Thornton practiced medicine at Merrimack (Londonderry) where he had come with his parents in 1718, at the age of four, from the Scotch settlement in Londonderry, Ireland. The Thornton grant was first made to accommodate fifty families, and comprised a total of 24,000 acres. It was later increased to 40,000 acres, and the number of families to ninety.

This was one of the earliest attempts made by the New Hampshire government to resettle a group of "colonizers" almost entirely from a single area to form a new community of individuals having the same native background abroad. In the grant were the Scotch-Irish families of Morrison, McNeil, Cochran, Gilmore, Gregg, Christy, Moore, Clendennin, and Montgomery.

Besides being one of New Hampshire's three signers of the Declaration of Independence, Dr. Thornton's fame was established by public service in many other offices. He was a justice of the Superior Court, speaker of the House of Representatives, member of the State Senate, delegate to the Continental Congress, and first president of the state under the regime following the Revolutionary War.

WARREN

WARREN was named out of respect for Admiral Sir Peter Warren, who won the admiration of the American colonies and his native England for his part in the capture of Louisbourg, Nova Scotia, in 1745.

The conflict that year was concerned with the colonial fishing and fur trading rights and the Louisbourg expedition was not only successful but did much to unite the colonies. The land forces were in command of Sir William Pepperell of Kittery, Governor Shirley of Massachusetts, and Colonel William Vaughan of Portsmouth. The fortress, known as "The Dunkirk of America," was taken largely through the skillful maneuvering of Admiral Warren's *Superbe* and his fleet of ships.

Warren went to sea at the age of fourteen. At twenty-four he was placed in command of the *Grafton,* a ship with seventy guns; and during England's war with Spain he had taken more than twenty prizes of considerable value. While stationed on the Atlantic seaboard Admiral Warren made many friends in New York, where he married a sister of Governor James De-Lancey. He invested his "prize money" in New York City land, and owned a three-hundred acre farm in what is now Greenwich Village and Washington Square. The British Government reimbursed the colonies for their expedition at Louisbourg and made Sir Peter a vice-admiral and a member of parliament. The Louisbourg victory was hailed in London by bonfires and bell-ringing in recognition of American prestige. Sir Peter Warren died in 1752.

The town of Warren, which includes the village of Glencliff, was granted in 1764 and consisted of 22,000 acres. The grant provided homes for forty families, each of whom was to "plant and cultivate five acres of land, within the term of five years, for every fifty acres contained in his or their share or proportion of land in the said township." Every settler was to pay for the space of ten years "the rent of one ear of Indian corn only per year" and after the expiration of ten years "one shilling yearly for every hundred acres he so owned." Warren, an area of large mica deposits, is today the location of a state fish hatchery and the Morse Museum.

WATERVILLE VALLEY

By an act of the General Court in 1967 the town of Waterville officially adopted the name Waterville Valley.

The town is said to have taken its name from its two rivers, called the Mad and the Swift. First settled in the 1760's, like many other north country towns, its peaceful countryside lay in a deep valley among majestic mountains, once known as the "Waterville Haystacks," and afterward to be named Tripyramid, Osceola, Tecumseh, Black, Sandwich, and Jennings Peak.

Waterville is among New Hampshire's oldest and best-known summer resorts. Its famous hotel, the Greeley House, gained success in part through the patronage of visitors attracted not only by the magnificent scenery, but because of the spectacular mountain slides at Waterville in 1869 and 1885.

Waterville's population was at one time almost equal to that of its neighboring towns of Thornton and Campton. The town was incorporated in 1829, and in the same year the Foss and Gillis families purchased state land there. They encouraged the erection of a schoolhouse and town hall, cultivated a considerable quantity of hops, and advertised it widely as a "vacation playground." The town, however, failed to continue in growth through the years and the transfer of considerable of its area to the government-owned White Mountain National Forest reduced it in size and population. The establishment of the

Waterville Valley ski area in recent years has done much to revive this picturesque town.

WENTWORTH'S LOCATION

New Hampshire's provincial governors, the Wentworths, were undoubtedly responsible for originating more town names in the state than come from any other source. They also left their own imprint in the names of two towns: Wentworth in Grafton County; and this small and sparsely populated town in the north country adjacent to the Maine boundary. Wentworth's Location was a grant set aside by the Wentworths for their own use, but for many years remained unsettled. More than a century later, however, when the town was incorporated in 1881, the name Wentworth's Location was retained. Situated on the road north to the Rangeley Lakes, it is one of the smallest towns in Coos County. Notable natural features in Wentworth's Location are Mount Dustan, Black Mountain, and Greenough Ponds.

WHITEFIELD

Whitefield was granted on July 4, 1774, exactly two years before the adoption of the Declaration of Independence. It was the last town to be chartered under the English provincial government, whose chief executive at the time was Governor John Wentworth.

The list of Whitefield grantees contained the names of Jeremy Belknap, the historian, John Cochran, commander of Fort William and Mary at Portsmouth, John Langdon, who was eventually to succeed John Wentworth as governor, and several other later American patriots.

The name Whitefield, chosen for the town, was that of George Whitefield, the famous English evangelist who, after a tour of New England, had died at Exeter four years earlier.

He was a friend of the Earl of Dartmouth, the Reverend Peabody and other New Hampshire divines, and had been the guest of the governor at Portsmouth.

One of the stipulations of the Whitefield charter was the provision of funds for the establishment of a "glebe" section for an Anglican church. To carry out the project the governor sent his personal secretary, Colonel John Hurd and Colonel Asa Porter, both fellow Harvard graduates, with the Reverend René Cossitt, afterward Episcopal minister at Claremont, in charge. This plan was vigorously opposed by the Reverend Peter Powers and others of Haverhill, and it was finally abandoned.

The town name was first listed as Whitefields, but changed to Whitefield when it was incorporated in 1804.

WOODSTOCK

THE GRANTEES of Woodstock, first called Peeling in 1763 by Governor Benning Wentworth after an English town, included no fewer than ten Cushmans, coming from the town of Lebanon, Connecticut, all neighbors of the Reverend Eleazar Wheelock, its minister. The Cushmans were descended from Robert Cushman, a Plymouth Colonist who has the honor of having preached, in 1622, the first religious sermon ever published in America. Other grantees, also from Lebanon, were Peregrine White, a descendant of the Mayflower Pilgrim of that name, the Trumbulls, Hornes, and the Demerits.

Governor John Wentworth renamed the town Fairfield in 1771, after Fairfield, Connecticut. It had not been settled under the terms of the charter and the governor, in 1768, gave a total of 2500 acres to Captain John Goffe in the hope of attracting new residents. Others apparently did not arrive, however, until the 1820's due to the mountainous terrain of some of the grants.

The town was renamed Woodstock in 1840, a name popular for other towns in New England, having originated from the historic palace of Woodstock in England.

Bibliography

In addition to general reference works of American history and many individual town and local histories of New Hampshire, the following books and publications were among those consulted in preparing the material included in this volume.

A.M.C. White Mountain Guide. Appalachian Mountain Club. Boston, 1955.

Anderson, John, and Morse, Stearns. *The Book of the White Mountains.* New York, 1930.

Batchellor, Albert S., Editor. *New Hampshire State Papers,* Vol. XXIV through XXIX, Town Charters. Concord, N. H., 1894-1896.

Belknap, Jeremy. *History of New Hampshire* (3 vols.). Boston, 1813.

Bigham, Clive. *The Prime Ministers of Britain.* London, 1922.

Carey, Mathew. *Carey's American Pocket Atlas.* Philadelphia, 1805.

Carrigain, Philip. *Map of New Hampshire.* Concord, 1816.

Carter, James G. *Map of New Hampshire for Families and Schools.* Portsmouth, after 1830.

Chamberlain, Allen. *Annals of the Grand Monadnock.* Concord, 1936.

Charlton, Edwin A. *New Hampshire As It Is.* Claremont, 1856.

Crawford, Lucy. *History of the White Mountains.* Hanover, 1966.

County and Town Index Map. State of New Hampshire. Concord, 1958.

Debrett's Peerage. C. F. J. Hankinson, Editor. London, 1959.

Doyle, J. E. *Official Baronage of England, 1066-1885*. London, 1886.

Drake, Samuel Adams. *The Heart of the White Mountains*. New York, 1882.

Encyclopedia Brittanica, 13th Edition. New York and London, 1926.

Fry, William H. *New Hampshire as a Royal Province*. New York, 1908.

Fuess, Claude M. *Daniel Webster*. Boston, 1930.

Gore, Effie K., and Speare, Eva A. *New Hampshire Folk Tales*. Littleton, N. H., 1945.

Harkness, M. G. *The Fishbasket Papers: Diaries of Bradbury Jewell, 1768-1823*. Peterborough, N. H., 1963.

Hill, Ralph Nading. *Yankee Kingdom: Vermont and New Hampshire*. New York, 1960.

Historical New Hampshire. New Hampshire Historical Society, Concord, N. H. (Issues 1945-1967).

Hitchcock, Charles H. *The Geology of New Hampshire*. Concord, N. H., 1874.

Holland, Samuel. *A Topographical Map of the State of New Hampshire*. London, 1784.

Howells, John M. *Architectural Heritage of the Piscataqua*. New York, 1930.

Hunt, Elmer Munson. Articles appearing in *Historical New Hampshire*, the journal of the New Hampshire Historical Society, Concord, N. H., as follows:

————. "Daniel Webster at Phillips Exeter", April 1946.

————. "Family Names in New Hampshire Town Histories", Dec. 1946.

————. "Daniel Webster and Our Foreign Policy", Dec. 1947.

————. "Spots Where History Has Put its Mark in New Hampshire", 1949.

————. "The English Background of the Wentworth Town Grants", Nov. 1950.

————. "Anniversary of the Inauguration of Franklin Pierce", Aug. 1953.

————. "The Origin of New Hampshire Mountain Names", April 1955.

Kilbourne, Frederick W. *Chronicles of the White Mountains.* Boston, 1916.

King, Thomas Starr. *The White Hills: Their Legends, Landscape & Poetry.* Boston, 1859.

The Lake Sunapee Area. Dartmouth-Lake Sunapee Region Assn., Lebanon, N. H., 1967.

Lakes Region Guide. Lakes Region Assn. Wolfeboro, N. H., 1965.

Langdon, Samuel, and Blanchard, Joseph. *An Accurate Map of His Majesty's Province of New Hampshire in New England.* Photostat from Ms. in Library of Congress.

Lecky, W. E. H. *History of England in the 18th Century* (seven volumes). New York, 1903.

————. *History of Ireland in the 18th Century* (five volumes). New York, 1893.

Leland, Charles G. *The Algonquin Legends of New England.* Boston, 1898.

Lodge, Edmund. *Portraits of Illustrious Personages in Great Britain.* London, 1823.

Mayo, Lawrence S. *John Langdon of New Hampshire.* Concord, N. H., 1937.

————. *John Wentworth.* Boston, 1921.

McCallum, James D. *Eleazar Wheelock.* Hanover, N. H., 1939.

Merrimack Valley Region Guide. Merrimack Valley Region Assn. Manchester, N. H., 1968.

Monadnock Regionnaire. Monadnock Region Assn. Peterborough, N. H., 1962.

Moore, Howard P. *A Life of General John Stark.* Privately printed, 1949.

New Hampshire: A Guide to the Granite State. Boston, 1938.

New Hampshire Manual for the General Court. Concord, published biennially.

New Hampshire Seacoast Guide. Seacoast Regional Development Assn. Portsmouth, N. H., 1967.

O'Kane, Walter Collins. *Trails and Summits of the White Mountains.* Boston, 1925.

Poole, Ernest. *The Great White Hills of New Hampshire.* New York, 1946.

Proctor, Mary A. *The Indians of the Winnipesaukee and Pemigewasset Valleys.* Boston, 1931.

Recreational Map of the White Mountains. White Mountains Region Assn. Lancaster, N. H., n.d.

Ruggles, Edward. *New Hampshire from Late Survey.* Walpole, N. H., 1817.

Saltonstall, W. G. *Ports of the Piscataqua.* Cambridge, 1941.

Six Regional Divisions of New Hampshire. Map. Concord, N. H., 1961.

Speare, Eva A. *New Hampshire's Historic Seacoast.* Littleton, N. H., 1967.

Squires, J. D. *The Story of New Hampshire.* Princeton, 1964.

Upton, Richard F. *Revolutionary New Hampshire.* Hanover, 1936.

Wentworth, John. *Wentworth Genealogy, English and American.* Boston, 1878.

Whittemore, Charles P. *A General of the Revolution: John Sullivan of New Hampshire.* New York, 1961.

Willey, Benjamin G. *History of the White Mountains.* New York, 1870.

Woodbury, Levi. *Writings of Levi Woodbury.* Boston, 1852.

Index